The
VOICE
and the
FALLEN

The VOICE and the FALLEN

MANUEL NARANJO DIAZ

The Voice and the Fallen by Manuel Naranjo Diaz

This book is written to provide information and motivation to readers. Its purpose is not to render any type of psychological, legal, or professional advice of any kind. The content is the sole opinion and expression of the author, and not necessarily that of the publisher.

Copyright © 2021 by Manuel Naranjo Diaz

All rights reserved. No part of this book may be reproduced, transmitted, or distributed in any form by any means, including, but not limited to, recording, photocopying, or taking screenshots of parts of the book, without prior written permission from the author or the publisher. Brief quotations for noncommercial purposes, such as book reviews, permitted by Fair Use of the U.S. Copyright Law, are allowed without written permissions, as long as such quotations do not cause damage to the book's commercial value. For permissions, write to the publisher, whose address is stated below.

Printed in the United States of America.

ISBN 978-1-955363-48-8 (Paperback)
ISBN 978-1-955363-49-5 (Digital)

Lettra Press books may be ordered through booksellers or by contacting:

Lettra Press LLC
30 N Gould St. Suite 4753
Sheridan, WY 828011
1 307-200-3414 | info@lettrapress.com
www.lettrapress.com

CONTENTS

Preface vii

Isaac Newton 1
    Blinded By Light 4

Adolf Hitler 8
    Oblivion 11

Vincent Van Gogh 19
    Essay Of A Portrait 22

Robert James Fischer 28
    In The Riverbed Of Oblivion 31

Sigmund Freud 57
    Anguish 60

Rafael L. Trujillo 70
    Death In Spring 73

Friedrich Nietzsche 80
    Importance Is Not Important 83

Ernest Hemingway 91
    The Briefcase And The Fury 94

Yukio Mishima 105
    Chronicle Of A Long Ending 108

Nikola Tesla 118
    Stolen Thunder 121

John F. Kennedy 129
    Sandcastles 132

Charles Darwin 143
    The Battle Of Ideas 146

The Unknown Soldier 160
    The Unknown Soldier 163

Galileo Galilei 178
    Raising His Gaze To The Sky 182

Franz Kafka 206
    The Mysterious Mr. K And The Worm 209

Carl Gustav Jung 229
    At The Lake House 232

Leonardo Da Vinci 260
    Obsession 263

Acknowledgments 285
About The Author 286

PREFACE

The characters of these stories have been chosen spontaneously, some because of admiration, others because of curiosity as in the pieces about Adolf Hitler and Rafael L. Trujillo. However, I have tried to present my personal vision as well as an exercise in creativity by inserting fictional elements in the middle of the depiction of real events that the characters have lived through in their peculiar and influential lives. To obtain the biographical information, I have relied on specialized biographies and audiovisual material from the Internet and other creditable sources such as BBC documentaries as well as history books where these characters have been studied by eminent researchers.

The structure of the stories consists in the alternation of plain dialogues and a narrator, forming a blend of fiction and reality after a thorough investigation into the life of each historical figure. The fictional elements are a speculation of what could have happened, as in the cases of Newton's investigations of esoteric subjects, the last days of Hitler, the final conversation between Vincent van Gogh and his brother Theo van Gogh, the fate of Hemingway's lost briefcase, some moments of Nietzsche's first internment in the mental institution, Jung's dialogues with two of the most influential women in his life, the conversation between Darwin and the cleric, the conversations between Galileo and his first biographer, and the conversations between Lisa Gherardini and Leonardo da Vinci, among other speculations.

The story about Kennedy is based on widely disseminated documentaries about that fateful day and other sources of information that support the conspiracy version, a situation that unintentionally highlights the prevailing controversy between the official version and the one referring to the conspiracy, which a large part of the public is willing to accept and defend.

In some of the stories—"The Battle of Ideas" (Darwin), "Raising His Gaze to the Sky" (Galileo), and "At the Lake House" (Jung)—a fundamental criticism toward the religious paradigm prevails, which is inevitable when one wants to be open and opt for a modern vision, which means giving way to the conclusions reached by the natural sciences and other fields of study that explain phenomena that occur on our planet and the universe through theoretical and experimental physics. Equally, a certain level of criticism toward religious ideas can be noticed in the field of philosophy in the story "Importance Is Not Important" (Nietzsche).

Despite the level of criticism mentioned, it is advisable to read these stories as a literary creation and not as a kind of protest song. I particularly consider literature as a forum open to the creation and free expression of ideas obtained from the fruit of personal observation and based on the characters who have shaped the history of a human being in a genuine or fateful way.

ISAAC NEWTON

(1642–1727)

In his book Ideas: A History of Thought and Invention, from Fire to Freud, the intellectual British historian Peter Watson told us that, in 1936, the auction house Sotheby's sold in London a collection of papers that belonged to the great physicist and philosopher Sir Isaac Newton that the University of Cambridge had considered as not having "scientific value" some fifty years prior, when the collection had been offered for auction for the first time. Subsequently, these documents were acquired by the distinguished economist John Maynard Keynes, who—after spending several years studying them—delivered a lecture about them at the Royal Society Club in London. Quoting Keynes, we read, "Since the 18th century, Newton has been considered the first and greatest of scientists in the modern era, a rationalist, someone who taught us to think according to the dictates of reason cold and devoid of emotion. I can no longer see him in that light. And I think no one who has studied the documents contained in this box retrieved from Cambridge in 1696 could either and despite having been partly dispersed, have come down to us. Newton was not the first man of the Age of Reason, he was the last of the magicians, the last of the Babylonians and Sumerians, the last great mind to contemplate the visible and intellectual world with the same eyes of those who began to build our cultural heritage almost ten thousand years."Following Watson's analysis, this astounding piece of information about this colossus of the natural sciences made us see a new and different

Newton, a man who devoted much of his time to alchemy, to the relentless search for the philosopher's stone, and to the study of the Bible's chronology, convinced that this would allow him to predict the apocalypse. He was a man fascinated by the Rosicrucians, astrology, and numerology, who believed that Moses knew about Copernicus's heliocentric doctrine and his own theory of gravity. After his great achievements concerning the invention of calculus and the description of the workings of the physical world and beyond in his Principia Mathematica, Newton was still striving to discover the exact makeup of Solomon's Temple on the assumption that this would lead him to determine the topography of the heavens.

All this makes us think of the enormous effort made by Isaac Newton to unveil the mysteries of the universe using biblical stories and precepts, especially the numerology contained in them, and applying his scientific theories and all his mental energy in a vain search for a coherent and explanatory whole, with the Holy Scriptures as an experimental basis. It is not surprising that his endeavor has not been successful, even for the exceptionally gifted mind of that great genius. What is certain is that this paradox in Newton's life—the adherence to strict scientific principles and the speculations of the occult—is a feature of the times in which he has lived, an epoch enveloped in darkness where any explanation has to include at least some of the Bible's teachings. This short story deals with Newton's concerns on that difficult and intriguing subject and takes place at the end of his long and fruitful life.

Life is really simple, but we insist on making it complicated.

—Confucius

Wisdom begins in wonder.

—Socrates

BLINDED BY LIGHT

1

The icy wind sneaked back through the cracks of the dark and desolate walls of the hall. He could perceive it as an omnipotent presence approaching through the labyrinthine and ancestral corridors embracing the soul of the inert objects behind the door of his laboratory, where in the past he had become the angels' executioner, inadvertently overturning the sacred laws of humanity while discovering the mechanics of the universe.

Many years had gone by, decades, more than half a century; and his discoveries, even though poorly understood by most of his fellow humans, were like legendary landmarks in the paths of reason. The plague had swept through the world; wars had ravished lands. The great loneliness of the genius—he had been holding the inexhaustible light of his deep understanding of things, essences, numbers, movements, and the truth that lay hidden in the vortex of the unknown, yet his achievements were not enough. He needed to dispel the greatest doubt, the truth of all truths—the perfect number.

2

"Useless! The truth has eluded me much more than before, back then during the time of the apocalypse, of confinement, the year of the plague. I was young and witty, and you hadn't been born yet. You must imagine that thinking in a vacuum hurts me. You know me well and know how hard it is for me to accept errors. I am not satisfied with the concept of nothingness."

"But, Professor, I don't think you are as misguided as you think. You should not trust the latest results."

"This calculus I have invented has been a fiasco. The divine figure has escaped me, and the big book has not allowed me to unravel its mysteries."

"Oh, Master, despite everything, I am pleased to have returned . . . but . . . I cannot understand the reason for your zeal. To tell you the truth, in all these years of being your pupil and friend, I had not seen you so distressed."

"Don't worry about me. None of this will be necessary when all is said and done. Later on, the secret will be revealed, and my words perhaps will make sense. In the past, when ideas flowed smoothly in my head as if they were dancing before my eyes, I deciphered the mysteries of movement, of the attraction of physical bodies, of light . . . and this problem simply eludes me. It has become a personal obsession, but . . . few of nature's arcana have discouraged me completely, and I will not relent now, believe me. Be my faithful witness."

"Master, I know you are a man of unshakable will and incomparable analytical acuity. I am sure you will succeed in the long run, but, Master, I must tell you that my presence here not only corresponds to my desire to see you again after so long and learning everything you would be willing to teach me. I am also here because the council has sent me. The members believe . . . it's not . . . advisable to continue this line of study."

3

The wind would not give in one iota in its escalation, slamming the soaring clouds scarcely illuminated by an accomplice and undaunted moon. He, more than anyone else, knew about its unchanging orbit around Earth, now interfering with his thoughts in the midst of the wild wind whistles outside the old enclosure. Nevertheless, this in no way would change the course of his ideas. Nature had been an ally throughout his life.

Images of the remote past, flowing into focus one after another in the stage of his existence, withered but were still rewarding, memories of the year of the plague—the confinement and terror that, like wings of a gigantic hawk, cast its grim shadow over so many European cities. However, he not only survived huddled in his distant nook but because of that, in the middle of the stillness and safety of his environment, also made the discovery of his lifetime—the law of universal gravitation.

His thoughts were taking flight in the warmth of his laboratory, but they were increasingly fragmented and less substantial. He was not able to reach a greater meaning, thinking of his quest as eternal and fruitless. Was he approaching a dead end? A singular maze reflected in an infinite mirror?

4

"Nicholas, the council must wait for my answer, which will be final. And if you harbor any doubts about my current research, I will confide this only to you, Nicholas, my work concerning the essential calculation, the measurements of the temple, the mathematical and physical parameters of the great book. But . . . the truth is that it slips away from my hands, and . . . I would not like . . . to stop."

"Master, I owe more loyalty to you than to anyone else in the council. Therefore . . . it is necessary to confess that nothing good awaits you in case you decide to hand over the fruits of this research to them. The council will betray you. Master, someone very powerful is envious of your glory."

5

The wind had subsided and turned into a languid whisper as in a melancholic ballad but still could be felt that night. And the moon, at its zenith, flaunted an unusual brightness. One could see from the window of the Gothic cloister, where time, with its leaden step, did not find the way through the mind of the octogenarian tormented by his indecision.

6

"It's late, Master. You must decide. They are waiting for an answer. Nooo! Master, don't throw them in the fire!"

"They will feed the flames. It is my verdict."

"For the love of God! It's the work of five decades. My soul cries! It was not my intention to induce you to do this, Master. How will I be able to confront the council? Everything will be useless."

"They are just papers, Nicholas. It is better to burn them now than to see them multiplied afterward, turned into the torture of an uncertain, and even doom posterity. Do not cry. I am doing you a favor. I will take all these numbers to the tomb with me, where they will never be recovered.

7

The small and thin curls of black smoke rose from the pile of ashes with an asynchronous rhythm while a tenacious rain pounded the windows violently, and the night was still young.

After all, he departed soon to the unknown horizon, leaving a trail of unanswered questions. Sometime later, someone with great authority would whisper at the foot of his tomb in the illustrious abbey, "The laws of nature lay hidden since time immemorial."

But another voice of equal authority would say, "But other realities will remain lost forever, mutating into vain smoke carried by the wind in a stormy night."

ADOLF HITLER

(1889–1945)

Adolf Hitler spent his last days in a bunker in Berlin. Historians' consensus about this period in the dictator's life assured us he died in there, his last stronghold; but unfortunately, the evidence that he committed suicide on April 30, 1945, was weak if we considered that his body and that of his wife, Eva Braun, were never properly identified. The story that would follow speculated about events that could have happened on that last day, when Stalin's troops were approaching rapidly at the beat of explosions and shrapnel, breaking through the remains of what once was the imposing and well-structured German capital.

There was no doubt that his body disappeared, either burned by his own collaborators trying to make his remains unrecognizable or in some other way. Some had suggested that, days before the capture of the bunker by Russian troops, he got out with his wife from the underground maze that connected his hideout with the outside world, and it would be worth pointing out that others with much less power than him managed to avoid arrest, like Martin Bormann, who finally found his way in a submarine to the distant and unfathomable South America—to Argentina to be exact. There was evidence, although not very precise, that a senior hierarch reached those far-flung places, and countless articles and books had been written and documentaries had been made speculating about the ultimate fate of the person responsible for the death of more than fifty million human beings. It would be worth the effort, considering the great loss in human lives, which became the imprint left by this unique, sinister, and singular person.

Another point of this short story was how a simple lance corporal without the ability to command elementary troops who lived as a vagabond before World War I and, on one occasion, was on the verge of dying of hypothermia on a forgotten park bench in Belle Epoque, Vienna, managed to reach the highest place in the German military hierarchy, making any similar biographical chronicle in the annals of history sound like a fairy tale invented by the feverish mind of some writer of previous centuries.

There was no doubt that this grim figure gave an unexpected twist to the history of the twentieth century, overturning the fate of all those who lived during his lifetime and causing social, economic, geopolitical, scientific, and religious repercussions long after. Therefore, this person would be important for us to try to understand human nature regarding the flexibility, resilience, political will, and boundless capacity to do evil as an extreme example of what humans, in their lust for power and control, were capable of achieving.

A political trial was still pending on this man who did not face the consequences of his actions, but the trial of history had ended and a verdict delivered by the future generations, who saw in him the embodiment of evil. But the greatest condemnation would be to be thrown in the dungeons of undesirable and absolute oblivion.

Pretend inferiority and encourage his arrogance.

—Sun Tzu

From the deepest desires often come the deadliest hate.

—Socrates

He who knows when he can fight and when he cannot will be victorious.

—Sun Tzu

OBLIVION

1

"Dr. Edmund Forster, don't be afraid. We are safe here. This is the Royale Café. No one can hear us. Paris is a city free from the clutches of your enemy."

"That's what I want to believe. You cannot imagine how difficult the situation in Berlin is. I am opposed to the regime, and they have me in the crosshairs. They couldn't care less about personal achievements or the careers of hardworking people like me. They only care about allegiance to . . . I don't even want to mention his name."

"It's okay, Doctor. As I said, we are safe here. Let's get into our business, please. How did you get to know him? You told me you had been his doctor. I'm not sure. It was not very clear in your short letter."

"Yes. For security reasons, I could reveal absolutely nothing. In fact, I won't do it. I will give you the documents, although I know I am putting my life in danger and my prestige, which I value equally or to a greater degree even, and then leave."

"But I insist. Give me some details, in case for some strange reason I'm not able to read the documents you will give me."

"I don't like this, but I will do it anyway. The die is cast."

"Thank you, Doctor. I'm listening."

"It was almost the end of the Great War, around October 1918, and this person was brought into my office. He was unremarkable at first glance, almost insignificant, and was suffering from a common ailment we call hysterical blindness, which was typical among certain soldiers who, at least subconsciously, do not want to go back to fight, this man in particular. Although his eyesight had been affected by British poison gas, the damage caused by it did not represent a serious health issue, and some of my colleagues and I had an effective method to treat that malady, which consisted in some degree of programmed humiliation to expose the main symptom—the psychological condition underlying the blindness. The general pattern of these patients was their desire not to face the battle, but . . . the character in question did not present the usual pattern. He did want to return to the front, which was puzzling even for someone experienced in the treatment of these patients. So after treating him for a few weeks with no results, I decided to implement a different method to achieve my objective, that is to say, to restore his vision. I used an elaborate psychological ploy and, in the end, was very successful . . . for everyone's misfortune." "You have me in suspense, Doctor. I find your success quite amazing, even though I hardly know what the treatment consisted of."

"Simple. In one of our sessions, after an alleged in-depth assessment of the damage, I claimed his condition was practically incurable, that maybe one in a thousand patients overcame the malady through enormous willpower. I used a powerful hypnotic suggestion to instill in him the idea that if his will was strong enough to see the light of a candle I had lit in an adjacent darkened room, he would not only recover his vision but would also be on the way to achieve whatever he wanted, that this demonstration of exceptional mental strength would enable him to change the course of history. And if he returned to his company of combatants, at some point, he could—if he set his mind to it—change the German nation's trajectory. The country desperately needed people of such competence. It would make him invulnerable, and nothing would interfere between him and the greatest glory. Needless to say, that day, he saw the light because, after all, his ailment was nothing serious."

"What you just told me is fascinating, Doctor. Sadly, your success doesn't fill me with joy, rather with horror. How is it possible to achieve such a metamorphosis in a person as weak as he was?"

"You have no idea how I feel right now revealing this for the first time, breaking the sacred ethical silence of my profession. Now having said that and to my chagrin, this interview is over. Do what you have to do with this information. I hope it might help reverse a little at least the involuntary evil I have done to my nation and the world. If the German people knew about this, he may lose credibility, and perhaps they would see him as I do—an insignificant being, a man without qualities as he has always been."

"Rest assured, Doctor. Your secret will be revealed in due course. And . . . trust me, before doing so, I will let you know in advance so you can make the preparations to go as far as possible from those people who have only come to release the monster that dwells in that unscrupulous being."

2

The dull and monotonous sound of heavy artillery reached his ears vaguely, cushioned by endless obstacles. For him, they were like sounds from another world; they no longer bothered him. He had decided to think about the good things of the past, like when he had discovered his love for painting as a child while looking at the northern city unfolding before him, a place full of life, a static life but cheerful at the same time.

3

"What do you think of this watercolor, Heinz? Isn't it wonderful?"

"Yes, my Führer. We are all very concerned about you and Mrs. Eva."

"You think it's wonderful, eh? It really is, impressively well preserved after more than a hundred years, Heinz. Please bring me the other folders. And . . . Mrs. Eva is fine."

4

Time was his scourge. The only way to stave off its leaden and inexorable step was putting good memories of his life in front of it and in his mind of a dark warrior winning relentless and unforgivable battles, and that was only possible through fire and blood.

At times, a slight tremor was felt throughout the whole enclosure, making all the others, occupants shake, although they belittled the importance of that unwelcome reality. The Führer, undaunted, had lost the ability to react; the volatility of his world would not touch him again. He was not concerned with the dismal instant.

5

"Gustav! Can you come to see this?" "Of course, Heinz. Is it recent? Mm-hmm, it seems so. But . . . could it be possible, in the middle of this chaos, to have the peace of mind to do this? A plan? Do you think it's a plan to—" "Be quiet. I'm afraid it is. A moment ago, the Führer asked me to bring his folder. That can only mean what both you and I know."

"How can something be sinister and sublime at the same time? Explain that, dear Heinz."

"Explain it to me. You know him as well as I do."

"You know very well that no one knows what goes through his mind. It is unfathomable."

"Always looking for frivolous excuses, deep down, you know what he wants, don't you? However, remember something—I will always be him until the last minute."

6

Many years ago, when he was like a simple blade of grass whipped by the winds of war, he became blind. It had been the magical turning point, like a fork on the road in front of the eyes of his instinct; in a malevolent instant, it boosted his life with a germ of will not experienced by any soul until then, directing him toward the dark path abounding with treasures and glory.

In his thoughts, an immense and powerful eagle welcomed him with firmness and motherly intention and made him soar with an iron determination. Unwittingly, Edmund—the doctor—by curing his blindness and imbuing in him more than confidence enabled him to dominate weaker beings than him, transforming that feeble person into the idolized and despised Führer.

7

"I have been at his service for many years, and I had never seen these works, Gustav. Clearly, they have to be recent. Probably nobody else knows about them. As you can see, they are very revealing."

"But, Heinz, are you implying that we should destroy them? There must be a way to preserve them. We should hide them in a safe place. They might be useful for us later—to get out of here, I mean."

"Don't talk like that, Gustav. We are like rats in a maze down here. Besides, the Führer has not discarded them yet . . . nor has given any instructions in that regard. He probably won't, I suppose. But this material is very important, and we'd be in trouble if we kept it. We should destroy it. If he hasn't kept it secret, it is clear that he trusts me. He always knows best anyway."

"That's your opinion. I don't see it that way. He has been acting strangely for some time now, and I think he no longer trusts his own judgment. I only dare confess this to you, of course. Logic tells me we will not have many possibilities to survive here, and in any case, I believe the world must know why so much has been sacrificed and—who knows?—maybe how to avoid a greater evil. Come to your senses, Heinz! Do not destroy them!"

8

His present situation brought back memories of captivity from more than twenty years ago. On that occasion, he had chosen the dark path in the world of the blind with an unshakable will. The bars of the cell represented the weapon of his martyrdom, propelling him to fame and prestige. Everything would be calculated on the fly, and in that way, he would seize power—with nothing to lose and the glory to win.

A new and burned-out skin unfolded over the kingdom of perfect beings he once created, willing to pour their blood in cities and countrysides by the dreams of greatness he infused in them, but now that dream was bitter tears, mud, and snow. Cities had died, and the enemies were at the gates. These were the thoughts occupying the leader's head while immersed in a chaos of collapsing roofs as a leitmotif of destruction coming fast toward him. He had done a lot trying to place his race on top of the others and, above all, to make war against the world in his obstinate obfuscation of power. It was not only a matter of survival but it was also complete domination that drove his most intimate yearnings.

9

"If you preserved these works, Gustav, it would be like betraying the Führer, to whom you owe absolute loyalty. And if some of the people here knew about your intentions, they would not forgive you."

"I think you are exaggerating. Did you hear that? The enemy is closer and closer, and I will become cannon fodder faster than you . . . and can't resign myself. I am a victim of his accursed charm myself, so as you understand, I will fight for my life until the last minute, and . . . I am not ashamed of being afraid of death. Aren't you as well?"

"We have lived with death before the war started, and it is impossible for you to get out of here alive anyway, even with my help or Martin's, who already fled, so forget about doing something you'd regret. I'll be against it until the end. I owe more loyalty to the Führer than to you."

"Oh, Heinz, you're so melodramatic. I'll tell you something—I don't want to die yet, and if I have stayed with the Führer until now, it's because I am faithful to him. I've had the chance to get out of this tomb for good, even before he asked me, but as you see, I am still here, although I will never forgive myself for staying."

10

Evoking a pleasant memory was not entirely impossible, just remembering the morbid sweetness of power, the capacity to influence people's lives and deaths, the dark pleasures unattainable for the vast majority of human beings, and above all being law incarnate. It was a matter of remembering and living again, forgetting what was terrible and inexpressible—the weight of guilt.

However, he could not decide. Pride, honor, his gifts as a leader, the devotion for the native soil? The act would be a harsh contradiction, he thought; but no matter how much he mulled it over, he didn't see another way. Living or dying? That was the question. Would he be willing to succumb along with his life's work? They had all sacrificed for him, even her, his brand-new wife. Why wouldn't he be willing to do the same? After all, he reasoned, life and death would mean the same for his final plan.

11

"Don't hesitate for a second, Gustav. You will be hunted down. You've snatched the paintings from me! Give me back the folders! It's only a matter of picking up the phone and telling them what's happening."

"Don't bother. I decided my death a long time ago, just when I joined the party. You too. Or are you so naive to think our 'kingdom' hasn't gone to hell yet? You heard me. No one comes out alive, not even him."

"Pure rhetoric. We'll see. Give me that now!"

"So that's how things are? Well . . . you won't stop me!"

12

The artificial fog of grenade explosions, the rattle of shrapnel, and the cloud of dust enveloping the debris never ceased while the vengeful troops of the enemy broke through the depths of the city; and outside through space, the tanks' vibrations entering the desolate city drowned the last whispers of the unfortunate, formerly invulnerable citizens of an unbeatable and predestined race, all the whispers except one, hidden deeper underground. It was almost unreachable, like an abyss in the middle of the sea. At the end of the day, nobody knew it, only the guardian who took the secret to the grave.

Sometime later, the lonely old man sipped his hot tea with a trembling hand and absorbed look, observing the extensive and snowy plain close to the sea, far off to the west and to the south, and exclaimed, "Oh! The drawing!" And he fell flat on the terrace floor, losing consciousness, finally forever, in the midst of an immense pine forest that stretched as far as the eye could see, where the silence was only overshadowed by the great oblivion.

VINCENT VAN GOGH

(1856–1890)

Vincent van Gogh was a Dutch painter considered one of the great masters of late nineteenth-century avant-garde. His works reflected a very particular appreciation of nature based on the intensity of colors and the distortion of the images. Although he only painted during the last ten years of his life, his oeuvre was very extensive, comprising around 900 paintings and 1,200 drawings scattered over the most important museums around the world.

His life was short but very intense. He left his native Holland and went to England and then Belgium until finally settling in France, where he did almost all his work. He was unfortunate in matters of love and, despite his genius and having rubbed shoulders with other masters of the late nineteenth-century avant-garde, was always misunderstood perhaps because of his low tolerance to frustration and the behavior caused by bad habits like the consumption of absinthe, very common in the time, and many other circumstances. He fared better when he was alone. In solitude, he honed his skills in the crucible of feverish creativity. His brother, the art dealer Theo van Gogh, was his protector and the person who always had unflinching faith in his talent in spite of having sold only one of his painting during the master's lifetime.

The Dutch master of color of the nineteenth century spent his last moments of agony with Theo. Little was known of what was spoken between them, but they certainly talked. Maybe they spoke a little about their childhood in distant Zundert amid a silent environment or any other topic of mutual interest—subject matters in his work, his final wish, his testament. Hard to know.

Portrait of Dr. Gachet (first version) was acquired by an eccentric Japanese businessman for $82.5 million. After his death, it was apparently sold to an Australian fund manager who, because of financial difficulties, sold it to someone whose identity had not been disclosed. Currently, its whereabouts were unknown. The second version of the portrait was in the Musée d'Orsay in Paris.

Sing like no one's listening, love like you've never been hurt, dance like nobody's watching, and live like its heaven on earth.

—Mark Twain

Not all those who wander are lost.

—J. R .R. Tolkien

ESSAY OF A PORTRAIT

1

"The first portrait is definitely lost. They know very well he painted two portraits of this man. I've told you already. One is in France, and the second—who knows where the second one is? Perhaps in Australia. Only God and the owner know."

"But, Professor, in the first place, why did he paint two portraits of the same person?"

"Please. We've talked about it before. He used to paint the same person several times. Remember that sitters don't work for free, never had done it. Only his friends posed for him, willingly and with no money involved. To thank them, he gave them a painting. It was not something necessarily agreed upon beforehand, but he did it. He used to send the other version or versions of a portrait to Theo in Paris."

"Professor, when you say lost, don't you mean . . . destroyed? What if the Japanese kept his promise and destroyed the painting?"

"No, no, no, I don't think he was so foolish. He needed a lot of money, and selling that painting, he could have paid off some of his enormous debts. Rather, it would be wise to think of something murky—tax evasion, dealings with the Mafia, money laundering, art black market. You pick one. Who knows?""It's a shame. Both portraits would look wonderful hanging on that wall."

"That's right. In a perfect world, they should be together."

"I can imagine where that painting might be, Professor—in some dingy warehouse, the owner waiting for the right time to raise the price through the roof and into the clouds. And perhaps that warehouse belongs to some organization whose aim is to profit grossly. Don't you think?"

2

The ineffable landscape fell under his gaze as a colorful and intangible scene hidden behind a curtain that suddenly dropped. Overwhelmed by sensations, he depicted it as best he can and painted it, discovering with no little perplexity that he was able to imitate nature but in his own way, just as he saw it. So begun a career in solitude during his last ten years, unstoppable and inexhaustible. No one had had such a prolific career in such a short time—an outpouring of instinct and virtues, even to him, who only thought, at the end of the day, he painted because he wanted to realize his vision of nature, not suspecting the enormous influence he would have and that his originality would give meaning to an entire period.

In his wandering palette, the vivid colors flowed like waterfalls in high relief and coherent contrasts, the brushstrokes always fresh. He knew the hard truths of life; he would live with them eternally. Pain, passion, remoteness, and above all loneliness would accompany him on the rough road; but at the same time, he would harvest a magnificent crop on that soil. His paintings, each one an agonizing and picturesque birth, revealed a clean, innocent, and transformed inner self as a concentrated product of his whole being; but even so, he did not mind getting rid of them. He did so as if shooting an arrow into a vacuum, not waiting for it to return and only seeing its reflection as it flew away.

3

"Lean a little more, Doctor . . . more. That's okay. Make a fist . . . rest your head on it. Good, and your hand on the table preferably. That way, you'll rest it."

"You pay a lot of attention to the details. I like that. You are a great artist."

"Try not talking too much, Doctor. The face, please—I want it sad . . . thoughtful . . . like that."

"It's not going to be difficult. You know what I will think about, eh? Oh."

"That's better. This torture will not last long. You'll see. Be patient, Doctor."

"I'm glad to be here, getting a portrait done and in my own home. You know I wanted it from the day you arrived."

"Doctor, the face, please. Keep it sad. Yes . . . don't forget it."

"Sorry, I'm excited. I know it will be wonderful." "Don't touch the branch . . . that's better. Good. A little longer, and that's it."

"Oh! Astonishing! I knew it . . . I knew it. You must make a copy for yourself. It is a major work."

4

His pursuit of love was always frustrating as if trying to take a train repeatedly and, when getting to the station, finding out it had parted a minute ago. One, two, three times was love, like a horrendous ghost leaving a mark on his soul. He was eager to be normal as it were—to have a family, children, work—but good fortune vanished long before uttering his name. Only in art could he snatch from life the gift of genius—forcibly; with contempt, hunger, and remoteness; and without the recognition of his contemporaries eager for sensationalism. That was why he didn't care for honors. All that was rubbish. He wanted to work and work, discover the wonders behind ordinary objects—a chair, a pair of shoes, a bridge, people doing their daily work—in other words, reality as he saw it, nothing more.

Despite everything, his life was not only filled with ochre. He had his dear brother, full of hope and foresight, a visionary tempered by past victories, the bearer of all the things Vincent was missing, a light along his narrow and short path, the indefatigable depositary of his masterpieces tossed into oblivion by his contemporaries, blood of his blood, a kindred spirit until death. Without him, nothing would have made sense. Theo was his fountain and sea. He didn't understand him, or maybe he did. It didn't matter because he loved him and would never forsake him. Vincent always would be his beloved.

5

"Here's your tea, sir. Is the child better?"

"Yes, Mademoiselle. The worst is over. Thank God and Dr. Clearmont."

"Such a test! Poor dear, so little. I am so glad for you and Mrs. Johanna."

"Thanks, Mademoiselle. Open the windows, please. Oh, and bring my correspondence if you would be so kind. Today will be a horribly hot day, don't you think, Mademoiselle?"

"Oh yes, sir, it's a boiling summer indeed. Here you are. Only this came in."

"Thank you. Put it there, on the desk."

"Sir, it's a telegram from Auvergne . . . from the doctor."

"Yes? It is from yesterday . . . nooo! Oh god! My brother has shot himself in the chest! It can't be possible! I'm leaving right away, Mademoiselle. Tell Johanna. I will not return today. Lord, this can't be true!"

6

Portraying life with an inexhaustible color palette, sad and joyous; translating his internal torments into them as if it were a daily exercise in any given sunset or morning; pointing to an indolent but beautiful south; discovering the bright yellow in a random vase full of sunflowers and right there deciding to paint or die; feeling strangely proud of his creation; in the end moving on with life . . . or not—everything would always depend on the circumstances of a single moment, the incomprehensible contingencies of existence, always there, just around the corner.

The idea of taking his own life was always present, hovering on imprecise spirals over his head full of failed aspirations. He was facing the horizon sometimes or looking at a complacent cypress or the village park or the multicolored clouds at dusk, but wherever he was, he looked forward to finishing a painting, like that last afternoon in the middle of a wheat field, the sky crisscrossed by vagrant ravens. He saw his fate clearly in his last abode in Auvergne, there in the field while looking up at the lofty heavens, surprised by foreboding black clouds. He would never escape from those clouds, present since the distant past. He thought of going to France; he would break away from them forever, but it was not so. They followed him mercilessly, catching up with him in that desolate field where he realized that creative inspiration had abandoned him, or at least he thought it had.

7

"Does it hurt, brother?"

"No. I don't feel anything."

"Why don't you rest for a while? I will stay by your side, I promise."

"No, please. Don't leave me. Give me a cigarette."

"You must not smoke, Vincent."

"Give me a cigarette, Theo, please."

"Okay, brother."

"Do you remember how our life in the house was like? Tell me about that. We almost never talk about it."

"I always remember how you used to take me by the hand . . . take care of me. You taught me to appreciate nature, and . . . do you remember our pact?"

"Yes, I remember it. Thank you."

"You're my brother . . . part of me. If you go—""I'm not going anywhere, brother. I'll always be with you. Don't be sad. I am not sad now."

8

Time did not betray him. Art poked its curious and fertile head in his creation and uncovered the desperate and great genius hidden in every trace of color and his brush, like a magic wand exalting simple realities and twists of life, a god of that existence hidden behind the shadows of seemingly insignificant everyday events, a masterful distortion populated with life and meaning.

He turned the bewilderment of his inner self into art, and over time, it has been appreciated by people—a work created with tears, blood, loneliness, and oil paint mixed in the laboratory of a genius only understood by his brother, capable of carrying on his shoulders an untimely disappeared world and happy of his prowess; he would have carried it until the end. Yes, a drop of blood from the chest was enough to reveal to the world the artwork of a real human being—a gift in the eyes of posterity.

9

"Isn't it beautiful? Definitely worth an inconceivable fortune. And since it has been kept hidden all these years, the value has increased even more."

"Sir, I made the estimates, and our data shows that as many as twenty families from where you know . . . could buy it." "Good." "And I must tell you, sir, that some of them have shown—to use the right word—excessive interest in acquiring the portrait of the legendary doctor, and . . . why deny it, sir? It will go to the highest bidder, so to speak. We need a lot of money."

"I totally agree. It's only a matter of time and of pulling some strings."

"I think so too, sir. Oh, your car has arrived already. Sign the authorizations, please. I will see you at the congress in a while. And come back to put the painting in the vault. We wouldn't mind if it stayed there for the next ten years. But . . . we'll see."

ROBERT JAMES FISCHER

(1943–2008)

He was better known as Bobby Fischer. According to many experts, he was considered the best chess player in history. He learned to play the game at the age of six and from there on did not stop playing obsessively until becoming the world champion in 1972. It must be pointed out that that championship was considered the match of the century because of its inevitable political implications, a battle between the Western bloc and the Eastern bloc, where the latter had dominated the scene since 1948. Another important component of this match was how Bobby Fischer's controversial personality was more noticeable and where he finally agreed to play when pressured by the U.S. government.

The chess world was taken by storm by his triumph and influenced positively the perception the Western bloc had of the game of chess. Dethroning the Russians in the middle of the Cold War, Fischer proved to be a genius, and his victory represented a milestone in modern history. After reaching the top, he quit playing professionally without apparent reason and disappeared from public view.

He reappeared after twenty years as a completely unrecognizable and resentful character. Defying the United States government by playing a friendly match against Boris Spassky in a country vetoed by the UN for a large sum, he won once again the world title held by Spassky in 1972. From then on, he became a pariah and moved from one country to the next, fleeing from his homeland and, in a sense, from everything he had once been. After spending eight months under arrest in Japan, he was rescued by the government of Iceland, where he was granted citizenship. Finally, he died in complete oblivion, away from the glory he had achieved.

Let your plans be dark and impenetrable as night, and when you move, fall like a thunderbolt.

—Sun Tzu

If you know the enemy and know yourself, you need not fear the result of a thousand battles.

—Sun Tzu

IN THE RIVERBED OF OBLIVION

1

"What do you see from this point on the road?"

"Well, I see a nice but solitary landscape next to the icy sea and a small church. Beyond it, I can see those green hillocks and far off in the distance a huge valley, mountains, ice-covered peaks, which if I'm not mistaken will be active volcanoes someday, God forbid. And even farther away, there's something similar to a lake."

"Now look toward the church. Haven't you noticed? It's Laugardalur's church, yes, where his grave is. Apparently, you didn't recognize it at first glance."

"Oh, you fooled me. I didn't want to get to know him this way. You are cruel."

2

He would conclude that life was but a complex game against the world, from that remote beginning when, as a child, he discovered the game, and the only possible door would open before him not as a prodigy, more like someone obsessed going down a fast-paced and labyrinthine path toward a goal marked by impossible battles packed with lucid variations.

His childhood ended one day, beating random opponents, applying fine reasoning on the inert squares populated by sagacious warriors. Only he would have that meteoric start, beardless and arrogant with deep eyes and an indifferent gaze toward the world. He would succumb on the board only a handful of times, showing great frustration and pain. Only he would dominate the board of his own life.

3

"I spent years looking for him, my friend, as if I were the only person who did such a thing."

"Don't get discouraged, Claudia. You always find what you're looking for. I know you well."

"Yes, but he disappeared . . . after becoming the number one, as high as he could possibly go, just vanished."

"I understand your frustration."

"Listen, I tried to follow in his footsteps. You know how I idolized him. I started very early in life to play that endless game, just like him. And he was—or rather, he is a sort of guru to me. Besides, no matter how much I study his games, its mechanics elude me, especially his middle game, so malevolent and forceful, not to mention his endgame. Ah! I had to find him someday."

"What a shame he is, and he isn't here with you in this instant."

"It's better this way, and I'll tell you why."

"I'm more than ready to listen."

"I just need a moment to appreciate him in his final resting place. May I?"

"Sure, dear. He is all yours."

4

"Good afternoon, Sebastian. This is an unprecedented battle for the title in the annals of this prestigious competition. I'm sorry for you, but the facts are clear, don't you think?"

"There is no doubt. This has been the match of the century. Gone are the classic clashes between Russians—Botvinnik, my favorite; Tal; Petrosian; and others. I have a lot of sympathy for them, but I wouldn't like to be in their shoes right now."

"No . . . nooo. What this young man from Brooklyn has brought to those sixty-four squares is the product of genius, and by himself, he has won a spot as the contender for the crown, and what a way to do it, going to war on the board against the mighty Soviet Union, invincible since 1948."

"Admirable, admirable, the work of a titan, although he is a bratty kid that well deserves a reprimand. But with your permission, Gabriel, it's time to introduce our special guest, GM T. J. Johnson, who's come from Britain to help us analyze today's game.

"Good afternoon, Grand Master Johnson."

"Good afternoon, ladies and gentlemen. Thanks for having me. It's a great honor for me to join you for game 21, which—as you mentioned, Sebastian—could well be the last one. I will try to analyze the moves from my humble perception, but before that, I'm willing to answer any questions you may have concerning these two great players."

"We thank the grand master for his wise comments. Without further ado, let's begin with a brief rundown of their careers. Why not to call them what they are? Warriors, both representing a respective corner of the civilized world, the Western bloc and the Eastern bloc."

"Indeed, Gabriel. This is literally a war between the two great powers that govern the world, and the battlefield is a board with sixty-four squares and thirty-two pieces. Without further delay, I'd like to begin with the champion, representing the Soviet bloc but who strangely is not a member of the Communist Party as many of you may know, a ferocious player with a very personal style, unbeatable until the beginning of this match, very self-confident, although some believe he has neglected the theory, and that deficiency may have reflected in the games he's lost in this match up to this point. We have all witnessed his power of penetration in the last ten encounters, where he has forced the opponent to draw most of the games. And he showed what a gentleman he is when, at the end of the magnificent sixth game, to everyone's surprise, he stood up along with the audience and applauded the American in a gesture of humility. Fischer was overwhelmed by that expression."

"By the way, Grand Master, we heard that when Fischer was leaving, he commented, 'You saw what that man did. He's a real gentleman.'"

"Yes, Gabriel. It was an absolutely unexpected comment, coming from someone who usually rants against the Russian delegation."

"Don't forget, gentlemen, that the champion showed more than finesse on the inaugural day and during the first three official games. He has nerves of steel and is a champion not only on the board but also in diplomacy with a great spirit of competition, unlike the challenger."

"Let's remind our audience that the challenger didn't show up at the championship opening day here in Reykjavík, and his participation was still uncertain until the last minute, when Kissinger himself called him on the phone and basically spurred him to play."

"Yes, the fact that the champion sat patiently, together with the whole world, looking with horror at his opponent's empty chair as if it were a bad joke was embarrassing for everyone but even more so for the United States itself. That's why I think that phone call wasn't that extraordinary."

"And his complaints afterward about the prize being insufficient. What a nerve!"

"We know how you feel, Sebastian. It was very unpleasant. But, my friends, everyone at this point in the chess world knows how unpredictable the American is. The information has filtered that the champion has nicknamed him 'the leader of the Union' and rightly so."

"Yes, that's funny. What humility and wisdom the champion shows. For good reason, he is the undisputed holder of the title—until this match, of course—and a champion at the board and in life."

"I totally agree with Sebastian. Now let's continue listening to the grand master."

"Thank you. The experts have pointed out that the pressure of the first games definitely shattered the champion's concentration. It may have been counterproductive to have won the first game by forfeit, and that's not surprising since the champion is so motivated by a spirit of competition, and that might've put an unduly pressure on him. Despite having won the second game, the apparently puerile complaints of the candidate having to do with 'mysterious noises' in and around the stage where the games are taking place supposedly affected his concentration, and he requested that the match be moved to a more enclosed area and without cameras. This definitely upset the champion. I don't have the slightest doubt about it."

"Grand Master, we've received information that the Russian authorities have asked the champion not to accept the change of rules proposed by Fischer."

"But Spassky, showing his good sportsmanship, for better or for worse, ended up accepting. I could notice his disappointment while leaving the game pavilion. Many people believe it was a key psychological move by the contender. I've also been tempted to think so, but as the following games have developed, it's obvious that the battle has mostly been fought on the board. We must be fair and give credit to the young contestant who has been playing with the determination and intensity of a champion himself. It's necessary to emphasize that his position in this remarkable tournament has been won with tooth and nail and after humiliating both the Russian Taimanov and the Danish Larsen. We'd never had a 6–0 win in the candidates' tournament during this century, and the young American has achieved it, plus his victory against the former world champion Petrosian 6½–2½."

"That's correct, Grand Master. We heard that the Russian grand master Taimanov didn't have a very pleasant reception in his native Russia. Maybe he won't continue playing at a highly competitive level, but I understand that he is a gifted pianist."

"Indeed. And as far as we know, Gabriel, there are rumors that the Danish is planning to retire from professional tournaments. It's quite a loss. I would like the Russians to prevail as you know, but I have to give credit where credit is due, and the contender has been playing astounding chess."

"That's nice of you, Sebastian. This man has turned the world of chess upside down. And to think that, at thirteen, he had become the United States champion already. It is no secret that he considers himself to be a disciple of the Russian school. Ironies of life."

"Yeah, what an irony. Destiny often fulfills itself in unsuspected ways."

"That's right, gentlemen. Fate has brought us together in these distant lands, and the Icelandic people have prepared a wonderful setting, and according to the polls, people in the streets were a little disappointed at how the event was going at the beginning. But for the great joy of everyone, the competition has developed at the highest level, thanks to Iceland's splendid effort, and it will set a historical precedent whoever wins."

"We fully agree with you, Grand Master. This has been the best of scenarios, full of emotion and suspense both inside and outside the 'combat zone.' We have all been biting our nails during the last games and for good reason. Sometimes the air could be cut with a knife as the tension between these two superpowers was reflected in the players."

"I am with you, Gabriel. Pure electricity fills the room. It's surprising how the players manage to concentrate in the middle of so much tension."

"Yes, gentlemen. Finals like this can destroy the best-tempered nerves. I confess I've been a victim of the pressure in more than one candidate's tournament. And the champion has to bear the pressure of possibly losing the crown."

"But let's not get ahead of ourselves, gentlemen. The game is about to start. The microphone is all yours, Sebastian."

"Ladies and gentlemen, this is the moment of truth. The challenger only needs a draw to win the event, but the champion must win this game and four others without draws to retain the championship. The players are ready. Let the game begin!"

5

"Listen carefully, my friend, just a bit of a recap. The man had been preparing, without exaggeration, since his early teens to be the world champion. He prepared thoroughly for every clash, in countries near and far, for many years. He played against Americans, French, Germans, Argentineans, Russians and defeated most of them."

"Wait, wait, and that does not make him, in fact, a world champion?"

"No. In this game, the rules are more complicated. In a nutshell, this is how it works. The best professional players in the world compete against each other in a candidate's tournament, and the winner challenges the reigning world champion. This takes place every three years."

"Ah, and he finally got to that point?"

"Of course. Let me explain it once and for all, and don't interrupt me, please. As I told you, he achieved it in a very impressive way. He beat everyone and became the candidate. The world championship was held in Reykjavík, receiving unprecedented press coverage. Up to that point, the Russians had dominated the sport for over fifty years, and the Cold War was at its peak. He, bold and at times even disdainful of the international rules of the game, irreverently proclaimed his own code, so to speak, capricious at first glance. And FIDE officials were about to declare him defeated, without having even begun the first game."

"Really?"

"Don't interrupt me. In short, with his apparently senseless and erratic tactics, he won the psychological battle over his opponent before starting the match. Well, they say wars can be won before starting by using good propaganda. In the end, he beat his rival after twenty-one games, with seven wins, three losses, and eleven draws, that way ending the Russian hegemony. But if I told you this was just the beginning of another race, rougher and more difficult to win and which would mark the absolute end of his brilliance, would you believe it?"

6

"Slow down, Mark. Look to your right, at two o'clock. See?"

"Jamal, Call Central. I think we've got a 10-66."

"This must be the man. Look at him. Looks as if he's wearing a costume, a horrible one by the way. He gotta be the one we are looking for."

"Central . . . here, Patrol 56. Mark Pendleton speaking. Got a 10-66. We heading down Sunset Boulevard South."

"Central station here. Do you need reinforcements?"

"I don't think so, but we'll let you know."

"Look, Jamal. He still hasn't noticed our presence."

"Yes, striding along as if possessed. Speed up a little. I don't wanna give him any chance to escape."

"Switch on the siren to see if he notices us. Park there, a little ahead of him, to see how he reacts."

"Sir! Sir! Stop, please."

"You're talking to me, Officer?"

"Yes, sir, I am talking to you. Stop, please."

"I can't. I'm in a hurry."

"Jamal, be alert and ask for reinforcements. The man definitely looks suspicious. For the second time, sir, stop. It's an order." "An order? And what have I done? Have I broken any law? Can't I walk freely on the street?"

"All right, Pendleton, let's get off the car."

"Sir, cooperate, and everything will be okay. Stay to the side of the patrol car. Your identification, please, and put your hands where I can see them. Do not make any sudden movements."

"I repeat, Official, I haven't done anything. My name is Robert James Fischer."

"Oh yeah? Show us your identification, please. I will not repeat it."

"Here it is. Don't you know who I am?"

"Yes. You already said it, Robert James Fischer. We aren't deaf."

"But you don't recognize me? Well, I guess not. I am the world chess champion."

"Yeah, right. And I am Kareem Abdul-Jabbar. In any case, Mr. Fischer, you have to come with us. We'll sort things out at the station."

"No, no, I refuse." "Don't make matters worse, Mr. James."

"I've done nothing wrong, Officer, and also, I'm in a hurry."

"It's just routine, Mr. James. We are not asking you. It's an order. Please understand. Jamal, proceed."

"Come on, hands behind your back. Things will be easier if you cooperate. Good. Watch your head."

"This is an injustice. You have no idea who you're dealing with. I will sue you. You can count on that."

"Sir, you have the right to remain silent. Anything you say can and will be used against you in a court of law. You have a right to an attorney. If you cannot afford an attorney, one will be appointed for you."

"Shut up! In your dreams, sons of bitches! You're minions of the Russians. They sent you. They've been after me for years, but they will pay for this!"

"Let's go, Pendleton. Don't listen to him anymore."

7

"Hey, Bobby. Where the hell have you been? Everybody is looking for you."

"Shhh. Don't say my name. Call me James. Oh yeah? They are you looking for me? Do you know who they are?"

"Everyone, Bob—sorry, James. But rest assured, my friend, with that look, no one will recognize you, with that long beard. You haven't shaved in years. Come on, let's go to my house. I'll give you some clothes if you want, and you can take a shower."

"Don't be silly. Wanna know who is looking for me? The Russians. I humiliated them. They never have forgiven me. And everyone is their accomplice. Do you know what they did to Mark and Boris? Imagine what they would do to me."

"You mean Spassky and Taimanov?"

"Who else?""My friend, you are exaggerating. That's history. You beat them in good faith. Also, you're here, where they have no influence."

"That's what you think? You really think so? The Russian motherland's arm is long. You know it. You've been there. On the other hand, if you only knew what they've done to me here, where you claim I am protected."

"James, can't you walk more slowly? I'm panting. I'm not trained to stride around as fast as you."

"I feel sorry, but we can't take the subway or any other public means of transportation at the moment."

"Oh gosh. Luckily, my house is not that far from here."

"Try to keep up my pace, please. We're almost there."

"Yes, I'm losing my breath. You have me intrigued, you know. What did they do to you?"

"They got me arrested . . . for no reason. They threw me into a miserable dungeon for forty-eight long hours and didn't give me any food. Those bastards! Of course, if they had given me some, I wouldn't have eaten it anyway. I'd probably be dead by now."

"And why would they do that to you, Bobby? It's okay, nobody can listen to us here."

"Yes, they can hear us. Goddamn it, you don't understand what the stakes are here.""It's okay, James. Look, let's go into the house. What do you want to do? Would you like something to eat?"

"I need money. I have to make some calls. My mother's pension is not enough for me. Can I use your phone? Oh, and I need a Coca-Cola if possible."

"Yes, you can also take a shower and change your clothes. Would you like a drink instead?"

"None of that is necessary. I only want a Coca-Cola."

"Of course. And I insist. I'll find you a more presentable jacket at least, and if you want to shave off or trim your beard, the bathroom is in the corridor."

"No, no. Are you crazy? My appearance is part of my protection, although those damn cops took me for a bank robber. That's why they arrested me. I will sue them. I'll show them they can't mess with me."

8

"Now you are the one that surprises me. It's hard for me to believe that from such an important triumph could come out a defeat like the one you're talking about."

"Literally, as you hear it. After that triumph, which wasn't only his but of all the West against the Soviet bloc, eventually, our man vanished from the face of the earth.""But . . . that's impossible. No one famous and still alive can disappear from the face of the earth."

"Well, he did. Just a handful of people saw him in twenty years. He was totally unrecognizable, looked way older than he really was, and worse of all was a little crazy and on one occasion was mistaken for a bank robber."

"Crazy. Yes, I believe you. You have to be a bit nuts to jump into the void from such heights, but mistaken for a bank robber? That's outrageous."

9

The board lay suspended before the world, enemy glances converging at a point far north in a neutral land, at the mercy of the competitors who, absorbed in their own universe, denied others' existence. It was a Machiavellian strategy, audaciously elaborated as if it were a web woven in the night; nevertheless, the plot was unnecessary. Sufficient talent and fortune accompanied him in the battle. His genius was demonstrated in the game. What turned out to be inexplicable was his rejection of a welcome in the style of

Lindbergh in the wide boulevards of the Big Apple, his homeland. His contempt for the joy his fellow men felt for his prowess would be a bad omen. Since then, he would become a hermit under his own influence, buried under the rubble of an absolute and long interwoven triumph—oblivion.

10

"Yes, gentlemen, after seven consecutive draws, this last game has been a crucial setback for the champion."

"That's true, Sebastian. Every draw is a setback for him."

"What do you think, Grand Master?"

"No doubt, Gabriel, that the champion is losing ground more rapidly despite the fact that, in the last games, he's played at the usual level. Even so, he hasn't been able to break the challenger's defenses whose technique has marked the rhythm of the game and has not made it easy for the champion."

"Do you think that is part of the American's strategy? Taking a less offensive approach and waiting for more convoluted and bizarre endgames?"

"I'm afraid that's not the only factor, Gabriel—long hours of study in quasi confinement. Rumor has it that, in his long preparation for this match, he analyzed each and every one of the champion's games by himself—admirable, in my opinion."

"I'm not sure about that, Gabriel." "Don't underestimate that assessment, Sebastian. However, colleagues, I wouldn't like to be part of the Russian delegation right now nor be walking in the champion's shoes. But despite the mishaps, he has shown class and an excellent spirit of competition."

"Yes, after returning to his usual pace halfway through the match, it's undeniable that in the first few games the challenger's psychological tricks affected his concentration."

"From a grand master's perspective, I've seen the development of every game move after move and must say the level of these two contenders is sky high. In them, we see the pinnacle of excellence achieved in this game science, except in the first game, where Fischer lost. And in my view, it must've been a draw, especially for a player of his stature."

"That defeat didn't affect him in the least. The kid has prepared well, although that's not saying much since he has been preparing for this match since he was seven years old, so to speak. That is important to emphasize."

"Yes, and let's not forget the challenger's decisions when he has refused to take part in important international tournaments throughout his career, not taking advantage of those opportunities, claiming they were not profitable enough."

"I agree, Grand Master. And with no real valid reason, he has declined his participation in prequalifying tournaments, first in Amsterdam and then his premature withdrawal in Tunisia."

"He is a very capricious young man, Grand Master. That's a reason why he hasn't moved forward as he should have. Thank god. If he had been less arrogant, he would've faced the Russians at this level a decade ago. Although with his current strength in the game, we could see these results coming down the pike eventually."

"Precisely because of that, gentlemen, I have a theory about it. I dare say that, deep down, money doesn't rouse him as much as it seems. Rather, he is motivated by certain internal conflicts that intermittently have kept him away from major competitions, perhaps an irrational sense of insecurity about his preparation or another darker reason. Remember the protests against the Russians and how he managed to change the rules of the game to the detriment of his opponents, who in one way or another used to play as a team. That has had its repercussions."

"The truth is that he is a controversial character, don't you think, Sebastian?"

"I do, and the rest of humanity thinks so too, Gabriel. This American is made of a material unknown even to his own compatriots."

"Maybe the absence of a father figure throughout his life and an unusual mother, to say the least, have caused in him a natural wariness. As the saying goes, 'There are people born to wreak havoc.' I don't doubt this person might be one of them."

"Probably so, Grand Master. But we must give to Caesar what is Caesar's and to God what is God's. This young man is a wizard on the board. Nobody denies it, and in the last few weeks, he has exceeded everybody's expectations in terms of performance and, as though unwittingly, has disarticulated not only the champion's offensive but also the entire Soviet Union's, delighting the American people in the process."

"A shame for Russia. First his victory, 6–0, versus Taimanov and then 6½–2½ against Petrosian."

"A milestone. Besides, he obliterated Larsen with a result of 6–0. There had been no such feat in the history of chess."

"Some are already talking about the Fischer's syndrome, something unacceptable to the great Russian machinery but irrefutable nonetheless. Others are calling him the new Einstein. However, we don't know what his opinion is about all these comments. I can imagine that his level of concentration doesn't allow him to stop and think about those details. It's exactly where he wanted to be—on top of the world."

"You can say that again. Also, consider how the games have been unfolding, especially taking into account several no less important details, such as the immense media coverage, even surpassing that of FIFA World Cup. Isn't that right, Sebastian?"

"Absolutely. And the most significant part of all this—what is at stake, meaning which of the two great world powers will prevail in this miniature war within the Cold War? It is a little frightening but . . . comforting at the same time to know that this war is being fought on a chessboard, where for decades the Russians have dominated."

"Well, Gabriel, Sebastian, game 21 is about to start. Will it be the last? Let's see. Fischer has the black pieces, and to my surprise, he's chosen the Sicilian defense on this occasion. Needless to say, he's very skillful with this opening, which involves an aggressive strategy."

"Yes, something unusual at this point since the champion is the one who needs to play more aggressively. But look, he has advanced a pawn. What does that mean, Grand Master?"

"It can only suggest that the American wants a close game. He has thought it through, I'm sure. Maybe he's looking for another draw. From here on, everything will be more unpredictable. He is excellent dealing with uncertainties. It represents an apparent disadvantage for him, but he's just throwing the champion off balance, trying to dismantle any scrupulously planned attack by the champion."

"Oh. Grand Master, we are on move 40, and nothing is clear yet. They'll take a break now. The Russian delegation has left, but before going, the champion has written his next move in a piece of paper and put it in an envelope."

"That's right, Gabriel. We're about to reach the decisive moment of the championship. Hold your breaths until tomorrow, folks. Will we have a new champion?"

"The phone lines are congested. We are receiving reports from all over the world."

"Yes, Sebastian. In America, they are already celebrating. And here in the streets of Reykjavík, there's an air of festivity. We've got reports that people have gone out on the streets to wait for the result. But we will have to wait until tomorrow. Thanks, Grand Master, for being here, sharing with us your analysis and the excitement we've experienced in the last few weeks."

"Thank you, esteemed colleagues. Tomorrow is the big day. And I predict that if the game turns out to be a draw, the champion will not show up. It would be an unbearable pressure for him if he has actually lost in front of the whole world."

11

"You say only a handful of people knew about him. And didn't they tell anyone else of his whereabouts?"

"No. Those people were not connected to each other. He wandered and wandered through the United States, and no one recognized him. He looked like a hobo."

"I can't believe it." "But . . . if I tell you it'd have been better for him to continue living that way, would you believe it?"

"Let's see. Explain yourself better. It seems you are exaggerating."

"When he came back from his self-imposed exile, after decades lost in his own land and friends, family, associations, private and public institutions, the relentless media, and others searching for him, he made a big mistake by agreeing to play in a country banned by the UN . . . for money . . . a lot of money. You have no idea. He played against the man he had defeated masterfully and dramatically, that one Russian, and beat him again. The Russian claimed Fischer was still in great shape. Bobby's bravado cost him his citizenship. The American authorities took away his passport."

"What a pity! A disgrace!"

"You're alarmed, and no wonder. That's how we, his followers, reacted back then, saddened and alarmed."

"I can imagine the rest."

"He became an outlaw, paranoid, and elusive, drifting furtively in and out of some countries of the Socialist bloc, ending up in the Philippines, where he supposedly procreated a daughter. It was necessary to wait until his death to know if it was really his—you know, matters of inheritance."

"A daughter! It already seemed strange to me, but . . . was she really?"

"You have to wait until the end of the story."

"I guess I have no other choice."

"Then he went to Japan, after a woman, it seems. He came and went as he pleased, with no one knowing his true identity. His appearance was completely different from that when he became famous. It took a little scandal at an airport for him to be finally recognized, and you can't imagine the hoopla."

"Yeah, like any celebrity going incognito, the paparazzi and everything else."

"No, not at all. He was a fallen star, yes, but it has been his own choice to go away. The issue here was the extradition to the United States."

"Extradition?" "Of course. Remember, he was considered an outlaw by the American authorities. He spent many months detained in Japan, awaiting imminent extradition."

"And . . . finally, they sent him back to his country?"

"No, the Icelanders, by virtue of the past glory, finally rescued him. He was granted citizenship. Ah, and by the way, it was determined by DNA testing that the girl wasn't his daughter."

12

"Oh, child. The way you found me is worthy of admiration."

"Well, when I put my mind to something, I usually get it. Since you evaporated from the face of the earth, I've been looking for you, and this is the result."

"It seems you got into my head . . . and I don't know how the hell you did it. You deserved all the credit. That ad in the newspaper was outstanding."

"Was it? I got a little help, you know, and it was worth it because here we are together. If you weren't in front of me, I wouldn't believe it."

"Well, here I am. This is me and not me. I've had to hide from my enemies all these years and been roaming here and there. You can't imagine the vicissitudes I've gone through so they wouldn't recognize me. It's as if I kept playing chess with the world. Besides, I preferred to live in a very precarious situation as long as the Russians couldn't find me. They haven't forgiven me yet."

"They haven't forgiven you? I think you exaggerate, Mr. Paranoid."

"Girl, don't talk to me like that. You don't know those people. They are everywhere. They would've been able to retrace my steps through my mother, but I didn't allow it. Not even she knows my whereabouts."

"Hmm, convince me."

"You are naive. They couldn't stand their defeat, which was fair, and everybody saw it. You see how they treated their people. Those whom I defeated unfortunately have been relegated to oblivion. Also, I have confidential information that says they are looking for me, and I don't think for one second their intentions are good."

"Please. Of course, they are looking for you. We all are looking for you—to admire you, to get to know you, to learn from you. To me, you are officially unbeatable and, despite everything, still the world champion, even though you declined to defend the title. Absolutely no one can claim having defeated you."

"Yes. For that and other reasons, I decided to become invisible and suffer hunger and all kinds of deprivation instead of endorsing mediocre products and putting myself in a position where they could catch me."

"From what you tell me, I understand you're having financial difficulties. And to be honest, you don't look good."

"Thanks for the compliment. But I already told you this is the best disguise, and the proof is that nobody recognizes me. And yes, my financial situation is not good, and that worries me."

"I'm sorry to tell you, but it shows."

"But . . . not long ago, I published a pamphlet about how badly the police treated me here in California. Would you believe those bastards took me for a bank robber? To my surprise, it sold some copies but not enough."

"And don't you think you have the potential to make all the money you want?"

"Yes, yes, I've received offers to give interviews, but I've asked for enormous amounts of money so they wouldn't bother me again."

"Oh, I didn't know that. And . . . wouldn't you like to earn a lot of money doing what you're good at? The best by the way."

"What do you mean?"

"To go back to professional chess. I know how. I have the best contact. My father works for that organization I told you about in my letters, and he'd be pleased to help you."

"I see. Go ahead."

"He knows a lot of wealthy people who would die to bring you back to the arena. I'll write to him, and he will definitely get you a good contract so you can play again."

"I'm going to think it over, but if possible, I'd like to play against someone of my level."

"Are we thinking about the same person?"

"If he agrees to play, I would go for it in the blink of an eye as long as the organizers comply with my conditions. FIDE doesn't pay much, and I won't play for peanuts."

"I don't think it'd be hard. Everyone is eager to see you play again. And if the match is against him, people would go above and beyond to raise a good sum. In fact, my father has told me he knows people willing to pay anything to put together a new match of the titans twenty years later."

"I'm glad you found me. You're a very sweet and smart girl and had the guts to come to see me."

"You flatter me. See? It was worth crossing half the world to find you."

"I appreciate that, Zita. You have a strong will, and I liked you since I received your encrypted letter. That was a real feat coming from someone so young."

"Thanks, Bobby, for letting me find you."

13

On the horizon of his life, an endless formation of stormy clouds awaited him. Turning away from glory had always had a high price—death in life. His erratic steps buried him incessantly. He fled from the flattering and interested glances and believed them to be calculating and perverse, like poisoned food for the warrior of a thousand battles.

He didn't know it for sure yet, but he felt it; something broke inside him. Perhaps the gear of his great machinery had suffered a dislocation, exhausted by the recent journey on a perilous road full of rugged mountains and tortuous paths, having crossed them all with cunning and determination without a minute's hesitation, to the detriment of all the rest.

He thought and felt he was playing against the world and hid as in a game full of risky strategies and false moves that turned into complex circumlocutions to evade his executioners, who turned out to be his victims. He revealed his game at last and, in doing so, became sullen and coarse, pushing everything aside, even his own roots. He fled with the false belief that distances existed, that everything was at the reach of the persecutor of a thousand eyes and hands. You didn't play against Big Brother without losing. So with a good dose of indulgence, inflamed by past glories, the already hunted prey was released, ending his comings and goings sheltered in a cold corner of the world—on the banks of the endless river of oblivion, where he was prematurely returned to Earth.

14

"Ladies and gentlemen, listeners around the world, we have witnessed one of the greatest feats achieved in any sport. This young American, of humble origins and against all odds, has achieved what the most powerful army on the planet could not accomplish—defeating the Russian machinery—something unprecedented in the history of chess championships, which are held three years ago."

"That's right, Gabriel. And for humanity's sake, this encounter has ended in this sublime way and not in another less benign. This young man from Brooklyn has defeated the Russians by his own means, in a very exciting tournament with a shocking and unpredictable start. It had never happened before. What a way to do it! Give us your opinion, Grand Master. What's your take on this match, which apparently has marked a before and after in the history of chess?"

"I agree, gentlemen. Let's recap the most important moments, first that uncertain beginning, where the challenger's capricious personality prevailed. That's not entirely surprising because we've gotten used to his antics during his last decade, appearing in important tournaments. The question remains whether the psychological game at the beginning was the preamble of an elaborated strategy as some critics have pointed out. In my opinion, the opposite was demonstrated as the games developed. There is no room for doubt here. It was a battle of giants, where the best player won."

"Don't you think, Grand Master, that the dislocation in the Russian champion's concentration played an important role in boosting the challenger's confidence?"

"That's likely, Sebastian, but we all saw how the champion recovered his footing and played at his accustomed level in most of the games. But as in boxing, this was a battle of endurance, where the strategy and genius of the challenger triumphed, only allowing a few losses, applying his long and solitary hours of training. Apparently, we'll have Bobby for a long time. Don't you think?"

"And for good reason, Grand Master. Are you of the same opinion, Sebastian?"

"I am. Now the new champion has the arduous task of defending his title, and we all know that his Achilles' heel is not exactly at the chessboard. But let's find out what the Grand Master's perspective is on the new champion's future."

"Now begins a new and equally uncertain phase for him. Let's not forget he feels an enormous pressure in these types of competitions, which could affect his performance. Therefore, I would say his future is inevitably unclear and probably will be characterized by controversy."

"However, Grand Master, he is the absolute monarch of chess now. And in your own words, that is what he has always longed for. We assume he'll be received as a hero in America, and that will possibly keep him in the scene for a long time."

"Probably. They will welcome him as he deserves and, thanks to his great accomplishment, take chess to many, many homes."

"Correct, Grand Master. Sales of chess sets have skyrocketed not only in the USA but also throughout the West."

"He has earned the title of 'hero of the West' and will always be remembered."

"Allow me only a few more words, dear friends. While it's true that the achievements of this young American are a milestone in any sport, let's not forget that the personalities of many sports heroes can damage that person's sanity and therefore their brilliance, and I think this applies for most of the great geniuses in art and sports and even science. We've seen many towers fall, brought down by mere trifles in their peculiar lives. Psychological pressure is proportional to the personal success achieved in a specific art, including chess. I don't want to be a bird of ill omen, but behind this chess genius, there is a very controversial personality prone to disputes. Come on, he has shown that side many times, and I'm not trying to take credit away from what he's done in this unforgettable championship here in Reykjavík."

"The grand master is right. Our role is to be reporters and analysts of all aspects of the game."

"Not only of what happens on the chessboard but also of situations outside the game as the grand master clarifies. Anyway, our congratulations to the new champion. Cheers!"

"Well, with this last comment, we close our transmission, hoping our audience enjoyed it as much as we did throughout these weeks of tension."

"Thanks, Grand Master, for your analysis and thoughtful comments."

"Thanks for the invitation, and congratulations to the West."

"Congratulations."

"Yes, congratulations."

15

"We are waiting for the prime minister's order."

"Well, let's go. The order has been given. Hurry up, he's already boarding the plane."

"From what I know, we'll need a battalion. This guy might be a handful."

"Okay, go." "Sir, are you Robert James Fischer?"

"Yes. What can I do for you?"

"You have to come with us, sir."

"And why should I do that?"

"Orders, sir."

"And you need so many guards? One is not enough?"

"Sir, come with us, please."

"What if I don't want to?"

"You must. It's for your own good."

"It is better for me to leave your beautiful country, sir. Don't you understand? Are you stupid?"

"As you wish. Guards! Execute the order!"

"Hey, hey! This is an outrage! You can't treat me like this. Animals! I will sue you all, the airline, your government. Don't touch me!" "Okay! Put him down! See, Mr. Fischer? We were going to put you down anyway. You are breaking the law, and the immigration authorities need to ask you some questions."

"I won't answer any of your questions unless a lawyer is present. You have mistreated me. Look at my arms."

"It was your own fault, sir. You will be charged for resisting arrest and attempting to travel without the proper documentation. Your passport has been revoked by the authorities of your country, where you have an arrest warrant."

"Bullshit! That's a lie. This is nothing more than kidnapping. Who do you think you are? You'll have to face my lawyers. You are nothing but servile henchmen at the service of the United States government."

"Sir, anything you say can and will be used against you in a court of law, so in your best interest, you should remain silent."

"No, no, no, I will not be silenced. This is an abuse of power. I need a lawyer!"

"Don't worry, a lawyer will be appointed for you. Keep silent."

"Let's see. Do I have a choice? Tell me! Do I have a choice?"

"Gentlemen, don't argue with him. We will take him to the interrogation room."

"The torture room—that's what you mean, don't you?"

"No, sir, there will be a doctor there."

"Don't forget that I need a lawyer."

"You'll get it."

"You have no idea who you're dealing with. Despite appearances, I am the world chess champion, and you should treat me with respect and not like a beast. This is a plot of the US government and your prime minister, who is just Uncle Sam's puppet, but you'll see.. You'll see."

16

"And turns out you are the one who is surprised now."

"Yes, but I wanted to give you the opportunity to see his grave . . . and experience all this on your own."

"Okay . . . but . . . that story about coming to explore geology, I never believed it anyway."

"Sorry, but I didn't see any other way to get you interested in coming to this place without suspecting. Now I'll leave you alone with him."

"No, wait a second. I confess I feel the need to talk to him as if he were alive, but I want you to stay and listen."

"And what would you say to him?"

"Dear Master Bobby, you were the best chess player in history. Your passage through the world served as an inspiration to many people. You take the best of me with you. Despite not having met you

The Voice and the Fallen

in person, each of your games has given joy to my life, and you taught me a lot through them. They say you were selfish, that you betrayed your country, that your achievements were overshadowed . . . by your contentious personality and gave priority to material gain and not to the spirit of good competition, but . . . to me . . . you were nothing but a human being, a product of your time. You didn't receive the love every child needs in this unpredictable and unjust world. You fought against fate, and maybe that's why you couldn't appreciate those who wanted the best for you. Some would say you received what you deserved—glory and oblivion. Goodbye . . . from the bottom of my heart."

17

"Mr. Fischer, are you comfortable? Do you feel better?"

"No, Gardar. I still feel weak, and it's as if the cold were drilling into my bones."

"I'll stoke the fire."

"Good. Would you be so kind to bring me some tea, please? I don't know where Miyoko is now."

"Yes, Mr. Fischer."

"Gardar?"

"Yes, Master?"

"When are you going to call me Bobby?"

"It's out of respect. You know how much I appreciate you. You're my best friend."

"Call me Bobby then."

"Okay, Bobby. Here is your tea. I feel strange calling you Bobby."

"But you're my friend, and that's how you should call me."

"As you wish."

"Gardar." "Yes, Bobby?"

"I feel like I have little time left. I no longer have the strength to get out of bed."

"You don't have to do it now. That's what Mrs. Miyoko and I are here for, to take care of you."

"Thank you."

"Always at your service, Master—I mean . . . Bobby."

"I already told Miyoko, but I want you to know as well. I don't want many people at my funeral, and please . . . celebrate it in the church cemetery, if it isn't too much to ask."

"Don't talk about that, Bobby. Everything will be done in due time."

"And another thing, Gardar. If someone asks you about me, tell them I was the best chess player that ever existed. Go now. Miyoko is back. Thank you."

"To you, Bobby, I will do so."

SIGMUND FREUD

(1856–1939)

Freud was an Austrian neurologist whose theories about the unconscious and deep psychology became an intellectual staple of the twentieth century. He was known as the founder of psychoanalysis. Of Jewish descent, he spent most of his life in Vienna, where he formed a family, treated all his patients over decades of practice, and wrote numerous books, taking as their basis his experiences with patients, his reflections, and his studies in collaboration with other researchers. He was considered one of the most influential intellectuals of the twentieth century because of the multidisciplinary approach of his research, striving to encompass psychology, anthropology, sociology, human sexuality, art, philosophy, and other fields.

However, despite his attempts to make his methods compatible with the requirements of science, he did not succeed, a situation that, in itself, did not diminish his merits in the eyes of many followers, who consolidated and expanded the school of psychoanalysis after his death.

At the end of his life, besieged by the ravages of palate cancer, he found himself trapped in Nazi-occupied Austria shortly before World War II. He didn't want to leave his beloved Vienna, where he had lived all his life and had harvested the fruits of his long investigations, but there was no other choice; he must leave or else suffer the cruel fate of his entire race—the concentration camps. Finally, he went to London, where he would remain for a year before dying, overwhelmed by the most absolute pessimism about the ruthless reality he had to live in until the end, far from his homeland. He passed away at the beginning of the Second World War, with the blitzkrieg falling over Europe, perhaps believing that the end of civilization was near when the German dictator ascended to power.

There are two ways of spreading light: to be the candle or the mirror that reflects it.

—Edith Wharton

ANGUISH

(THE ROADMAKER)

1

Vienna, 1938

"This is the café. From here, we'll have a better view. Besides, he frequents it."

"As many of his kind."

"So it seems, but that's coming to an end anyway. The old man's days are numbered, don't you think?"

"Yes. His fame is not going to help him this time."

"I hope not. But who knows? There is the remote possibility that higher-ups accept to negotiate."

"It must be something substantial, I think, considering the stature of the target. In any case, if it happens, I hope it won't be just a briefcase full of money for someone."

"Don't ever dare think out loud again. Here, for a few years now, the walls, the tables, and even the glasses can hear. You understand? However, I agree with you. There are several people interested in that charlatan, and they may offer a lot of money. Hey, boy, tell Freddy to bring us another round! Do you understand what I'm telling you? Shut your mouth, keep your thoughts to yourself, and be alert."

"I will, Hans."

"Mmm, the wine is great here. Look, I'll be back with a definitive answer in a few hours, and remember to call me every hour. Stay put."

"Understood. Thanks for the advice. I won't make the same mistake again. No worries."

2

Judging from the fruits of his life, he had been fortunate. Life had been an inexhaustible engine of lasting influences over a century— coming to the world in the center of Europe far away in time, emerging from nowhere through his studies in the midst of great human curiosity, organizing central ideas from scattered concepts on the dark side of the mind and its meaningful empty spaces. He could recognize the imprint of the quotidian and isolate the terrible, unspeakable, and irreverent as if it were a dangerous germ, raising storms of sharp and unbearable criticism and, to the same degree, admiration and respect for his courage and creative imagination during long and painful decades.

His immense intellectual enterprise was worthless in the eyes of the official hordes willing to snatch from him and his race the air they breathed by virtue of an inhuman and totalitarian creed, the arbitrary condemnation to a slow death oscillating like a pendulum over his and his people's heads. Burning his work in a dishonorable pyre was the payment for his efforts, a vision ahead of his persecutors by decades or even centuries. Avid inquisitors were commanded by the so-called Angel of Death and his master, the Führer; but an upcoming surprise would overshadow their designs.

3

Vienna, 2013

"I wanted to tell you the story in the right place. Do you know that he used to take his famed Viennese coffee here? It's been a long time, but they've managed to preserve the place very well. I'll order a traditional cup of coffee for you. Sir, make them two, please. He's pretty old, don't you think? The famous Freddy, he has spent all his life around here and makes the coffee himself."

"Yes. Uff, it's delicious. I think I'd get used to this coffee very quickly. This man is awesome. Now . . . what is it you want to tell me about him?"

"You see, he tried harder than anyone else to unveil the secrets of the mind—the unconscious, sexuality at an early age, the functions of the human psyche, among other concepts. That you already know. Nevertheless, his true passion was the investigation, through his patients, of the mind's depths from a scientific point of view, the search for the other self that lies underneath every one of us."

"But . . . from a scientific point of view? I wonder how he would do that, psychology being so speculative, at least back then."

"That, unfortunately, is one of many questions that has remained unanswered. Here's the detail—how to connect the internal world of the human psyche with the scientific tradition, that is to say, to find a rational explanation for the whole thing, which was what he intended. And despite being considered unanimously as a genius, the task exceeded his capabilities as a thinker. He organized scattered concepts of depth psychology, which were already commonplace. It's one of his fundamental merits rather than being the discoverer of the unconscious, just to mention one of the more important concepts."

"What you say is even a little painful to me, considering the degree of influence his ideas have had over more than a century. It's like building a whole city on quicksand. If so, would his ideas be more akin to art than to a scientific discipline?"

"That's a way of looking at it, but . . . it's not less painful to think that, after so much effort, he was unable to prove scientifically the nature of that internal self, if not its very existence."

"I wonder if it'll ever be possible for someone to do it."

4

With an inquisitive gaze and creative curiosity, he crossed barely known oceans, carriers of one revelation: the dream, an unfathomable sea, uncharted, recurrent in itself. He imagined himself to be the great admiral, audacious and understanding, mastering immense and enveloping waves, traversing them in a flow of unreal cinematics, and projecting them into his masterpiece, a charmer of intellectuals, The Interpretation of Dreams.

He mapped the mind with cartographic precision, framing the unknown in his convoluted but comprehensible verbosity, discovering in turn dichotomous characters around the self and its mystifying inner world full of protective mechanisms, establishing a new dialogue filled with silence but rich in meanings—a healing symbology in itself, persuasively influential throughout the century.

5

Vienna, 1938
"I've got bad news. They finally accepted the money."
"No!"
"It is an important sum and comes from good hands."
"Don't tell me the—""Yes, the princess. The old man wasn't very persuaded at first, but after locking up his daughter for an entire day, he didn't think twice."
"Capturing her was a mistake!"
"I don't think so. He's worth more alive than dead. Besides, it's better not to damage our image more than it already is, although in the end the Führer doesn't care."
"You're right to some extent, but the physical permanence of the insatiable and weak Zionists is not convenient."

"I know your reasons, but I think our superiors made a good decision letting him go. In any case, sending him away from everything he values and loves might be a fatal blow for the old man. Doesn't seem like sweet revenge against him and all his people? And we get paid anyway."
"I'd rather not answer to that. My hands are still thirsty for vengeance."

6

Reminiscent of a better past, he sought in the lost gaze of contemporary man, finding only the individualistic yoke of those erroneously oriented drives. He felt with his own life the miserable condition of an era, of a whole continent and only perceived a thick and endless fog covering the surface of the disposable society. In the end, there was nothing left to analyze.

But what if there was something linking the internal and the external? Wouldn't this be enough to continue the search and, above all, to prepare a fertile path for more gifted people in a more attainable future? It was what he aspired, knowing deep inside the hardships of the enterprise—knowing the soul, knowing humankind.

7

Vienna, 2013

"These concepts and ideas we've been talking about, spread in everyday life, refer us directly to the Greeks—to Aristotle and Plato rather."

"Why those two figures specifically?"

"Can't you see the connection? They differ somewhat in their fields of study. While Plato opted for the inner being, the inner search for the soul, and its immortal nature and perennial ideas, Aristotle went after the same truth but in matter, in external things, in what he could feel, measure, experience, in short the material world."

"The old dichotomy between matter and spirit."

"Yes, the city of man or the city of God."

"Oh, Saint Augustine."

"Body, mind—is there really a limit between the two? Are they consubstantial? Interdependent? Can't the mind exist without a body?"

"But . . . what is it all about? It might be possible to reconcile these two universes someday?"

"I'm afraid I don't have an answer to that. And if he, after writing rivers of ink, trying to elucidate the deep psychological realities of the individual, couldn't reconcile his theories with science, neither will I do it from this café, which by the way was a witness of his time."

"I'm going to order another one. Don Freddy, another coffee, please! That man is a marvel of the human race. Since we're already here, why don't we talk with him a little? What do you say?"

8

The curtain opened slowly for him in London, the city of fog. He strolled along the port with weary steps and the assistance of the world, like a perennial symbol finding himself adrift. Resigned irrevocably to leave everything behind, the tears were in the inside, and he went along, sustained by the firm arm of his daughter. Looking back, he felt a yearning to forget, like the traveler crying in pain after almost reaching the end of a tortuous journey. His achievements were not enough to appease the pain in his soul, and the achievements were plenty, but so was the pain. A vast dark cloud lingered over his head.

9

London, 1939

"Daughter, I have made a decision."

"But, Father, you don't know how painful it is to live without you. You have been everything to me . . . for all of us, someone important even for many people around the world, people you don't even know."

"I would like to believe it, daughter . . . but many hate me deeply too."

"But that is not a reason for leaving like that. Please reconsider. I beg you.""The war, daughter, it has already begun. That man will destroy our world."

"This war will not last long, Father. When it ends, everything will be the same or better than before. Don't be discouraged, please."

"Our people will be annihilated, and there is nothing we can do to change what is coming."

"Father, we also have people on our side. They'll help us in this war."

"Anna, this is no longer my war. Don't you realize I'm dead? I am dead! I can't take it anymore. Also . . . I have everything prepared. Max knows what to do. Trust him."

"Father . . . if that's your wish . . . I respect it. But for the life of me, I can't share it, and I respect it because I love you."

10

Vienna, 2013

"Actually, another reason I brought you here is that you can know someone who knew him in person—Mr. Freddy, who has been serving us all afternoon."

"Yes. Don't tell me he—""Yes, he met him, and he served him coffee just as he has served us. I've heard he likes to talk about him and has many histories to tell. It would be good to ask him a little bit about his experiences from that era. Let's see if he's in the mood. Mr. Freddy!"

"Hello. May I help you?"

"We are foreigners and have heard many good things about this historic café. We were wondering if you'd be so kind to answer a few questions about your most distinguished patron. We know from a good source that you knew him. You might already know who we are referring to."

"Yes, of course, I know exactly who you are talking about. It would be a real pleasure to answer your questions."

"Well, Mr. Freddy, would you like to join us? We won't take much of your time."

"Certainly. I have all the time in the world. Would you mind if I get served some tea? Stimulates memory and exalts humor."

"By all means. The pleasure will be ours."

"Hannah! Please bring me my tea. And hurry, please. They take good care of me. But they think I should not strain my memory for sentimental reasons, but that is not right. Remembering is living again."

"Great. Our first question is, what was that time like—I mean, when he used to frequent the café? Before the war?""Well . . . uh . . . if you mean before the Anschluss, everything was normal—you know, he would come alone in the mornings to take his coffee as usual. Sometimes he read the newspaper for a while. Or occasionally, he came with someone. He did not spend hours here as many other customers."

"It's amazing how he made time for everything."

"Yes, we knew he was a very busy person but always made good use of his time and liked to come here to recharge his energies, so to speak."

"And didn't people bothered him often?"

"Well . . . before the Germans came, you could say no, only his friends. And apparently, he enjoyed their company."

"And later?"

"Well, later, his visits became more sporadic. Besides, you know he was a Jew, and his fame did not help him much."

"Do you remember any anecdote?"

"Yes, of course. Nazi militants began to show up in the café. It was not difficult to spot them. They were—how to put it—boastful and noisy. On one occasion, they asked me if he was a regular here. But since he barely left his house anymore, I said no."

"And how did they take it?"

"As you'll understand, I was very young at the time. They did not waste a second and started threatening me that if I did not tell the truth, there would be consequences. But I, like many others, did not agree with their methods, so I sent him a note surreptitiously, warning him that for his own good, he or no one from his family should come to the café. He took the advice seriously and, days later, thanked me when he found out they were looking for him that day."

"Grandpa, it's enough. It's nap time."

"As you see, gentlemen, they take care of me way too much, I'd say. Wait, Hannah, I haven't finished yet.""It's time, Grandpa."

"I told you to wait, girl. Don't be rude. As I was saying, where was I?"

"You sent him a note, and he thanked you."

"Oh, yes, he let me know through a friend in common, another regular patron. But on another occasion, shortly before his departure from Vienna, two Nazi hoodlums appeared. Their intentions were perverse, I'm sure, and with all the insolence in the world, they stationed themselves here. It seems as if they were going to apprehend us and shut down the place. As you can imagine, we felt totally helpless. I am convinced that they were looking for him. But what they didn't count on was that we had already warned him, and we did everything in our power to boycott their intentions, without them noticing obviously."

"Give us an example."

"Eh . . . we served them our worst wine, also disconnected the phone every time they wanted to use it. We gave them terrible food and did other things I wouldn't like to repeat now. Anyway, they did not realize what we were doing. You see, I'm still here. It's kind of funny in hindsight."

"You were very brave."

"The old man deserved it. He had not hurt anybody. And he was an Austrian."

"It's comforting to know that."

"Unfortunately, many others were not so lucky, including some of his relatives who died in concentration camps. After the war, we learned he did not live long after leaving Vienna. Well, you already know the rest."

"Yes, everyone knows what happened to him."

"That's right, young man. I hope what I have told has been of some use. They are already coming for me as you see. You are so diligent, Hannah. Thanks for your visit, gentlemen. I hope it will not be the last one."

"It won't, Mr. Freddy. Thank you for this interesting conversation."

"Ah, I almost forgot. I remember clearly the last time I saw him, which was also the last time he came to the café. Leaning on his cane, he pointed at me with his cigar and said, 'A man becomes wise only through his own personal experience.' And he left, never to return."

11

The decision had been made some time ago, when he saw everything distinctly as a crescent flash in his consciousness, suddenly struck down by knowledge. He did not see it coming in an explicit manner; rather, its vision affected him as the contemplation of the gradual but inevitable metamorphosis of a cloud high in the sky. So he learned to deplore life, a temple of pain, and to embrace death as the end of prolonged torment.

Everything was ready, and sorrows were put aside. The end of the pain came before death, just before the rupture of time, in the hiatus between life and death—that disembodied lapse under the stage of consciousness in its endless path to absolute disintegration, if you will. He knew it but could not explain it, even less now, when he saw himself tracing the long and luminous route toward the unknown.

12

London, 1939

"Are you ready, Master?"

"Yes, Max, go ahead."

"It was an honor to meet you, Master . . . to have been your patient, your disciple, your friend."

"The honor was mine, Max."

"Thank you. I'll never forget." "Now . . . end my misery. Auf Wied . . ."

RAFAEL L. TRUJILLO

(1889–1961)

Trujillo was a dictator of the Dominican Republic who stayed in power for thirty-one years. He built the infrastructure of the whole country with a progressive and martial will, winning the respect of both poor peasants and many intellectuals of his time; nevertheless, he achieved this with an iron fist. His mandates were infallible. He was idolized like a king; his family and friends enjoyed for decades the honey of power at the expense of the freedom and dignity of a people who didn't ask to be oppressed by a strange and whimsical ruler.

Nobody could eclipse him, and those who tried paid with their lives; likewise, an offense toward his person was inconceivable and became an unequivocal offense against the state. "L'état, c'est moi" became his motto, like a Louis XIV of the Caribbean proclaiming himself benefactor of the nation, not only guided by his increasing narcissism but also uplifted by the most brilliant and ingratiating writers at the service of the state; for that and many other elements inherent to the behavior of dictators, he became less and less tolerant of criticism, and those who dared criticize him sometimes paid with their lives for dissenting about the way he governed and dominated his people, who were humble but deep down very courageous in the face of growing adversity.

So in the night of May 30, 1961, on a lonely road on the west coast of Santo Domingo, he was intercepted and riddled with bullets by a group of men who spoke on behalf of all those who had suffered because of this self-appointed monarch of the Caribbean. This story took place during the last half hour of the dictator's life and told what happened in several contexts as revealed by the main witnesses and surviving participants of the event and a new source who, by the vagaries of fate, was in the right place at the right time.

Wherever there is a man who exercises authority, there is a man who resists authority.

—Oscar Wilde

Nothing strengthens authority so much as silence.

—Leonardo da Vinci

DEATH IN SPRING

1

"How's the night, Zacarias?"
"It's cool, sir."
"Time to go." "Yes, sir." "The streets are dead tonight. Turn on the radio, but keep the volume low."
"The usual station, sir?"
"Yes. I'd like to take a nap on the way there. Take it easy. Don't drive too fast."

2

A long time ago, he'd had the same stature of any other human, a child among other children. Games, disagreements, joy, sadness, hopes were all part of his life. He was a normal kid born in a land ravaged by the dereliction of an era—an old colony liberated by battered and exiled heroes, long gone by then, lying inert and invisible on a map of islands swept by sea winds from the East. A native of that island was the man who, one day, would wield the scepter of his own false glory, yielded by destiny's dark hands, always ready to engender chaos.

3

"I can't fall asleep, Zacarias. You're jolting the car too much."
"Excuse me, sir. Maybe the road will be less bumpy farther ahead."
"Yeah, yeah, take the usual route, Zacarias, please."
"As you wish, sir, but that road might be very solitary tonight."
"Sure. Remember that today is Tuesday, day of the dead."
"Yes, sir, Tuesday."
"A little adventure is always good, eh? I think I'm not going to take that nap because of you, Zacarias. Turn up the music a little."

"Excuse me for not letting you rest, sir. It won't happen again. Do we go through that street then?"

4

A stroke of luck showed him that turn in life that he knew how to take at the right time. He did not see it at first, but one turn led to the next, over dead bodies and weak-willed contemporaries. He was still young when he took the political scene by assault, virile and irreverent, imbued with fashionable ideas—crush and live. It was an outrageous motto, contrary to civilization. He never showed another face other than that of a mysterious harlequin in the scenario of terror called his homeland, a place of absolute but ephemeral expediency, full of beings addicted to the mere pleasure of usurping God's workings on Earth and of condemning a whole people to pay tribute to another human being as fragile as a serpent's egg.

5

"How was the food?"

"I loved it. Every time we come here, its taste stays with me for a while. Thanks, love."

"It's worth coming from San Cristóbal, don't you think?"

"Yeah. We should come here more often. By the way, I love the name, El Poni. Do you know why they gave it that name?"

"No clue, but I can ask. Hey, waiter, please."

"Yes, sir. How can I help you?"

"Do you happen to know why this restaurant is called El Poni?"

"Well, hmm, I'm new here, sir, but I can ask the manager if you like."

"Hey, did you hear that?"

"Sounded like gunshots. Right, Linda?"

"Yes . . . and there's more." "Couldn't they be fireworks, sir?"

"I don't believe so. Is it a holiday today? It's May 30."

"Not to my knowledge."

"Wait, wait . . . that was a barrage of bullets. Linda, I think we should pay the bill and leave. I don't like this one bit. After the shooting, we should wait awhile just in case and then get the hell out of here."

6

He possessed everything, from perpetuation in a dazzling throne sweetened by the flattery of inferior beings to cries of peace in mouths frozen by fear and hunger in every corner of the island, from torrents of luxuries sprouting from marble columns supporting his personal palaces to gloomy dungeons in the shadows of the empire, warmed by the inclement sun.

His personal motto was walking with the silent gait of a cat in heat, dazzled by his own reflection, showing ostentatiously the title of the benefactor of a submissive country incapable of reacting for a long time, its thinking men in chains, tied to their servile pens and prose. He erased from the annals of a young homeland the name given to the city by history to impose his own, a cruel and embarrassing stamp on the back of an innocent society; but history being a patient lady, a placid weaver of the human condition, would make sure that the infamous name would not last long because those submissive people were already alert to the silent murmur of brave and hidden voices lurking in the background. He did not see it coming but sensed it. There was no time for laments in that long tropical spring night, in which death, hidden behind a lightning bolt, claimed without mercy what was its own, exchanging the dictator's route of pleasure for a blind alley.

7

"What do you say, Zacarias? You think that woman lied to me?"

"I don't know, sir. Maybe it's true that . . ."

"She had her period. I hope she didn't lie."

"If she lied to you, I pity her, sir."

"Her wimpy husband will pay for this. I'm gonna fuck him up, lying to my face like that."

"You propose, and God complies, sir."

"It's okay, Zacarias. Let's go straight to San Cristóbal. I want to get this crap out of my head."

8

Gone were the enemies, blown away by a strong wind like pieces on a board, a powerful swipe rather, until he was at the top on his own, with blood on his heels, without a look back or remorse, always heading forward with a haughty attitude, full of cruelty and bloodlust. As he was taught in the army, "Shoot to kill. You do not spare the enemy. You do not leave loose ends because you might regret it later."

9

"Those are definitely gunshots."

"It doesn't seem they're going to stop, Linda."

"Oh dear . . . and people are standing on the tables."

"Isn't that Arturito, the general, a friend of mine? He's also leaving."

"We can't stay here. I'm so scared. Let's go now, please."

"Yes, yes, just let me ask something to the general. General! General!"

"Oh, Doctor, this is getting ugly. I'll go out with my escorts to check what's going on. I'll let you know at the club. I'm going there tomorrow, God willing. See you then. Good night."

10

His coffers were full to the brim with extraordinary riches, swollen by the profits of powerful companies snatched away with impunity from public patrimony, with no trace of decency and uncontrollable greed. With the sheer force of his power, he spurred the efforts of those whose mission was to augment his inexhaustible and zealously guarded fortune; but perhaps someday, some around him would think. Someday his house of cards would suddenly collapse, burying him along with his offspring in the rubble of oblivion, when the great fountain stopped gushing out.

11

"Sir, it seems someone wants to get to San Cristóbal first."

"What do you mean?"

"Two cars are approaching, seem to be racing each other. They're catching up with us quickly and are flashing their headlights at us. What are you going to do with these drunks, sir?"

"Let me take a look at them . . . Damn it, Zacarias, don't let them reach us! Drive faster! Shit! I'm wounded!"

"Where did they shoot you, sir? I have to stop!"

"Take the submachine gun and defend me, goddamn it!"

"Another car is coming, sir. I hope it's some of our people. Don't get out of the car yet! Boss, nooo!"

"Antonio! Here is the man. He's fucked up!"

12

First, it was that infamous student who had smeared him by publishing a big lie. He had to pay. The naive offender did not expect that the longest and most powerful arm in the Caribbean could catch him. There was no barrier between him and his revenge though. The transgressor would become shark food soon. It served him right.

The illustrious heroines would also succumb in the grip of his power, butterflies trapped in a nefarious web.

Not one offense would be forgiven, no matter who had committed it. Arrogance would come wrapped in its own poison, and he would taste it at the appropriate moment. He went too far when he cut those flowers disdainfully and untimely. The people—mute, deaf, and blind—suddenly came back to their senses after being subdued for so long by fear, apathy, the credo of every man for himself and jumped over the hurdle of dismay to arm themselves with the necessary courage to put an end to the ignominy once and for all.

13

"Go more slowly. I'm very scared."

"Calm down. It seems that the shooting was over there, where those cars are, but it's over now."

"Ah, I see. Leave them behind, please. It's so dark."

"Hmm, there was a tragedy here. Shit! I know that car. Oh, Linda! We have to get away from here!"

"What is happening? Did you see the general's car? He is driving as if the devil were after him. What's going on?"

"Listen, Linda, that car in the middle of the road . . . riddled with bullets . . . is the boss's car."

"What? His car? We have to get home as soon as possible and . . . keep our mouths shut."

"Let's not talk anymore. Just let me drive, love."

14

As time went by, historical facts were narrowed down or enlarged, always depending on the convenient inclinations of the pen delineating them. His death evidently belonged to the realm of imponderable events. There was no turning point.

The fall of the tyrant filled a people hungry for light and bread with a false grief, crying for vengeance against their humble but brave saviors, not knowing or not wanting to know that a better future would dawn because of the sacrifice of a small group of men who proved to be more powerful against the capricious clarion of a rare and inhuman specimen than a whole army of quivering pens. Society would not forget it.

15

"If they killed the boss, Linda . . . we're lost."

"I don't think so, love. People are very important to others but not necessarily indispensable."

"But . . . he is the provider of this country. There are so many people whose lives basically depend on him."

"You're wrong. What people need to survive is food and shelter. Everything else is secondary. I'm sure everyone will find a way to survive."

"I am speechless, love. You were so attached to him. You were so nervous earlier, and you're so peaceful now."

"Maybe it's because we are already safe at home. Listen, love. The only ones I'm really attached to are my children, to you, my family. And I tell you, no one really suffers the tragedy of others. Each one has his or her own cross to bear, and mine is heavy enough already, mine . . . ours. So let's go to sleep. Tomorrow will be another day, with or without the boss."

FRIEDRICH NIETZSCHE

(1844–1900)

Nietzsche was considered one of the most influential thinkers of the twentieth century; his works had marked the political and cultural ideas of a whole era. He was a philologist, musician, poet, and above all philosopher born in Germany who delved into the main problems of philosophy, namely, ethics, morals, and human will to deal with the contingencies of life. He identified the possibility of the existence of an Übermensch or superman in his famous book Thus Spoke Zarathustra: A Book for All and None.

He was a controversial figure in the world of philosophy and beyond, even after his premature death, probably due to the ravages of tertiary syphilis, although some researchers didn't rule out the possibility of a brain tumor. He never married or had children, was in very poor health throughout his life but possessed a strong will, and was extremely intelligent and definitely well ahead of his time. He was a professor first in Leipzig and then in Basel at a very early age. His philosophy was imbued with a high degree of individualism, and some historians attributed it as part of the German cultural impetus that led to the two world wars; of course, this was nothing more than a sociopolitical and cultural conjecture.

In his midforties, he began to suffer from a degenerative brain disease that progressively incapacitated him for the rest of his days, first being taken care of by his mother and then after her death by his sister. He also spent long periods in mental sanatoriums. This story focused on one of his first stays in one of such institutions, in Jena in 1889, and how—despite the rampant evolution of his illness—he may have had flashes of lucidity worthy of his genius, determined not to leave the world without first revealing himself as the disruptor of an entire epoch.

He died at the age of fifty-six, although for all intents and purposes he had been dead for society for ten years already—but not his great works, which had lived on, influencing philosophers of all levels. There was still speculation about how his ideas would have developed had he not suffered from this disease that happened to attack the core of his being as it were, namely, his brain. Had such tragedy not happened to one of the greatest bearers of human ingenuity, we wondered where his deep and controversial ideas would have led us. We'd never know, but we did know that each one of us, beings capable of challenging the mysteries of life, harbored small parts of the whole, and the legacy of each individual exalted and gave nourishment to all humankind.

Life isn't about finding yourself. Life is about creating yourself.

—George Bernard Shaw

IMPORTANCE IS NOT IMPORTANT

1

The critics of an era had said the word had been lit once again. A singular light illuminated the darkness, like a lighthouse in the proximity of a threatening coast warning the ominous reality of the future absence of truth. That strange light burst forth in abundance, sometimes simple like a flower, other times harshly, like a rock stuck in the cold and wildland but always deep like truth itself, which arose from mystery, anger, or loneliness, unveiled through creative inspiration, through blind and meticulous intellectual effort and determination.

Eternal adversities crossed his path from very early on. His world was plagued by primordial absences, leaving an inevitable imprint of loneliness, misfortune in love, and fragile health like a silk thread stretched by life itself. His half-extinguished eyesight scarcely contained light's flow at the bottom of his boiling mind and illuminated the depths of a well that was his life.

2

"I have a bad feeling about this situation, Karl. It's been a long time since I last saw him. I told you I didn't want to come here. I think it will be the first . . . and the last time."

"You are so ungrateful to your father. If he wasn't my brother and didn't asked me in such a heartfelt manner, I wouldn't have brought you to this place."

"I understand, Uncle Karl, but you need to understand I do this only for you. You have given me everything in life. He only did his part and Mom, as you know, hers."

"I did what any good brother would have done, but that's not the issue. He wants to see you, and I do my share by bringing you. He has been through hard times lately and unfortunately cannot get out of here."

"Well, it's not as if I have many things in common with him, but I'll do my best. Okay?"

"It's a start. Here we are. I'll leave you both alone."

"Hello, Walther."

"Hello, Friedrich, my son. It fills me with joy to see you again. A while ago, your mother came. Her visit made me so happy, despite everything. I thought you would come around that time too, but I know you live in Basel now, and it's not that easy coming all the way here."

"That is so, Walther . . . Dad. By the way, you look quite recovered. It seems the sadness is gone. I hope so."

"Yes, son. I think the worst is over, thanks to the doctors who always make their best effort, despite having a lot of work and some remarkably difficult cases to treat even for the most qualified of them. I wanted you to come to see me when I was feeling better, but I also want you to take a look at a very special case. I know you're very busy . . . and . . . I'll get to the point. I'd like you to see someone else. They brought him a few months ago. He has the same name as you—Friedrich."

"What a coincidence!"

"This gentleman was an eminent professor. He has written many books, mainly about philosophy and about other things too, I believe. I would like you to meet him. Perhaps you could help him."

"Oh, Walther . . . Dad, you have so many expectations about me. Anyway, I think I may be interested in the case. I've heard something about it. He is famous, but I did not know he was here."

"His situation is so sad. They say he went crazy in Italy defending a horse. A horse—can you believe it?"

"It's hard. Madness is not a simple matter by any means, but . . . how do you think I can help?"

"I'm not sure but maybe if you talk to him. You're a good listener. In his youth, he was a teacher in Basel. Here in Jena, it's as if he'd never existed. Do you understand? A doctor told me he is wiser now despite his madness. I don't know. He only greets me when he feels like it."

"What else do you know about him?"

"As I was saying, I have not talked to him much. We've only exchanged a few words, greetings, things like that. I haven't been in the mood to talk to him either. Besides, my ailment is very different. If you saw him . . . sometimes he is in a good mood, eager to talk to everyone, seems very cheerful, excessively I'd say, but . . . suddenly withdraws, goes to a corner, and starts mumbling something. He talks to himself constantly. They say he always talks to a woman in his mind."

"A woman? Who?"

"How do I know, son? Maybe you could find out. You are a doctor of the mind and know how to treat cases like his. Besides, I suspect you'll find this very interesting."

3

He was singled out as a prodigy when his first inclination was to decipher the letters and ideas lost in the dawn of culture. He penetrated magnificently in ancient Greece the matrix of a select group of thinkers in the world's history whom he understood like no one else, admired in equal measure by scholars and freethinkers of his time.

He was bold in thought and action, and the thirst for knowledge, the depth of his research, and perhaps shyness clouded his ability to conquer love.

He was an inveterate iconoclast engrossed in ideas that had been taken for granted, swaddled in cocoons, grasping the essential in concepts that were always there behind the German numen, the pinnacle of abstract thought. He grasped the ideology of willpower immersed in a Darwinian dialectic as if such a thing were possible in a world still subjugated by the monarchs of faith, not foreseeing the reaction of generations ahead—powerful but erroneously and fatally oriented. *He took causality as a codified and sterile simplicity for true knowledge and made the wise hermit descend from the mountain.*

4

"Good morning, Professore. Can I have a moment of your time, please?"

"Naturally, Doctor, naturally."

"I want to introduce you to a colleague. He came to visit us from Basel, and if it isn't too much trouble, he would like to ask you a few questions."

"Yes, yes, of course, Doctor, he can do that."

"How are you feeling, sir?"

"Call me Professore. Professore! I feel great."

-Yes, Professore. They tell me you are a music lover."

"You've been informed well, Doctor. I also like buns and ham. And my wife . . . yes, my wife brings me buns and also books."

"Oh, by the way, Professore, I have also been told you have written many interesting books."

"Yes . . . interesting books."

"And what are your books about, Professore?"

"Well . . . uh . . . about things . . . this and that, you know."

"Oh, I see, and don't you write anymore, Professore?"

"Yes, I write and read. I read more though. And listen, between you and me, Doctor, I read the Bible. Excuse me for whispering, Doctor, but I know everything about the Bible. Ask me what you want but not now. I cannot speak. Listen, the sow is listening to us . . . but I am protected, very well protected."

"Does someone want to hurt you, Professore?"

"Shh, I know everything. That's why they pointed the gun at me. They don't want me to reveal their secret, and I will not. I will not do it. I put glass shards behind my door and smeared myself with excrement to keep them away and make them believe I was crazy, and if they continue to annoy me, oh . . . I'll disclose everything."

"It is not necessary, Professore. Rest assured they will not bother you anymore."

"Do you believe it?"

"Yes, yes, I'm sure. Everything will be fine."

"You are very good, Doctor. I'll get along with you. Now I am leaving. In your next visit, please bring me buns, and you can tell my wife not to come back."

"I will do so. Bye, Prof."

5

He declared himself a Hyperborean, a different being from other intellectual dimensions and latitudes, without modesty, rather with mettle, and conscious of carrying forward the ancient torch of Aristotle, who like him had scorned the nothingness that lay in the future known only by the hypothetical immortal. That same nothingness was the object of Christians and their paradoxical morals, dismissing as a weak puppet the unsuspecting subjects of incense and obsessive chanting. He did not give up in his struggle to outline the true Antichrist, the one who lay incomplete halfway between the valley of tears and the fool's sky.

"God is dead." He hoisted that remark as a solitary flag, making it his particular religion. He did it without fear, like a child throwing a tantrum, and didn't consider the consequences. Indeed, he died for those whose target was far above the heads of the weak, meek sheep led by protected wolves in their sumptuous lairs, clad in golden cloaks and flashy garbs, facing the powerful ghost, with their backs to the doomed people.

6

"Hello, Doctor, good to see you again. Now your friend is worse than ever. Maybe he'd agree to talk to you."

"It's a real shame. Is he still talking about his wife?"

"No, no. He has been very incoherent and argumentative, also aggressive with other patients and sometimes does not want to shut up. Let's see if listening to you calms him down a little. It was necessary to keep him in solitary confinement for a few days. You know how it is. Oh, here he is. Professore, look who came to see you."

"Yeah, yeah. Go ahead. Who are you?"

"I'll leave you with the doctor. Good luck."

"Thank you. My friend, I came to visit you a few days ago. We talked for a while. I brought you a gift."

"Oh, yes, the doctor. You brought me buns. Thank you. It's so kind of you. What a nice surprise! Do you mind if I eat one now?"

"No, no, please. Do me the honor."

"If you had come earlier . . . hmm . . . you'd have met my mother. We were . . . reading the Bible a bit . . . and she touched my face with her sweet hands, and . . . they say I kicked my roommate, but I do not remember doing so. I only know I have been reading some passages of the book of Proverbs, but I don't know why I can't read beyond the first page. Can you explain it to me, Doctor?"

"Certainly. Maybe you were angry, Professore, or you were interrupted while reading."

"I don't remember, Doctor, but . . . I'd like to confess something, only to you. Sorry if I lower my voice, but . . . we are being listened to. Him—He listens to us. He is a ghost, and He does not exist but can hear us. Don't you believe me? Ah, you don't believe me. You think I am talking nonsense."

"No, Professore, I believe in what you're saying. I have great respect for you."

"Respect is important. Yes, very important. What I am saying . . . the bun, oh, it's delicious. Can I eat another one? Yes, another one?"

"Absolutely. Of course, you can, Professore. They are all yours, but I would like you to tell me more about Him, the ghost that listens to us."

"Oh, yes, Him. You know what? It's not important after all. It's like everything in life. My conclusion is that importance is not important. Do you understand? That is fundamental."

"What do you mean by that, Professore?"

"There is nothing important on the face of the earth. Only the observer believes that something is important."

"I still don't follow."

"Doctor, I am talking about your God and also about the bun. Don't you understand yet? It is absurd to sacrifice one's life for a vague nothingness, to kill indiscriminately life's instincts in pursuit of the promised nothingness. That's why I maintain that importance is not important faced with death . . . inescapable . . . empty . . . and neither my buns, well . . . just for me."

"Now it is clear what you mean. I see you liked the buns. Will you grant me another interview?"

"Why not?"

7

The thinker's twilight was outlined on the horizon, slowly but surely. Misfortune can be a sword directed toward him unimpeded; thus, the illness dug a hole in the helpless body of all equally. Nevertheless, our thinker was a living dead many years before his actual death, burying his unattainable ideas under even bigger heaps of soil, to the great lamentation of future thinkers, eager for the knowledge that may illuminate the dark paths bestowed by sinister ancestors through blood and fire.

Our restless nights in search for answers were made of moons and stars, winds and dust sheltered under a roof enveloped by light, by the heat of a fire caressing our skin. So brutal, necessary, and unavoidable were the ideas that sprang from silence in the forging of thought liberated from superstitions, like sudden and vivacious sparks in contact with air—ideas that can be terrifying, some full of rage, others intimately profound, developed without ornaments, whose aim was to create a rift in his era as a glass broke from above noisily, giving us a strong sense of the inevitable and irreversible. Oh, thinker! He walked the earth and accomplished his mission. Long live the thinker!

ERNEST HEMINGWAY

(1899–1961)

Hemingway was one of the most acclaimed American writers of the twentieth century, a representative of the Lost Generation, a term coined by Gertrude Stein to refer to the generation that came of age during World War I. His prose was very evocative of his time, setting the pace for the literature of that period. He took part in the World War I as an ambulance driver and saw with his own eyes the pain of the fallen. He worked as a war correspondent, and the experiences in that job would be useful for his creative process.

He often wrote about his own life experiences but did so in an innovative and attractive style. The success of his books made him a public figure, and he lived life in his own terms. He married multiple times in search of an inspiring muse. He was an adventurous man with innumerable stories to tell, ranging from bullfighting in Spain to participating in the Spanish Civil War to fishing in the high seas to hunting wild animals in Africa. We may say he did a little bit of everything.

However, in an unfortunate twist of fate, he lost the manuscripts of his youth, which he entrusted to his pregnant wife to take to Switzerland, where he was working as a correspondent, but she lost them at the Gare de Lyon railway station. The fact that she was pregnant was a factor for her noncompletion of the delivery without mishap, and as Murphy's Law stated, "Anything that can go wrong will go wrong." The manuscripts disappeared forever. This event represented a hard blow for a writer as promising as him, but in addition, in the briefcase containing the manuscripts were the carbon copies he had made of them. There were many theories about where the manuscripts could be, but none had determined its whereabouts. Hemingway's scholars considered these manuscripts as highly valuable, and it'd been said their cost could be weighted in gold. This story offered a fictitious account of what could have happened to those manuscripts and offered a general outline of the life of this important figure in twentieth-century literature.

Live in the sunshine. Swim in the sea. Drink in the wild air.

—Ralph Waldo Emerson

There are far, far better things ahead than any we leave behind.

—C. S. Lewis

THE BRIEFCASE AND THE FURY

1

1922

"Pierre Derlain brought this one. Yes, Pierre, the same old idiot. He has no luck. At first glance, you can see this briefcase contains nothing valuable. How could he have taken the risk of being arrested for so little?"

"Mm-hmm, you know how it is. Beggars can't be choosers. That poor wretch would steal from a nun on her deathbed."

"But it's no excuse. He should've been more careful, and then showing up with a briefcase full of crap written in English? Who'd come up with something like this?"

"Speaking of the devil. Here's your booty, you moron!"

"What was I supposed to do? The opportunity presented itself, and I took it. That woman got up from her seat as if she'd forgotten something outside and left the briefcase right there just in time for me to take it and go out the next door. I only saw something that could've had something of value inside."

"But someone could have seen you. You were such a sucker, taking the risk for nothing."

"How was I to know the briefcase was packed with papers in English?"

"Oh, you aren't that stupid apparently. How do you know it's English? Do you speak it?"

"No, I don't speak it, but I can recognize some words. It's nothing special. And now if you don't want the briefcase, I'll take it."

"There you have your treasure. You can take it . . . and use it as firewood."

2

1940

"After the Germans occupied the country, I don't know what I'm doing these days."

"If you haven't noticed, it is happening to all of us, Pierre. The children are frightened, especially after you ordered them to check the whole house and make an inventory of our things and theirs. We should do that ourselves."

"It is exactly what you and I are going to do. We'll only have two days to complete that work."

"You know very well two days are not enough. There's so much garbage stored in there that not even two years would be enough to make an inventory of it all. Maybe we'll have time to call Paul and ask him to bring his truck at midnight and take the most compromising material to the countryside."

"It will be difficult, but . . . let's do it. Call Paul."

"Dad! Dad! Can we keep this?"

"What is it?"

"It's an old briefcase. It's got a lot of mold on it, but we can wash it and use it."

"Ah, it's the one with the papers in English. Okay, you can keep it as long as you wash it thoroughly. Marie, you speak English well. You should check the papers in that briefcase."

"Let's see as if we had time to waste."

3

1955

"Going to the police would be useless. That particular theft was not reported, and if it was, there is no record."

"Yes. Also, even if there was a record, that does not necessarily identify the thief, much less the final whereabouts of the briefcase."

"Looking at it that way, it's almost impossible to recover."

"The owner never claimed it. He didn't put any ads on the newspapers, and the idiot who took it was more interested in finding some jewel or something of value, but since he only found papers . . ."

"And in English! Such an idiot. God only knows in what hole he had put it or if he threw it in the Seine or burned the manuscripts in the fireplace to warm himself."

"There's another possibility though. The thief might have gotten curious about the contents. Or he could have been living with his wife or a lover. You know how curious women can be."

"Well, she might have not spoken English. Who knows?" "And not knowing that now, many years after the war, the value of those manuscripts from a writer awarded with the Nobel Prize for Literature must be exorbitant. Can you imagine finding that booty in an antique shop or at a street sale somewhere in Paris?"

"To tell you the truth, I don't lose hope. Few writers' manuscripts are as valuable as those."

"I wouldn't like to stop searching either. If I have to go through all the streets of Paris, I will do it. And you will come with me."

4

He emerged as an urban legend brought from America by the winds of war. He had left resolute and hungry for adventure and heroism toward a continental conflict, hoping to put a great stamp on his worldly manhood and finally escape the tedium of his native Midwest in the other half of the world. And he did it, with his limbs wrapped in a bloody gauze, like a hero.

That was how the legend was created, overflowing with alcohol, love, passion, and dancing at night. He had his way with words, the ability to write in clear and precise prose. He discovered battle after battle, feast after feast when foes and allies succumbed, more out of exhaustion than thirst for blood, and even so was subjugated by that ferocious, picturesque, and bohemian continent, full of life but wearied, anguished, and hungry, harboring life, attempting to forget the pain and infinite grief suffered in the last four years of relentless wars. He was always trying to forget the fragments of soul left in the ineffable meadows full of scorched grass, ravaged houses, rivers turned red with the blood of thousands of unknown soldiers. That was where all the carousing came from—wanting to forget having to die. All this gushed out of his pen and blood just like the sun, a faithful companion of the fallen and the victorious, rising unfailingly in the east.

5

1925

"I don't think I can get over it. Deep down, I feel it's pointless to continue talking about it anymore."

"I have asked you to forgive me dozens of times . . . hundreds of times."

"It has nothing to do with forgiveness. If it was for that . . . I forgave you from the beginning. I'm the only one to blame for not having foreseen what finally happened. I shouldn't have left you alone . . . my love."

"Now I feel guiltier. I was a fool. I don't know what I was thinking at that moment. I went to buy a bottle of water, and I swear it didn't take two minutes. It's as if they had been watching me or, worse, got me hypnotized."

"Don't torment yourself anymore. You've told me that story so many times I feel as though I lived it myself second by second. I would rather torture myself now that I have the strength to do it."

"But you don't have to do it either. You should not do that. I feel terrible because there's no way in the world to comfort you. Just ask, and I'll return to the Gare de Lyon and go door to door, searching for the manuscripts."

"You know that would be useless. Let's talk about something else. Give me a shot of whiskey. Bring the bottle instead, and let's drink if you wish. In the morning, we'll have forgotten everything."

"We could go to San Fermín. It'd be good for us. And the child loves it there."

"Excellent idea. We're going to San Fermín. We will call Bill and Stewart and ask them to meet us there."

"It would be the best way to forget, love. Life is too short to choose to suffer. Let's drink."

6

1928

"You know very well I love Paris, and I've decided to leave because you want to. You miss your country, that's all. I, on the other hand..."

"You don't know how much it hurts me wanting to leave the place you so love and sometimes hate so much. But there are other things at stake. You know what I mean."

"Yes, Pauline, there are many things at stake. And I think you suspect which is the fundamental one. Lately, the city has been cruel to me, but... I was also happy here. We were happy. This city has brought out the best in me. Why the hell can't I forget the manuscripts?"

"A good way to deal with that is to cross the ocean and put many, many miles between us and this place. But above all, you must keep writing."

"Do you think that will work? I'm afraid it won't be enough."

"We will come up with something. We'll go fishing every day. We'll go on safaris as often as we want."

"Aren't you forgetting the bullfights?"

"No, we'll go to the bullfights as well. And we'll drink all the whiskey of every bar."

"That's how the stories will flow. Those that were stillborn will be reborn, I'm telling you. Even the last comma will be revived... until the last breath."

"On we go."

7

1935

"If you look closely at the photo, the Marlins look stunning behind us. And to think that, hours before, they were at ease in the sea, following their path, hunting, unrivaled . . . until we appeared."

"Yes, what a pity. That's life. Some have to die for others to live or simply to exalt their vanity."

"I don't think that applies to us. Well, in reality, that applies to men who live in the shadows. Look at them, how dour their lives are, sitting on the sidelines, silent."

"They really belong to the shadows as if they didn't exist. Instead, we smile joyfully. It seems that fishing had been invented only for us."

"Hmm, don't make fun of me. You know how much effort I put into catching those. I don't like half measures. But I admit the boys were very helpful."

"I thought you were not gonna say it. I've learned from you that not everything should be said, but sometimes you only say what's necessary to make yourself understood. I know you well, dear."

"Thanks for understanding, darling. Going back to the photo, do you remember our promise when we left Europe, to do all these things, to live life to the full so we wouldn't remember the bad times? It has worked out pretty well."

"Oh, love, it was about time you gave me that surprise. I can appreciate your smile in the photo even more now. You seem at peace with life."

"You think so? I didn't say that. I can be at peace with life when the earth opens up beneath us and swallows us. I don't want peace with you, honey, I just want to . . . open up the earth beneath us myself so it can swallow us."

"Ahh, you are a pervert, douchey. Turn off the light."

8

Wars had passed over him like an immense and threatening bank of black clouds, leaving actual physical scars here and there. Those indelible scars only lasted forever, but they traced for him the inevitable route of one who clamored in the desert with a chorus of voices, echoes of the doomed, dying, exiled, dismembered, and children of the nobodies tossed into the dark passages of anxious hopes in their dubious futures. War taught him that. It was vital to forget through his writing.

After that hiatus of oblivion, he returned to the blank page, standing and naked as he used to do, like a hardened gladiator recovering from mortal wounds healed only by time. He resumed the march with new vigor despite the hindrances—alcohol and adventure—and the lacerating pain that life itself, in its comings and goings, inflicted. His flesh eroded untimely in a slow hustle toward a boat that didn't return.

9

1968

"Dad, this situation is unsustainable. You can't keep us hidden here any longer. Also, you have your past. Do you think we don't know? All the more reason to come here, if you have two young children."

"But, Paul, you shouldn't get out. You would be arrested for sure. Who knows what they would do to you? And Max couldn't resist it."

"Oh my god, don't exaggerate. Both Max and I know how to take care of ourselves. Here, uncertainty will kill us faster than hunger."

"Yeah, Pierre. It's been a while since Mom died. Everything would have been easier if she had been here. You are more . . . emotional."

"I hate when you call me Pierre. Call me Dad as Paul does. And it's an order! You are not getting out of here! You see how the antiriot brigades are treating the students. They have created great unrest along with dissatisfied workers. Hypocrites! They say they've never had a coup in mind, but what they want is the general out of the picture. Let's see, what's that called? Coup d'état, here and in China.

"Oh, Dad, don't be so naive. You know they'll come here eventually. And what are you going to tell them then?"

"I know a person in the office of . . . well, to whom I revealed something once. That person is definitely on our side. I have something he desperately wants. It was a while ago. I was drunk when I confessed it."

"What's that mysterious thing?"

"Yes, come on, at least tell us your little secret so we won't die of boredom."

"All right, I'll tell you. Listen carefully. A long time ago, some documents fell into my possession. I'm embarrassed to say this, but . . . I've had them for the last forty-five years. I never suspected the value they could have someday, but I ended up keeping them. They reminded me of happier times, when your mother and I met. Maybe that's why. In reality, the briefcase consisted of unpublished manuscripts by a writer who, in time, would become famous and celebrated.

"Now comes the curious part. I was in the deputy chief of police's office and taking a look at his bookcase. What do I see? Well, there was a whole collection of books written by the author of the manuscripts I had at home. How did I know? It was as if a light bulb had been turned on in my brain. Something inside me reverberated like an alarm. 'It could not be possible,' I said to myself. What if I was wrong? I spent entire days mulling things over. Where did I get that strange idea?

"Then . . . I remembered your mother. Of course. It had been her who told me what was written in those manuscripts. She knew. But she was very ill by that time, and unfortunately, I didn't pay much attention. After thinking about the matter day and night, I judged it necessary to share my discovery with my friend, the policeman who, to my surprise, knew of the existence of the manuscripts. What a small world! To be more specific and also to confuse him a little bit, I said the briefcase was among the belongings of my brother Paul when he died, and they fell into my hands, like everything else, because he had no offspring. My friend was quite excited about my story and promised to help me in everything I could possibly need. I just had to give him the documents, he'd authenticate them, and everything would be arranged conveniently for both. He would offer me protection and support whatever my version of the facts was. I didn't tell him the documents in the briefcase had been stolen, but at this point, I considered it an insignificant detail, given the importance of the manuscripts.

"A detail, which is very significant, is that it's been a long time since I last saw the briefcase in the house, and we've moved so many times I don't remember where I put it. I need you to help me find it. Do you know what I'm talking about?"

"Eh . . . Max, you . . . uh . . . sit down, Dad, please. I think we know, or rather, we suspect the whereabouts of those papers, but . . . it won't be so easy to find them."

10

1961
"You are so quiet, darling. What's on your mind?"
"I miss the island, the boat . . . fishing."
"Me too, taking a nap on deck under the afternoon sun."
"I wonder what they'll do with the house on the island."
"I don't know. I guess they'll take care of it."
"I was so happy there. I'd like to get home. I feel as if my memory has been erased."
"I want to get there too. It's been a long trip from the hospital. How are you feeling right now?"
"Not that bad. I'm only looking at the landscape. I'd like to travel farther north and hunt a caribou."
"What I'd like to do is go fishing in our favorite bay. How about that?"
"Yes, I would hunt it with the twelve-gauge."
"Oh, don't mention that thing, please. This conversation is over."

11

1968

"Do you have the manuscripts?"

"Not yet."

"But you told me you kept them in the house. I need to see them. I'll be frank. If you get them, you're going to be rich. Both of us are going to be rich rather. And if you need to turn the house upside down, I'll help you."

"That's not the problem."

"And what is it then? You still don't understand what this is about. If you want an advance, I'll give it to you. Just ask. Ask what you want."

"Max, come here. Tell him word for word what you told me earlier."

"Sir, we haven't had those manuscripts for a long time. My brother and I sold them for a trifle to an antiquarian in the twelfth arrondissement, not far from the Gare de Lyon, near where we used to live. But . . . the shop doesn't exist anymore. The owner must have died. He was a very old man already back then."

"They lost a treasure! I can't believe it! Those were the manuscripts of . . . it's not worth mentioning anymore. They are lost! Absolutely lost."

"Maybe if we look better in the twelfth arrondissement—I mean . . . a more conscientious and . . . discreet search, we could find them."

"Don't play the fool, Pierre. It's been years since those papers aren't in that area for sure. With luck, they are still in Paris. You have lost the opportunity of a lifetime. How long have you had those manuscripts, Pierre? Thirty years? Oh lord, sitting on a treasure trove for so long, and you didn't even notice. That's what I call a dirty trick of fate. He who wrote them is as if he had never done it, and you who found them—it is as if you had found nothing. It's damn funny to me. I wonder how many absurdities like this history is made of. I'm leaving, Pierre. If you know something, don't forget to call me."

12

He woke up for the umpteenth time in his reality of more placid waters, but unwanted, he was a man of an inquisitive look who preferred troubled waters, tired from carrying on his back the burden of hectic years and the indolent ghost of all his past losses. He longed to keep going anyway until finding perfection through an epic marine dream, in the center of which was an old man with an unbreakable will, claiming for the writer the highest of honors. But he stoically accepted his destiny and, with determination, crossed in his thought the depths of the abyss within a hand's reach.

Now looking back, the picture was clear. The flow of his consciousness brought him the understanding for overcoming hurdles and crossing frontiers, the natural ones and those that magnified thought, and he understood once and for all that life cannot be tamed at will forever, that a point would be reached where the best times, the irreplaceable ones, would be gone, and the crest of the wave was definitely behind a long time ago. Bliss and sorrow would no longer be a problem; after all, he'd lived through heaven and hell. Now, he thought, he'd face the emptiness of being, where there would be neither joy nor pain. And in the final instant, he'd do it in his own style, full of fury. And like a lightning bolt wrapped in a fleeting thought, the memory of his briefcase irremediably lost would come to him.

YUKIO MISHIMA

(1925–1970)

Mishima was considered one of the great Japanese novelists in the twentieth century. He wrote about love, sexuality, death, and the samurai tradition, among many other important issues. From a young age, he excelled in literature, and his work became universal during his lifetime and for many years was one of the favorites to win the Nobel Prize in Literature. Despite being an unwavering nationalist, he was influenced significantly by Western literature.

He spent his early childhood with his grandmother, a temperamental and domineering woman. Although at the beginning his father didn't support his literary work, his mother encouraged him. He wanted to participate in the Second World War but was unable to do so because of health reasons, and this fact marked his life because he wished fervently to become a kamikaze pilot and thus have what in his eyes was a highly dignified death serving his homeland. His most important works possessed a tragic sense and were highly stylized, reflecting the level of his craft.

He traveled the world, got married, and had two children; however, his literary career and imperialist ideas dominated his will. He was obsessed with death for most his life, and it was an essential part of his personal ideology, which led him to create a kind of personal militia called the Tate no Kai or Shield Society. Through that organization, he perfected the imagery of a symbolic but very real death, rejecting the glory achieved as a first-rate writer. Some critics claimed the awarding of the Nobel Prize to his mentor Yasunari Kawabata animated his decision to practice seppuku, a form of Japanese ritual suicide by disembowelment originally reserved for samurai, which mystique had influenced him. Also, he was deeply disappointed by the direction toward westernization Japan had taken. He planned his own death for several years in complicity with a few members of the Shield Society, assaulting the Tokyo headquarters of the eastern command of the Japan Self-Defense Forces, attempting unsuccessfully to raise awareness of what were, in his view, the dangers for Japan if the country continued on the same path, that is to say, adopting Western culture more and more. However, his claims were ignored.

Death may be the greatest of all human blessings.

—Socrates

To see a world in a grain of sand and heaven in a wild flower, hold infinity in the palm of your hand and eternity in an hour.

—William Blake

CHRONICLE OF A LONG ENDING

1

The dazzling edge of the sword crossed the short space up to his neck, like a beam of sunlight in a single straight direction. A final movement was enough to break the already precarious flow of life, like a thread hanging from nothing. A second before, he sat in wait and felt possessed by an iron determination that the next second would take away, when his head, detached from his neck, fell in front of his body, chopped off by the brutal inertia of the sword's heavy blow, rolling on the floor like something out of this world, unspeakable, and lying in a small sea of irretrievable blood. If only time could be rewound just a few minutes to retrace the steps of chaos, but it was impossible. It was as inevitable as having been born.

2

"What's going on? Why have they summoned us at such short notice? And with this cold?" "I have no idea. Nobody knows yet."

"But . . . there is a great commotion in the commander's office."

"In the general's office?"

"And the chief?"

"He's not here, but it doesn't matter. It does not affect the command at all. I know him well. He's one of those who prefer to die rather than make a false move."

"So . . . don't you think we should worry?"

"I didn't say that, but . . . it's kind of strange what is happening up there. Everything was very quiet ten minutes ago."

"Hey, did you hear that?"

"Yes, something serious is going on up there. The commander has been taken hostage in his own office and tied up to a chair with a sword to his neck."

"What? That's unheard of. It's an insult . . . and in our own headquarters."

3

Of imperial lineage and a neglected aristocracy, he came into being during a cold January in the most bellicose land of the East. He inherited the sword of an inflexible samurai and the pen of a scholar in the mists of a forest surrounded by a wild sea, unaware of human sorrows but capricious and beautiful as a poem never recited. As a child, the beauty of an old painting hanging in a wall of his childhood home portraying a falsely masculine equestrian figure made a powerful impression on him. He would think and later on reveal his childhood as a disappointing period, absurdly trapped by a willful grandmother who intended to live his life for him no matter what, a fragile seed although inexpressive and stoic.

He discovered his gift very early as the dawn of spring revealed the dew lying on the grass before dawn and was happy despite the scorn his insensitive father felt for his talent, surmounting the obstacles of life in a single flight of discipline and genius. The written word opened a trail in him like the edge of a machete in the virgin forest. Nobody could stop his intense inward look, neither the sun nor the moon, as if he was an irrepressible poet whose intensity grew in solitude.

He knew success from early on and used it for his own purposes— to open himself through the mask, bold, reckless, and dreadfully profound—and continued with imperturbable gait, his sights set up high from the beginning with impudence and self-confidence, seeing in the mirror the reflection of his unmistakably double erotic nature.

4

"Your son says he is tired? Was that what he said, woman?"

"Yes. You find it strange, don't you? It seems strange to me too, but . . . he looks exhausted lately. He's been involved in so many activities that I feel sorry for him."

"That's your son. He is not satisfied with his success, so he always wants more."

"Remember who shaped his character."

"Yes, I admit my mother is to blame for many things, but you have to recognize that, deep down, he has always been very independent."

"I see we are about to start the same old argument. You know that if your mother hadn't taken him away from me as an infant, our son would be different."

"Didn't you get him back? And he has never abandoned you, neither me nor his siblings."

"Because he is strong willed and, although he doesn't show it, full of compassion."

"Yes, we have to give him credit . . . but come to think of it. Have you noticed he has changed in the last few months? He's been spending time with people we don't know."

"As usual. But I must admit that his activities have changed considerably. I hope it's not for the worse. As a father, I worry about him, even if you don't believe it."

5

The pen used as a sword was his trademark, red as the sun itself with his imaginary cast of discontented warriors, defeated by their mythical vicissitudes. He was obsessed with a death that didn't come and that was necessary to find—the hero in search of nothingness.

The brutal war brought with it the defeat and humiliation of the people, and death razed the air with its breath of chaos, but in him, it kept igniting a creative inspiration again and again, like a river overflowing with tragic words and merciless sorrows, sublimating within him a fatalism that one day would reach the climax in his own being, when he would meticulously devise his long-awaited end.

6

"What happened with the speech? You finished too quickly."

"They didn't listen. It's like crying in the wilderness. I understand the biblical prophets now. After all, humanity does not listen. They only do it when there is blood involved . . . a lot of blood."

"Surrender! Stop this farce!"

"Ignore them. Everything must go on as planned. There's no turning back. I'll take off my windbreaker and proceed with the seppuku."

"If they wouldn't listen, I will not talk either. They don't deserve it."

"Well said, Morita. Now . . . I need silence. I just need some silence. Let us honor those who have fallen before us. Long live the emperor! Aaargh! Aaargh! Stop!"

"Do it, Morita! Again! Strike again, I tell you!"

"I can't! You do it, Koga. Cut off the head. And then do it to me, just as we planned."

"Give me the sword. Quick!"

7

With eyes lost in the horizon and a soft wind caressing his face, he can see the modern walls built by man and the great torch at the entrance of the harbor—a warm and hopeful welcome. The touch of death was still far from him; he stood before small boats full of restless beings who, like himself, looked in amazement at the prosperity of others, which was his too because he was a representative of civilization's peak. The metropolis opened its arms. Others did as well. He attended a great carnival in South America; went from one Mediterranean island to the other, a region he had always dreamed of visiting and that captured something beyond joy and mystery; and sailed the seas at will in search of the fleece that would serve as an inspiration in his intense career of ink and paper. He saw everything;

hears everything, suffered everything with an artist's sensitivity—the artist he was and had always been.

8

"Did you hear that?"

"Huh? No, woman. I was asleep. What time is it?"

"I don't know, but it's not morning yet. Didn't you hear that sound?"

"No, I didn't. And the truth is I don't want to get up. I heard nothing. Maybe you had a nightmare, woman."

"It could've been. But I tell you, I heard something like a scream. You know I'm a light sleeper."

"Look out the window toward the house if you want. Probably your son is still up, writing or something. Check if his light is on."

"He told me he was very tired and was going to bed early."

"That's unlike him, don't you think?"

"Yes. It's strange, and I don't like it, but apparently, it's the power of habit besides. And already, his body refuses to sleep at this hour."

"What do you see? Something unusual?"

"No, but his light is on. Poor son, a slave of his own genius. The muse will never leave him alone. I'll try to sleep. I'll ask him tomorrow."

9

The prose within him never slept. During the day, he wore the garments of fiction yearning to grasp beauty, force, and rich sonorities in a ritual of exhibitions that bestowed to his creations something close to life. At night, he entertained the world in Western-style parties, wishing to exist, to be different, but he only managed to move further inward to his own roots, becoming a distant creature even to his own brothers, discovering at last the practicability of death in the fountain that was his inspiration.

The Voice and the Fallen

He did not know the details at first but was very aware that tragedy lurked in the background of his work, like a demon manipulating his soul through steel threads. But he neither avoided nor resisted them; instead, he let himself go adrift to the end of a sterile sea. And he felt as if a powerful voice deep inside wanted to roar, but he still didn't know it and would never know it—that its foolish and empty cry would only echo disappointment and pain.

10

"We arrived right on time at the command. It's only ten fifty. Keep a straight face and follow me very closely."

"Good morning. Where are you heading, gentlemen?"

"Good morning. The general is waiting for us in his office. Guide us, please."

"Just a moment. Let me confirm . . . Come with me, please . . . Attention!"

"General! "

"Hello, distinguished gentleman, gentlemen. Hmm, I'm impressed by your military gifts. I didn't know that side of you, well, just by hearsay actually. You look splendid in your outfits."

"We're well trained, General."

"I see you have excellent swords. Are they sharp? And have you allowed to carry them here . . . in the compound?"

"This blade is endorsed by the prestigious swordsmith Seki no Magoroku. It is welcome everywhere. Koga, a handkerchief, please."

"Yes, sir!"

"But what are you doing? You can't do this! Don't tie me up, please! Come to your senses! You won't get out of here alive. What is all this about? I don't understand."

"That's the intention, General. Life is fleeting, like a flash of light lasting a second for the human eye."

11

Drums of war can be heard in the depths of his thoughts, filled with bloody and senseless stories once again and forever. They were soft at the beginning like a subtle symphony that went deep inside and became thrilling and unattainable. And he enjoyed it like no one else, as if he had been born for it—to die continually.

By crossing alien seas crowded with unlikely stories, he became more conscious about his own story, filled with forgotten heroes that went back in the past of his people, each more glorious and heroic than the next. He imagined himself riding a white horse of mythological proportions cutting the mist of dawn as he descended from the mountain as a quasi-real divinity that grew bigger with the blood of soldiers poured out for him; in turn, he became ecstatic as he inhaled the breath of death directly from their mouths. That was what he was looking for as he daydreamed, the road to true existence, not through words but by the sword—maybe someday.

12

"What year is this model from Chibi-Koga? It doesn't seem too old."

"From '66. It's beautiful and modern. In addition, it has style and is appropriate for the mission. Oh, how fast we got to the house!"

"Here he comes. Looks imposing wearing the society's uniform, don't you think?"

"Yes. And he is carrying his favorite sword. He looks impressive . . . and happy. How much I admire his martial bearing!"

"Good morning."

"Good morning!"

"You arrived on time. Let's go immediately. Here you are. This is for attorney's fees, and this is a letter in which I take responsibility for everything. Keep it safe. Chibi-Koga, turn right in the next corner.

We will drive by the School of Nobles. Hmm, my daughter is a student there."

"Would you like to stop for a moment, sir?"

"No, there's no time for goodbyes. I want to ask you a very serious question. What kind of music would start playing if this were a gangster movie?"

"'The Good, The Bad, and The Ugly.'" "That's hilarious."

13

Seen from the distance in time and space, we observed the daily landscape of a being who inhabited the land of vast and complex culture, who knew how to incarnate a character of his own creation, a character whose acts and thoughts were rigorous from early childhood, marked by an inflexible matriarchal imprint from which he couldn't escape.

Life went on its indolent course in the middle of the chaos of the war and his impossibility to take part in that war because of the fragility of his being, but it was not in his nature to fight for absurdities then. His great conflict was the search for purity in the language of his own squalid and hopeless life as the evil of many who succumbed to the moment, involuntary heroes who did not survive like him. Perhaps it would be his fault to remain alive beyond the unthinkable.

Success was his implacable punishment. It would become unbearable over time and the burden of having everything at the expense of the freedom allowed by a healthy anonymity; the happiness of being just another person in a pure and inalienable society, not the one given to the victors, ignorant of the millenary traditions of a truly combative people. In time, he would raise his voice in protest.

In that state of quiet vehemence, he outlined the intricate path to follow, planned rigorously and not devoid of an iron will, with a passion shared by a handful of men, equally blind and deaf to opposite reasoning. He would achieve his mission, like staging a surrealist and mythical play in a world enveloped in the individualistic vortex of meaningless consumption, like an inconsequential fashion in the flow of everyday life. No one understood the supreme act of wasting his life's riches. Only he would do it in the most indolent and theatrical manner.

14

"Son . . . thank you for taking care of me . . . and drying my sweat. I don't think I can stand the pain for much longer. I would be dead already if not for you."

"No, Grandma. Don't say that. It hurts me as much as your pain hurts you. I'll stay here until the last pang of pain is over."

"Thank you, my love. Thank you . . . you won't be with me for long. The last pain is near."

"How do you know, Grandma? I don't want you to die . . . nor suffer. There isn't a middle ground?"

"There's no middle ground. That's fiction. We are always on the verge of death, but we don't realize it. It is bad to die in pain but . . . not always. The best thing is to die with honor and placidity but, above all, consciously. That is true glory.

15

The day had finally arrived. It would be the last. He thought the sun would continue its march without noticing his absence, but this was always the case, even in wartime, in times of disasters, despite the achievements and failures of mankind. That was his consolation. But people would not be indifferent to his ultimate deed. His action would be seen as meaningful in the future, although difficult to understand. Questions would reverberate in the collective unconscious, but in the end, there would always be a reason why.

It was arduous, perhaps impossible, to grab by the tail the mystery of death. The knowledge of the end was reserved for the last second. Would it be as he had thought, that at that precise moment life would

The Voice and the Fallen

be filled with a meaning that eluded us throughout? Was it true that, at the very last moment, life would express itself in the final blink of the eye, and consciousness, before vanishing, would delight in the timeless instant? Was it possible he had kept his life in suspense until that point, when the sword ended its trajectory? The questions would be too great to be answered, but it was worth asking.

NIKOLA TESLA

(1856–1943)

Tesla was an inventor in the field of electrical engineering. He was of Serbian origin who moved forward the knowledge of electromagnetism at a practical level, being the first to develop remote control technology; he investigated extensively the practical qualities of radio waves, electricity, and its wireless distribution and also invented the famous Tesla coil in addition to the first alternating current motor, among many other devices, of which he left only the plans, and enthusiasts had finished them later on. Generally speaking, many of his creations were surrounded by mystery, and some were merely urban legends; however, the exact scope of all his discoveries—those taken to completion and those found in plans only—was hard to determine given the aura of mystery enveloping this character in the last forty years of his life and many decades after his death.

Undoubtedly, he was a misunderstood genius who—in addition to being far ahead of his time with regard to matters such as electricity, electromagnetism, the transmission of wireless energy—was also considered a polyglot; he spoke eight languages, was an amateur philosopher, was very gregarious, and was considered a great humanist despite being in favor of altruistic eugenics. His vast accomplishments could have made him one of the most powerful men in the United States. But unfortunately, he had a compulsive-obsessive personality and considerable mood fluctuations that, at some point, led him to hold outlandish beliefs improper of a scientist of his stature and to profess an ultraidealism that ended up threatening the interests of powerful people; therefore, he was gradually excluded from those high spheres, where he could have potentiated his financial gains, presumably due to some mental health issues that, although did not prevent the expressions of his genius, might have affected his trajectory in such a highly competitive world.

This story highlighted some of the most important moments of his life, and an intriguing element concerning the alleged plot to keep his legacy out of the public eye, something that was surprisingly achieved for a long time, despite the fact that his contributions literally changed the world, and throwing his legacy into obscurity was an unforgivable act.

Do not go where the path may lead, go instead where there is no path and leave a trail.

—Ralph Waldo Emerson

It is during our darkest moments that we must focus to see the light.

—Aristotle

STOLEN THUNDER

1

In the depths of a country that no longer existed, surrounded by mountains, peaceful at the time, in the middle of a remote and laborious land, a fragile seed was planted. Someday it would bear fruits in the form of a shining and magnified light, an energy unknown until then. Once as a child, he dreamed he would change the world; in the dream, he saw an image clear and precise, like a mathematical truth but without the numbers, only the image of an immense body of water, which in its current dragged the power of nature controlled by his will—the power of a colossal waterfall.

2

"I've met two geniuses in my life, sir. One is you, and the other is that young man I mentioned in my last telegram. He has managed to master the flow of currents—in theory, of course. I thought I wouldn't see it in my lifetime, at least not in this life."

"I'm not as gullible as you. I sent you to Paris to work hard, I know. But . . . why are you so passionate about people? What you claim he did is impossible."

"It was impossible, sir. The boy is brilliant. And he's still just a kid."

"Where you got that from? I see you have become attached to him as if he were your own son."

"He is a Serbian, but his genius is extraordinary . . . flawless. He is sure he will build the induction motor and achieve control over alternating current."

"Really? That is very dangerous, don't you think?"

"Absolutely. It would be enormously useful though. Think it over, sir."

"There's one problem though. I didn't invent it. You understand?"

"Well . . . hmm . . . but we can benefit from it."

"Oh well, I don't think he'll do it after all. In any case, hire him. Let's see where all this leads to. If he is as clever as you say, we can use his talents in other projects."

3

"What's going on?"

"Security staff tried to throw a stowaway overboard, and some passengers stopped them. This is ridiculous."

"Don't you mean it has been necessary to do it to set a precedent?"

"No, that's not what I mean. You and I are also part of the security staff, and we can't—rather, we shouldn't do something like that.

"Let's ask Smith. Hey, Smith, what happened? What was all the fuss about?"

"We caught a stowaway, but in this case, the charlatan insulted the security people because they didn't believe the story of his boarding pass and all his belongings being stolen, and he made a scene. He treated them like trash."

"What was their reaction?"

"They were about to throw him overboard. I don't think they would have come to that, but they were eager to give him a lesson. A group of passengers prevented them from doing it. According to him, everything he had was stolen. And to top it all off, he claims to be a scientist on his way to New York, where he'll run a great experiment, something about electricity, one of those crackpots that show up on board from time to time."

4

Once, a man wished fervently to turn night into day, darkness into radiant and inexhaustible light. He wanted it more than any other person born before or after him, to overcome the natural barriers hidden to the ingenuity of humankind behind a mysterious veil for millennia. And he, along with the effort of many other people, pulled aside that simple veil and discovered for a humanity anchored in a millenary past the immense flow of nature and in the process, like the simplicity of an idea in the trajectory of humankind, transformed villages into cities, small factories into industrial plants at the service of a humanity that knew only one possible direction—the luminous but evasive horizon.

Success was a trickster—that was clear to him and for those who accompanied him. Success was an invisible pendulum but with concrete and sudden effects, a train running at a staggering speed that could get derailed, and events would take an unexpected, ominous, and impersonal turn. That was success—a stone thrown at your head while being at the top, where destiny had elevated you through your own efforts.

5

"I heard the meeting was ruthless, but none of us had access, only the bigwigs and not all of them."

"You may imagine who they were—all the heads of industry, the rulers of this country."

"As always."

"Yes, the owners of everything, beings from Olympus. They are the ones who decide who keeps the head above water in the world of finance."

"In short, they have vetoed the young genius."

"He's been blacklisted, so to speak?"

"Kinda. And please keep your mouth shut. Spilling the beans could endanger our positions."

"No worries. I have mouths to feed. They've gotten away with it. Let's see how long their farce lasts."

"The lord of lords, JP himself, he has no intention of giving them one more penny, even though the genius's project was decidedly ambitious, far reaching, and already well advanced. Poor guy."

"Building those huge towers to send wireless signals to everyone and, in addition to that, electricity in abundance—for free. Unacceptable."

"Yes, it is intolerable for the group. They believe the project will affect them all and their industries as such in the long run."

"Yes, it's a commendable initiative but no less outlandish."

"As executives, we are protectors of their interests, and it's equally unacceptable for us."

"Do you think it'll be necessary to do what we can to block the little genius's projects?"

"I think so, and it is also necessary to undermine any credibility in any other of his plans and inventions."

"True. I don't see a more effective way to attack him at his core, that is to say, his theories. It should be easy in some cases because of the quirky nature of some of his initiatives. Who would come up with the idea of contacting the Martians?"

"However, the world would be a better place if someone could achieve such a feat. Don't you believe so?"

"But if you take a closer look at it, other large industries would be in danger, and a myriad of jobs would be lost."

"No, no, no . . . it's unacceptable. Besides, humanity is not prepared for such a sudden change."

"He must be silenced once and for all. And I don't mean, you know, his physical disappearance. Just by supporting his detractors, who are many, and not giving him more money is enough."

"The process will be long and tedious. Hmm . . . have you noticed something curious? After our conversation it's easier to agree with the point of view of the demigods, meaning our bosses. Well, finish those coffees, and let's start working on our plan."

"Indeed, let's silence that voice once and for all and let history go on its course."

6

The enveloping fog advanced a short distance from the coast; he never saw it coming, immersed as he was in discovering the world, in unraveling the rays and sparks hidden in nature. His senses, enraptured by the glare of light, didn't perceive the harsh reality approaching at a slow but steady pace; everyone else can see it coming, except him who fell along with his work when his throne was usurped by that bold young man who claimed to have discovered the way to propagate radio waves wirelessly at will. This overwhelmed him; it made him foresee a very uncertain future and, worse of all, feel that future as the most probable. They had stolen from him what he valued the most.

Since that moment, his destiny could not have been worse. His old mentor avoided him as if poisonous sparks came off him. It was better to go away and not look back. He fell, and there was no way to avoid the fatality when the fall was from such a height, when he didn't see the abyss appear under his feet. He didn't know it yet, but his misfortune would be marked by ostracism, hardship, and finally long oblivion until his strange and lonely death in a hotel bed, his body discovered by a maid three days later.

7

"First of all, we must know the schedule of his last outings, starting from the last weeks before his death."

"I think it's fair, but you know very well what he did."

"Yes. His papers are scattered in different places. Only in the last warehouse we inspected, he had forty trunks full of truly sensitive material, even though we don't know what the majority of it is about."

"The ray of death—that is our main concern. If the Germans find the plans first, we lose the war. You can be sure of that."

"Experts have reviewed that specific one already, and they concluded it is not feasible."

"Come on, they don't know everything, and this guy was light-years ahead of us. Besides, our enemies are still searching. And if they find it first, you won't want to know if it's possible to build a ray of death or not."

"Yes, you're right. If they develop it first, you will be derided. Some would want to retaliate against us. We must hurry, but if we get to a point where we just can't find it, there's the possibility they will not find it either. And after a while, if nobody finds it, we can claim it never existed."

"In that case, we must protect our reputations and continue to understate the importance of his achievements. It will be necessary to perpetuate his anonymity. Take him out of history."

"As if he hadn't achieved?"

"Exactly. That's what I mean."

"Perfect. We will consider it. Good thinking. We already have an Edison anyway."

8

Ostracism marked his life for a while, and weakened as he was, he worked on his projects like a dynamo powered by mysterious forces, never running out of ideas to feed his inexhaustible fountain of creativity. In aeronautics, in the way of distributing massive amounts of energy basically out of nowhere, he got tired of saying Earth itself—passive in appearance—was an endless source of energy and that air was also always volatile and full of electromagnetic emanations, but nobody listened to him. No one gave credit to the dazzling future he proposed, and intending to contribute to the antiwar effort, he collaborated with his country, which only proposed deceptive and misguided actions.

Misery, that great lady, ubiquitous in the life of those who did not reach the honey of fortune or who ultimately snatched from it a well-deserved success, had made an appearance in his life. Its shadow was persistent and ungrateful and full of anguish. It made him a nomad in the metropolis, going from abode to abode, from hotel to hotel, with his already slow step leaving traces of useless knowledge in subtle harmony with the faithful pigeons that accompanied him because he didn't trust people any longer. He went ever more deeply within himself and away from humanity, which had not rewarded his efforts and good faith. He preferred the company of these birds; they knew nothing about genius, but they recognized his sublimated tenderness.

Long obscurity awaited him, forged in one day. All the clouds had drifted away, like opportunities sliding between the cracks of time toward the center of the earth—the great oblivion. His feet had not walked the face of the world; electricity had not burst through his hands one day; villages had not been transformed into immense and impersonal cities overnight, thanks to his inventions; his shoulders had not been the support to a thousand people who had revolutionized the century. In short, his actions—as if dried fruits—became food for crows.

History was a war booty, the most valuable over time. Whoever held power owned the truth and everything else. With their vicious will, they buried the genius under thick layers of forgetfulness because he did not enlist in the ranks of power. But he thought he could set foot on clouds of glory beyond a mere mortal, the grandiosity of an alienated man able to reach the distant cosmos with his inventions or split Earth in half or end the war using a ray of death or convert Earth's vital energy into a resource everybody could use for free. The owners of the world exclaimed, "Simpleminded! Naive! You will be condemned to silence, and when your name comes up through some recess of reality, it will only be to magnify the vaporous mystery that surrounds you."

9

"Show me how much truth there is in that statement, and I will believe it."

"Isn't what you just said a little redundant?"

"Of course not. You just have to make sure to prove your statement."

"To begin with, the oscillator is a reality. He even mentioned it in the trial against Marconi and described its potentialities."

"Yes, but that was not very convincing and much less a definitive fact. People just laughed at him."

"But he made it! He did! Decades later, the project was developed in the most absolute secret . . . until now."

"Show me. Don't tell me. I need evidence, something undisputable."

"As you wish. I knew I had to prove it to you. Would you dare stay in the building while I start the device? It won't take long."

"You must be kidding. I believe you. I believe you. Let's go out. Why destroy this abandoned building or the Brooklyn Bridge or a country for that matter? You already convinced me. I don't want to die. Let's go to that coffee place you've been talking about so much."

JOHN F. KENNEDY

(1917–1963)

Kennedy was the thirty-fifth president of the United States and the first Catholic to occupy the Oval Office. He was the second youngest president of that country, coming to power at the age of forty-three. Considered one of the most popular presidents in US history whose policies went in favor of the civil rights movement, he stood out as a great promoter of the space race and opposed to his country's war policies. Precisely because of his way of dealing with geopolitics and the particular way of empowering himself in the role of president and as the absolute head of the armed, he made enemies within the main defense and intelligence organs of the nation such as the CIA and the FBI, as well as senior military commanders who were opposed to his antiwar approach, not underestimating his role in the failure of the Bay of Pigs invasion when he didn't authorize the air support so important for the success of that military action, which became a key point for the animosity generated against him in the CIA and the Mafia. Organized crime syndicates had been uprooted from Cuba by the success of Fidel Castro and his revolutionaries, and they wanted their business back.

Much had been said about what happened on November 22, 1963, in Dallas, Texas, at 12:30 p.m. in the Dealey Plaza. The Warren Commission formed by Pres. Lyndon B. Johnson to investigate the case decreed there had been only one shooter, Lee Harvey Oswald, known as Leon; however, in 1976, the United States House Select

Committee on Assassinations was established to investigate the death of President Kennedy. Its final report concluded, among other facts, that Pres. John F. Kennedy was probably assassinated as a result of a conspiracy involving several agencies of the US government. Rivers of ink had been written about this assassination, and the vast majority of authors agreed that there was a conspiracy to kill the president. There were many reasons for this assertion. He had many powerful enemies inside and outside government, so it was not foolish to argue that there was a conspiracy; and if there was, those responsible never paid for this crime committed in front of everybody and that became a cruel lesson stating that true power was invisible and had no limits when it came to enforcing the agenda that suited it best. The images of his death remained in the memories of those who hadn't been even born, and we'd see the death of this young leader destined to change the world as a sandcastle collapsing after being kicked capriciously but in a calculated way.

This story depicted that fateful moment on November 22, 1963, as well as other episodes no less important related to the event.

The only wealth which you will keep forever is the wealth you have given away.

—Marcus Aurelius

Greatness is not found in possessions, power, position, or prestige. It is discovered in goodness, humility, service, and character.

—W. A. Ward

The only thing necessary for the triumph of evil is for good men to do nothing.

—Edmund Burke

SANDCASTLES

1

It was, without a doubt, the great farewell of an era. Those gloomy sages, like so many lively birds, sighted the carelessness of their enemy with great anticipation that brought about the magic act—the unthinkable, a nonstopping moving scene of tragedy and bewilderment—in front of astonished eyes and those of posterity, forever amazed in a pain that no longer belonged to them as a laborious and poisonous thorn stuck in the hearts of those who, with innocent and confused eyes, saw all and absolutely nothing. A powerful specter had enveloped them in a macabre game, sheltering secret hiding places with the South Plaza as a stage, hiding nothing except sighs, terror, and anguish. How to know if the birds took flight too late for him at the precise moment before the sound of the first shot?

2

"It is a riddle wrapped in a mystery inside an enigma."
"Churchill."
"Do you know how many Roman emperors died by the sword or under other tragic circumstances?"
"No, I have no idea."
"Almost all of them. If you want to get yourself assassinated as commander in chief, make many changes. Win some personal enemies inside the highest levels of government and outside of it, commit your best effort to the benefit of minorities while remaining charismatic, and lastly, if you want a perfect and public death, wound the pride of the military. Above all, have your worst enemy disguised as your closest ally."
"I think that last one would be enough."
"Yes, but you'll only get them to put you to the sword in private, in a gloomy corner of your bedroom."

"But isn't it worse to do it in front of everyone?"

"No. The spectacle creates great confusion, which helps hide or simply get rid of evidence. Furthermore, it creates opportunity for blaming others."

"I see, but the successor runs a great risk."

"No, if he takes over quickly. Successful coups are those in which the perpetrator doesn't hesitate for a second. Of course, you must have the main details covered. There's no room for doubt. Hesitate, and you die."

"Ah, now I see everything more clearly."

"As I was saying, most Roman emperors died by the sword, the assassin's dagger, the poisoned food, a misguided passion, or any other tragic occurrence, but it's difficult to find a perpetrator acting alone. That is simply unacceptable, and when it happens, it is to be expected that the mastermind has enough power to make the majority believe that that is exactly how it happened."

"It's a perfect coup d'état."

"Not yet. To be perfect, the conspirators behind the plot must get many people involved, completely unknown to one another, working in concert. The assassins must be sought in far-flung places, very removed from the place of action so that it becomes impossible to trace him or them. No one will know their identities, and they would act disguised as everyday people. They will be ghosts that never existed. They will disappear just as they appeared, mixed with the shocked and bewildered crowd. They will be light-years away from the truth, and their code word will be an indecipherable mystery. If they don't proceed in this way, the truth will come out eventually and crush them."

"To achieve that, they must have all the power on their side."

"They'll have the media. Angry pundits will play their roles and pretend their truth is the only truth and will defend it as if it were a hidden cause and certainly will be, even if they are nothing more than pawns with no idea what they are defending."

"And all will be confusion, won't it?"

"Yes, exactly. Evidence will emerge by the score, by the hundreds, and all will be easily refuted with a good dose of chaos and, above all, distraction. This last will escape detection by even the best informed. Very few will discern the depth of disinformation, and in the end, they will be ignored. Time will take care of the rest, as always, by burying the facts."

"I feel nauseous just thinking about it, Oli. Better to know nothing and get on with life?"

"That's how conformists speak. Don't fall for it. Shouting in the desert has some effect. It doesn't matter that a fact gradually gets lost on the horizon as long as it's still visible. We know it is a tiny glowing ember that may take an erratic flight and may miraculously start a blazing fire in a distant forest. As the saying goes, 'The fluttering of a butterfly in Brazil . . .'"

"'Causes a typhoon in the Sea of Japan.'"

3

The last day would be the longest, full of receptive crowds. There was joy in his eyes on that sunny day. The previous night had been full of light jesting and fleeting premonitions, surrounded by the daily commotions subject to a promising future more permanent than the long sigh of battles already won. His benign fate spoke above all—the sun would darken before his defeat. His reelection was assured.

The airplane flew toward destiny amid glad conversations and promises. What would the sovereign couple talk about that morning while they lifted and crossed the clouds? Perhaps holding hands, whispering random thoughts, smiling openly, or gazing absently, he with the weight of a nation on his shoulders, the invincible young Atlas wrapped in an entirely protective aura, she sometimes watching the cotton-white clouds, other times giving him a little wink of contentment, waiting to be absorbed by the tasks of another day in her calendar of yellow and red roses.

4

"Is it cold where you are?"

"Not much. I can't get my mouth to speak the words. It hurts me so much to talk to you under these circumstances."

"Don't cry, please. You'll make me cry, and . . . I can't allow it."

"It's impossible . . . not to cry. This is killing me, your absence, what you're doing."

"There's nothing I can do. This is the point of no return for me."

"But there must be a way out of this for you. You can still get far away from here. Change your name. Flee to another country."

"I can't, even if I wanted to. The world isn't big enough for them, they will find me no matter what I do, and my end will be painful because . . . they threatened to kill my wife and daughters if I quit. It's inevitable. Please don't cry."

"All right, I won't cry because I love you more than anyone else in the world. These months together have been the best of my life."

"Mine too."

"But . . . while there is hope, we can find a way out. I want to have my children with you, only you."

"Don't torture me anymore, please. I feel as if the whole universe were unfolding and wrapping us in a warm blanket of stars. Your voice soothes me. Oh, how I wish I could be there with you."

"I miss you so much. I can't look at our streetcar without feeling like I'm dying. How did we get to this? Tell me."

"I don't know. From the beginning, this has been bigger than us. I didn't see it coming. It was my fault. Forgive me."

"I have nothing to forgive you. I wanted to be with you."

"Yes but not in this task. You must promise me something: don't forget the details I gave you. Remember the names and the three locations. The most likely place will be the plaza. The least will be the airport or the final destination. Escape wouldn't be difficult. The plaza fixes everything. It's more practical there and fast. The chaos will allow for an easy escape. If I don't make it . . ."

"Oh for god's sake, can't you make them abort at the last minute?"

"That possibility exists, but I'm not in control. They do. Perhaps if the weather—I know you're as much a believer as I am, but pray that it doesn't happen. In any case, my bullet will be one less."

"But can't I do anything to dissuade you?"

"It's too late now, fewer than thirty-six hours to go. It's impossible to look back. Now, my love, goodbye. But first, I'll ask you a favor. Have many children, the ones you and I will never have. Have them for me. I'll be happy thinking you will. Promise me."

"I promise. Goodbye, Leon. Don't hang up yet."

5

There was a large and amiable welcoming committee at the airport. A happy and patient crowd awaited them. With grace and elegance, she descended the steps of the airplane that had flown them to the Southern city. He, followed with just as much style as she, had a heartfelt smile on his face. His bearing was confident and satisfied, warmed by a generous sun as if it were also a part of the colorful crowd, defenseless in the light of his charisma. That was why he left his security escort behind and walked with spirited easy toward the small, controlled, and enthusiastic crowd a few yards from the airplane's stairs to make his first greetings.

The luxurious convertible limousine waited in the background, its former occupants the governor and his wife, she with her open, happy face, maybe thinking that she wouldn't trade places with anyone in the world, and him wearing a wide-brimmed hat as if emphasizing his belonging to that particular sunny space, holding the door open for his chief, who looked even younger and more vigorous in person, not to mention better dressed. His wife looked as if she had stepped out of a high-fashion catalogue, wearing a bright pink dress that matched her young freshness. She would be the envy of every woman under the midday sun. Someone gave her a bouquet of red roses before she entered the limousine with her husband. As the vehicle made a slow progress, its occupants waved mechanically at the diffuse faces who caught a fleeting glimpse at them through the sparkling arch of the sun. The security detail followed closely. A couple of hundred meters to go, and it would all start as they left the airport behind, together with the history of the past three years.

6

"Oh, darling, you managed to get an invitation for this exclusive party. The crème de la crème will be here. You can't complain."

"Yeah. You know me. I'm not half bad at this, just like you. Who would've thought?"

"Do you know who's going to be here or actually already is here?"

"I can guess, but I'd rather you told me."

"Well, hmm."

"Come out with it, you little idiot. Shoot."

"You already know the host. He owns this mansion and half the state—you know, the oil tycoon."

"I know him better than you do. Who else?"

"Dick. We don't know who invited him. Some members of the top brass, meaning an assortment of general. I heard that your lying boyfriend is coming, the interloper."

"That's a real surprise."

"Why do you think you were invited?"

"Oh, I heard that they're going to fete the Bulldog. Don't look surprised. It was impossible for me to remain out of the loop. Don't ask me who told me either. That's confidential."

"You're are an old fox. He must be on his way from the airport unless he's already at the meeting with them. I wouldn't be surprised."

"I think he's the main attraction. Can you confirm whether he arrived?"

"Wait a moment . . . Yes, is he here? . . . Confirmed, darling, he is here. I think you'll be surprised to know that there are a couple of

Jews at the party that I know very well. I don't think they're in the main hall. You know how those people are."

"Yes, that's quite strange. Oh, looks like their meeting is over. Here comes my boyfriend. See you in a bit . . . Hello, darling, what a nice surprise! Oops, you want to whisper something."

"Yes, darling, I'll say this. Those bullshit big shots won't bother me anymore. Hear me out, sweetie. That's not a threat. It's a promise, you hear me?"

"What do you mean by that?"

"Nothing, nothing. Don't mind me. Wait until tomorrow. Just wait."

7

The breeze was soft against their faces, but as they made their way in the open landscape, it became almost unbearable. He figured out that by sinking down into the back seat and not leaning toward the door, he could be more comfortable, even though his hair tended to blow over his forehead constantly, making it awkward to greet the crowds lining the road. He thought that once they reached downtown, it would be more agreeable in the shelter of the buildings. He didn't want to talk very much as he needed to save his voice for the luncheon meet and greet awaiting at the end of the journey.

The waves of people in the city awakened in him an unexpected but pleasant sympathy, and he felt it was his duty to reciprocate the greetings of all those kind, ephemeral faces that honored him. He thought for a moment about the hustle and bustle of the night before and how vulnerable he had felt in the hotel; the rain; the usual discomforts of travel, thinking that all this effort was just a taste of what awaited him at year-end; the campaign; the crisis of last year that seemed far away now. At one point, he wondered if he could cope with all these tensions for four more years. Would it be worth facing so many enemies at the same time? Then he thought, The enemies aren't human. They're the difficult situations I'll have to face. The greatest enemy of humanity was his personal nemesis—indifference.

So when they reached the city center, he felt a part of these people who welcomed him so warmly, seeing him a sort of proud father, one who happened to be in the most powerful seat in the planet, making the fundamental decisions for humanity—decisions they cannot make on their own. He got comfortable again in his seat, smoothed down his windblown hair for the nth time, and greeted the masses. He looked in all directions without focusing on anyone in particular, taking them all in as one body—his body.

8

"Do not abort! I repeat, do not abort! It was just a small incident at the contact point. All clear. Support team, over."

"One ready, waiting for big event, over."

"Two ready. All clear here, waiting for visual contact, over."

"Three. Front clear, no incidents, waiting. Have support. Request ETA, over."

"Control. Five minutes. Slow progress on Main Street, over."

"When they reach Houston Street, turn off radios and meet at contact point in one hour. Synchronize watches, over."

"Three. Some interference . . . one moment . . . all clear, over."

"Control. Don't switch off. I have visual on Houston. They're approaching the Book Depository, over."

"One. I have visual, over."

"Two. I have visual, over."

"Three. I have visual on Houston, over."

"Make ready in this order: one, two, three. Switch off radios in . . . three, two, one."

9

A cold breeze awaited them as they turned onto Houston Street. He whispered something to his wife, perhaps a banal comment about the sudden cold in the plaza or their proximity to the city center. His struggle with the constant wind blowing his hair was almost over. His wife looked pleased with the welcome from the throngs crowding both sides of the street. Living Houston behind, the three forward escorts spread out after turning onto Elm Street while slowing down for the long straight climb. Smiling broadly, he gave one last wave with his right hand, without losing sight of a long row of ladies waving their handkerchiefs as he passed by, some holding cameras. Perhaps he glimpsed the man with his back to them opening and closing an umbrella on the edge of the sidewalk, perhaps not.

In the background, the clear road leading to his final destination could be seen, but what was this? In a millisecond, he felt a sharp pain in his throat as if a filament of steel had suddenly pierced his body. He thought he'd heard the sound of a firecracker. I've been shot, he thought. His wife, with a quick move, wanted to help him as he began to faint second by second beside her, not knowing what was happening. He, between semiconsciousness and darkness, let himself be cuddled like a reflex, but it was useless; in the next two seconds, another impact would hit his head, fragmenting and blowing away the most important part of his being. He did not hear this bullet as he sank down in the seat, adrift already in the dark and eternal sea of death in its unambiguous approach.

What happened next defied explanation—fragmented light, pandemonium, a sense of speed, unintelligible noises, and above all weeping. In the background was a familiar yet incomprehensible voice. Suddenly, he was a child again; he saw everything but understood nothing. He needed no explanation. He saw a hospital, the ceiling of a long hallway, an emergency room. He felt no discomfort, no pain, nor was he afraid, just different as if afloat in an indefinable space. With no explanations, everything was clear somehow. Everyone seemed to be surrounding one body; they moved, they wept, and there was noise, but he had no sensations as such, no fears, no curiosity or anger. He was just there, present and absent, conscious and unconscious.

Then he felt something, like a fluttering as if a wave of bodily sensations invaded him suddenly and pleasantly. It was the last thing he felt. He heard the loud snap of an abrupt white light that he had never seen before, and just as quickly, it snapped off.

10

"Have you ever played chess?"

"Some."

"If you've only played some, you don't know that the game can be lost before the first move. It's the psychological phase of the game. In this phase, the advantage goes to the player who conceals better his or her aggressiveness and true intentions. Politics is the same, although the opposite strategy may lead you to the same results. The trick is when to apply the most favorable style."

"Of course, the moral is that you must keep playing even when the board is absent."

"That's it. The key is to never let down your guard. It's obvious now on that perfect day at the plaza, full of warm welcome, pomp, and contentment, that a checkmate was taking place."

"How was it possible when power always has the advantage?"

"Not when they let you believe that you have the power. That is true advantage. As I said, it's like chess."

"Then . . . if according to your simple yet impeccable argument it's all a chess game, with whom was he playing? In other words, whose hand dealt the checkmate?"

"Can't you guess? Really? No? I'll grant your doubts in face of the impressive number of opponents, but the answer is easier than it seems. Others have solved the problem with no small effort. Just remember the Occam's razor, which suggests that given equal conditions, we should choose the simplest solution. For example, who benefited by his death, and at the same time, who had the power to cover his tracks successfully and conceal everything with impunity? Who, in short, had enough ambition to climb into the vacant post?"

'From your argument, I can make only one possible, extraordinary, and simple deduction: our candidate would be the next world champion of our imaginary tournament."

11

Death looked on the idolized icon at his most vulnerable moment. Just one gaze, and a chain of improbable events materialized as if everything had been foretold, from his ascension to the throne, his return from the war, his long-ago birth.

His body—inanimate, disposable, useless—became yet another common particle when it lost the essence that gave it life, leaving behind an elusive symbol of what could have been for yet a little while and what wasn't because death looked in his eyes and said, "All your hours have ended."

The truth was a great official lie. It had always been, but better the blissful innocent to perpetuate that lie than the one who dug for the mystery in the facts. It would always be that way, no different from that moment when the sun disappeared suddenly in that plaza in front of everyone deliberately, shamelessly. It was hard, maybe impossible, to determine what the future would have been had it not happened. Only conjectures remained, unnecessary illusions, sad allegations. However, in spite of his opponents' arguments about the reasons, his words—composed from reality—would echo for all time: "We all breathe the same air, we all worry about the future of our descendants, and we are all mortal."

CHARLES DARWIN

(1809–1882)

Darwin was an English naturalist considered the most influential in the natural sciences by virtue of deciphering, through his theory of evolution, the way all living species change over time, creating new species from extinct ones through the mechanism of natural selection. He published his controversial book On the Origin of Species in 1859, and from there on, the perception that humans had of nature was not the same, displacing forcefully the creationist conception, which stated that a divine entity had created spontaneously all living species. It was fair to point out that the view posed by the book of Genesis continued to be accepted by a large part of humanity; however, as far as science was concerned, there was no doubt that the extensive observations made by Darwin and his extraordinary final conclusion marked an unsurpassed milestone in the development of an entire scientific vision of why nature and everything that inhabited it was as it was. Secular reasoning had been the great engine in the advancement of knowledge about natural phenomena, and the supernatural explanations, little by little, had been losing validity to the point that, in the great universities of the world today, it was inconceivable to ignore a theory that had catapulted human knowledge like no other in history, constituting the foundational basis of modern biology.

In his famous journey around the world in the HMS Beagle (December 1831–October 1836), he discovered not by chance but rather by the overwhelming archaeological and geological evidence found throughout his voyage that species, for some reason, changed to other living forms or species more adaptable to a specific environment and that all of them somehow had a common origin. And another very important fact he discovered was that the species that didn't adapt simply went extinct. And in that process, as the capacity to measure long geological intervals comprising millions of years was being refined, the variability of the species increased proportionally and spread throughout the globe as well, changing according to the vital space they had to live in and their level of adaptation to that specific environment. He also discovered that our species was not separate from this overwhelming biological reality; we were the result of a highly complex natural selection process.

These concepts were formalized in the second half of the nineteenth century, were very controversial, and still are. Darwin's theory had many objectors but many defenders too who deepened and expanded his ideas to a point where it was impossible for us to deny the evolution of species if we wanted to understand nature as it was, with all its mystery and grandeur.

This story intertwined real situations with fictitious ones to dramatize and speculate about how the theory of evolution was attacked and defended in its beginnings with the echo of a voice clamoring for truth.

Life is a shortcut of light between two great darknesses.

—Vladimir Nabokov

See the world as it is, not as you wish it would be.

—E. Lockhart

Most people do not listen with the intent to understand; they listen with the intent to reply.

—Stephen R. Covey

The devil can cite Scripture for his purpose.

—William Shakespeare

THE BATTLE OF IDEAS

1

The light scorched the sphere in an eternal present, but the passage of eons was not in vain since that distant alpha that consciousness did not register. Earth turned like an inanimate and erratic rock under the blind influx of a dazzling sun fixed in its perfect orbit, breathing life into it—a minuscule ember in the primordial soup. And the light, the movement, and the attraction were creating form and substance—inseparable in its unexpected fate. The bubble of life broke through the hot mist and chemical elements and went on to multiply.

A ceaseless flow of shapes sprouted from the water, the land, the air to the crackling sound of fire. There was not a crevice without a sign of life. Time was the only requisite for life to diversify into infinity, and through Earth's seasons, the life cycle of all species from birth, reproduction, and death occurred, along the way changing back to its natural shape, previously selected by successful adaptation. Life was already invincible in its indelible expression. There was no return, only a steady state of flux out of time itself. What remained to be done was to discover consciousness, and after lifting the veil, humankind can marvel at the immeasurable complexity of its functioning.

2

"Well, son, I've told you how the world works. God created everything in seven days, in six rather. The last day, He rested. I've told you many times since you were four years old, remember?"

"Yes, Dad. God created the heavens and the earth . . . and humans . . . and animals too. You've always told me."

"Indeed. It's that simple, son. If you ever hear a different explanation, it's a lie. The Bible is never wrong. It's all in there. I've always told you that, and you know I wouldn't lie to you."

"I know, Dad. I've always believed you, but . . . I've heard certain things in school, quite the opposite of what you've taught me, that man created God, and God can't be omniscient and omnipotent at the same time."

"I can't believe this. Did they tell you that? But you didn't believe it, did you? Tell me you did not believe them."

"Well . . . no, Dad. Of course, I didn't."

"You don't sound very convinced, boy. Do you want to go to hell?"

"Never, Dad, never. But I think I'm confused."

"Confused? How? I thought I explained it to you clearly."

"Yes, Dad. You said I'd go straight to hell if I believed them, but . . . they claim evolution is not wrong either and that all species have been evolving for hundreds of millions of years, and we've evolved successfully because of our great capacity for adaptation, and that's why we are the dominant species on the planet, but we are just one more species among many . . . that the universe is—"

"Lies! Let them burn in hell!"

"I know. And that's not all, Dad. They claim we are a species of primates."

"Primates? So God is a primate too because the Bible says, 'God created man in his own image.' Oh yeah, the Bible teachings are false. Tell me right now if you believed them. And be careful not to get it wrong this time."

"I'm confused, Dad. Sorry."

"But everything is crystal clear, son. How can't you see it? The Scriptures are the foundation of our beliefs. God dictated them to holy men. He made himself flesh and lived among us humans, to save us from the consequence of the bad decision that cost us paradise. How can't you understand that?"

"But what if everything is . . . a myth? Understand, Dad. They are right when they say that what feeds the truth is doubt and that, in the end, it makes you reevaluate things."

"You know that through faith, you don't need to reevaluate anything. A myth! Like a Greek myth maybe or a Roman myth, and why not like an Egyptian one? That is what you think?"

"It can be, in this case the Hebrew myth."

"I see you've been deceiving me. You read books you should not have read, behind my back probably."

"Yes, Dad, and I apologize. I only did it because I wanted to have enough arguments to fight back and be able to defend my beliefs, the ones you have inculcated me, but somehow things make more sense to me now. You don't have the slightest doubt about what you believe, so . . . something must be wrong in your belief system. I see it now. I'd better go."

3

The ship finally sailed off after a long wait. It might be said that this unassuming and reserved man of science had been waiting for this boat in this same harbor in a cold and windy spring in the north part of the island all his life. This was the ship that Aristotle himself waited for in any harbor of ancient Greece and with him all the biologists and zoologists and entomologists who have populated the earth before him in search of the hidden mechanism behind nature's movements.

The vessel sailed toward terra incognita, a region abundant in triumphant life through eons. And on the journey went a young scientist, his mind open to new things, to the encounter of the tiny traces of extinct species that would reveal the underlying reality beyond the seas and the solitary plains to the exotic south of the New World and in islands, mountains, straits, jungles, archipelagos, and isolated beaches, digging through Earth's skeleton, finding at last what man hadn't discovered in thousands of years, thanks to his distraction with the soul. He found the way to demystify the ancestral tale, the light turned off by the sacred letter. He discovered evolution.

4

"Yes, Lord, we have reviewed it repeatedly. We are gathered here, as you have ordered, and our decision is unanimous. With your permission, the battle will be fought."

"And are you sure you will not make fools of yourselves again? He has good defenders."

"However, he will not get far in his aspirations, sir, because our truth is rooted in the people through blood and fire over centuries. It is impossible the people will give credit to a ridiculous theory."

"Anyway, something worries me greatly. That theory is very prolific, and in spite of concerning a matter completely different from ours, it is still very attractive for the group of scientists who have been our natural adversaries in this strife, so you must put up the greatest resistance by the most persuasive means. I want public debates with this man."

"Yes, public debates. Excellent idea, Lord."

"I want attacks on his reputation and, if necessary, also on those who dare to defend him. Mock him because God Himself will laugh off his ghastly theory."

"It shall be done, Lord."

"Besiege his editors. Do not let those ignoble words to be spread. If necessary, threaten with excommunication. Attack him with all the means at our disposal."

"You are inspired. Our Lord Jesus Christ has enlightened you."

"And for good reason. This type of threat, however simple, must be choked at birth. The battle the Lord has entrusted us is ruthless but fair."

"Wise words, my lord. God forbid that this false science takes root in the learned in the arts of nature of our Christian kingdoms and thereby pour their poison from within."

"That will not happen! I decree!"

"May God, in His most holy mercy and omnipotence, keep that evil from us."

"Do you have any doubts about His eternal and implacable will? Neither your eyes nor mine will see that calamity, and the endless generations to come will not either."

"Yes, my lord, I believe it. The ways of man are inclined to the adoration of God through unwavering faith, and without it, no peace can be sustained in the soul of those fearful of His Word."

"Well said. Now it's me who is glad to hear those divinely inspired words."

"Thank you, my lord. It is a great honor."

"Now let's get down to work on this holy battle and overturn those vicious intentions wishing to do harm to our church."

"The emissary has been sent to the north. We will stop his advance."

"The attack has begun. Let us pray. Kneel on our sacred altar with me."

5

He found a sweet refuge away from the battle of ideas, where—in the warmth of his family and the distance—he discovered what was subtle and profound in the perpetual motion of nature. His engine was inexhaustible curiosity poured into the constant variation of organic matter whose essence was not unfamiliar to his fine observation, his true and more powerful weapon; with it, he would bring down walls built with the sweat of slaves of the Word. With it, it was possible to lessen the influence of a church carrying dark veils spread over the bodies of suffering subjects during long centuries; with it, he would embark on a staggering path, followed by many others with open eyes and clear understanding in generations to come.

In his peaceful abode, sheltered from his stalking enemies—the backward conservatives—with hard work and strength of will, he would find what he was looking for, the connecting thread hidden in the specimens brought across the seas, that relationship that united all living beings transformed by the same sun with its life-giving light—the unequivocal sequence part of all living structures bound to the functions that supported survival in different geographies. He discovered that man was a simple but powerful species with a much deeper and immense past more awe-inspiring than the one created from inert clay by divine breath, necessarily mythical like a fervent fable traveling through word of mouth from a dark but relatively recent past.

A great wall of ignorance fell but slowly and with much resistance; in turn, other walls would be erected through fear and the perverse control of naive and exhausted minds in a world that did not accept death in any of its disguises. The wall fell slowly and, in time, would fall irrevocably.

6

"Thomas, have you seen the bishop's face? I would have liked to be draftsman to have depicted his enraged countenance. It was an enviable moment."

"I am extremely satisfied with the results. If he had known this before, I would have tried to prove more seriously which family of primates he had come from."

"That's amusing. Oh, Thomas, Owen's advice did not do any good to the unfortunate bishop."

"Indeed. It gives me great pleasure to debate with religious zealots like him because I know their arguments lack any scientific basis as you could appreciate."

"Unfortunately for them, they turn a scientific debate into a personal attack, attacking your ancestors. That was very low, but you knew how to counterattack with class and discernment, which surprised me greatly. I wonder how you do it."

"You know, Harry. I sharpen my claws before going out. If they want to play hard, I also know how to play hard. I think I was born for this."

"Will you tell Charles about today's results?"

"Of course, I will write to him detailing what happened. I do not know how he is going to take the way I attacked the bishop, but I feel that, deep down, he will be satisfied."

"I believe so too, but I'm also afraid there will be some kind of reprimand. You know he is not a belligerent man. Besides, he has affection for the clerics."

"That might be the case, but I suspect that, sooner rather than later, he will change his mind. He cannot imagine the uproar his ideas have unleashed."

"And don't you think that the intensity of your defense will influence him at some point and finally will make him follow your footsteps in your fight for his ideas?"

"He is not that kind of person at all. You don't know him. He is a man totally dedicated to science, lives for his family and the permanent study of nature. He has converted his house and the surrounding area into spaces suitable for his studies. He has created a world away from the hustle and bustle of the city."

"So you have become the hermit's bulldog."

"That's correct, and I will be for a long time."

"I admire you, and you know it, but I do not envy you."

"I find it amusing, but to a greater extent, it is very satisfactory to fulfill my duty since it is a self-imposed duty as you understand."

"I would like to possess the boldness and firmness of your position, but I feel that fear paralyzes me somehow. I fear enough the church reprisals and even more the blind and uneducated people who are capable of everything as long as they don't see their idols falling. Yes . . . yes . . . I know we're not in Torquemada's time, but it doesn't matter. They are as ruthless with their enemies as they always have been, and don't tell me that times have changed. You know how dangerous this situation may be."

"I know you are not exaggerating, Harry, but you must understand that since the Enlightenment and beyond, studious men have been breaking free from the yoke of Christianity, taking slow but forceful steps. We must call a spade a spade—control of the people, those who think and those who don't. Theological reasons proved to be a dead end since St. Augustine's time. Look for heaven on earth! Please! Consciousness is here on earth. It does not reach the sphere of the heavens, and if it does, it is impossible to know for certain."

"But unfortunately, you can't reach those conclusions in a debate about the origin of the species. That is another subject of an investigation that will always be inconceivable for legions of illiterate people. Those legions can even kill fighting against ideas they will never understand."

"Suit yourself. You can continue living in fear then. But I'll be Charles's bulldog and do my bit to advance the cause in the understanding of nature, which after all will dethrone religious conception someday."

7

Human origins dated from so long ago, so distant in the deep past that only an unstoppable, inexhaustible imagination can glimpse into it. Perhaps an immeasurable crack opened in the land of an old continent to the friction of incandescent plates in constant motion, outlining the landscape over a defenseless surface once more and on a whim, creating a valley as big as imagination itself, generating the breeding ground for the incipient but definite sprouting of consciousness. Perhaps a disconsolate species fled due to abrupt and harsh shifts in their arboreal home, the only escape route being the bare ground, a lair of predatory and opportunistic enemies.

A single step of an individual of the species can cause a leap of quasi-infinite proportions for that species lost in the dawn of time. His flight made him erect his body, which was not yet prepared to survive in the hostile plain, on two legs; and after thousands of savage generations had come and gone, he looked up, finding the true context of the landscape. His hands were free now, getting ready for defending and attacking; by assuming for good a standing position, the size of the belly would increase and hence the volume of the skull, which would hold, in a far distant future, the depository of ideas, the greatest achievement of evolution. The species started in the black continent, creating a diaspora, a creative process of races and peoples as diverse as the stars in the sky.

To change our reality would be simpleminded in the face of the astonishing evidence carved in stone. The search for an ethereal body within us would be a vacuous task. Our animal origin was as undeniable, hard, hostile, and random as survival itself; there was no creative divine breath in our ancient past other than a stubborn remnant of a primitive idea anchored in the minds of the slaves of the Word, in the minds of legions fearful of death, upholders of the inexplicable myth who denied the animal nature in human origins. Those would be displaced from the shores of knowledge someday.

8

"Thank you, Bishop, for kindly accepting my invitation. I must say you are the first cleric honoring us with a visit. I beg you to forgive me for any inconvenience you may have had on your trip."

"The honor is mine. It is a real pleasure to contemplate your nice gardens and cozy home."

"I hope the work area, the place where I make my observations, is to your liking as well."

"Of course, but more than a pleasing experience, it will be a challenge without equal to contemplate the crucible of your extraordinary observations."

"Your comment flatters me, Lord Bishop. I hope not to disappoint or intimidate you with my results. Please understand that I have tried to be as objective as possible in the search for answers. It would surprise you if I told you that during my sea voyage, I was still a fervent devotee. However, the findings I made eventually ended up—why to hide it?—undermining my traditional perceptions of the world."

"Yes, I have heard some of that, but you also have to understand. It seems to me that you have not made an effort in the spiritual aspect proportional to the one you have done in your studies of nature. Therefore, when you went on your exploration trip, you were a man of faith. I wonder what mysterious designs changed your mind. Forgive my insistence on this matter, but it is . . . it was a . . . remarkable change and, to some extent, an insensitive one, if we take into account the strong Christian traditions so well rooted in the spirit of all good people, be they clerics, serious scholars, bourgeois, or ordinary people."

"Bishop, I'm listening to your words attentively, and I assure you that the motivation that has driven me to cross the seas and go to distant lands in a research trip has not been to undermine my fellow citizens' beliefs. Believe me when I say my findings are the outcome of the tenacious work of many predecessors. I have only been putting the pieces together whether I have found them in some hidden place, on an abandoned beach, an island brimming with life, or on mainland. And regarding the preservation of religious traditions you mention, I confess that the direction that science traces is powerful and inescapable. It is not in the nature of science to get stuck in old patterns because evidence sets the way forward, and whoever denies this is ignoring the great effort made by many human beings over the centuries, ignoring culture itself, progress, and the innate inclination of humanity to find the answer to our most pressing questions."

"There is no doubt you are a tireless seeker, a true genius in what you do, but I insist that in a way you have strayed from the righteous path. The things of the spirit do not require finding out a reason why. Your enterprise and achievements are praiseworthy but at the expense of condemning man's soul to the endless pursuit of knowledge, to his doom. As the Holy Scriptures declare, knowledge of worldly things will bring affliction and the perdition of the soul."

"Well, if you see it that way, I will not judge you. But remember, the goal of science is to illuminate man's path, not to confuse him. And if it does, that confusion must be welcomed because it is what pushes forward inventiveness, creativity, and the search for answers in an utterly material world. That is inevitable."

"As inevitable as the condemnation of those who have no faith in the things of the spirit."

"I can live with that because I do not have an adequate answer . . . to your concern, but what I can assure you is that my findings make sense in the natural world. For example, look around. Nature does not lie, only hides to the human eye how the world's remote past has been, teeming with specimens like some of these right here, some extinct and somehow linked to today's species that have adapted to their environment and therefore have survived."

"Very interesting, very interesting. Do not think I dislike the subject of your investigations. In fact, I am an unconditional lover of nature and sufficiently curious to be enraptured by its mysteries. However, my level of curiosity is not such as to make me abandon the ideas and precepts that guide my spirit. Unlike yours, and I say this with all due respect, I don't have the guts to deviate from the path, even when I would like to. It is too late for me."

"I understand, Lord Bishop, but please don't misinterpret what I have been saying today. It has never been my interest to change your religious ideas or people's for that matter. My concern is merely scientific. The trip I made around the world lasted five years and involved great sacrifices and personal risks, not only for me but for the crew as well, and all would have been in vain if I had not published my conclusions."

"No, no, don't misinterpret my words either, Mr. Darwin. What motivates me is an interest in your soul, your spiritual well-being, that you cultivate an interest for what is beyond the material and what you deserve. And in the end, you do not tarnish your soul by the fruits of a life sacrificed for a legacy well intentioned but ultimately wrong."

"I appreciate your concern, Lord Bishop. But rest assured, I think I know where I am heading."

"Excuse my insistence, but I have the impression that is not so. However, I give you credit for being a brave man. I hope to God you know what you are doing, and if you repent, I hope it's not too late."

"Have no fear. I do not see perils where you do. I am a man of science, and my duty is with it. Where I see the real danger is in silence when it numbs curiosity for being a victim of fear and lack of instruction. Unfortunately, for some people, the pursuit of knowledge means abandoning the ideas and precepts they have been raised believing in. It is not my case. My father was a great physician who taught me not to be fearful of scientific truth. If I faltered now and embraced the precepts of the Christian faith with all they entail, it would be like betraying him and myself. So I will continue on this road until the end. It would be unwise to turn back now."

"I see. It is your sovereign choice. I shall not bother you with my insistence. Now if you would be so kind as to show me your little secret."

"It will be a real pleasure. This is my collection of orchids. I'll show you briefly how each tiny part of this flower has a very specific function related to pollination and therefore to some insects and birds."

"Astounding. I thought, like everyone else, that this manifestation of nature's beauty was only an act of kindness from our Lord Almighty toward us, but I see now that science has a different explanation. Let's take a closer look."

9

The battle of ideas had been long and fruitful, some denying the glaring evidence, others denying that position; and so the struggle went on and on, year after year, century after century. But at the center, in the heart of the labyrinth of ideas, beneath the surface underlay a question that reverberated but remained hidden infinitely, inexorably; it took a lifetime to discover it, but only the privileged ones—figures of the forgotten past, always unknown—tackled it, wrapped in the material of consciousness like an invisible flow that touched matter and transformed it forever. That question did not have an answer.

Mystery exacerbated fear, blind belief, and a false certainty about the existence of a glorious parallel universe; it was difficult to embrace what seemed to be unacceptable, to turn eternal silence into eloquent words of hope, to accept that we were here by ourselves facing the sun, that we listened to ourselves, that we asked the questions and provided the answers enveloped in doubts and certainties opposed to each other and that impelled us to prolong life in a more suitable manner. Survival was the only law that prevailed in nature; the vast universe was indifferent to everything else. This had been the pale reflection seen by a great intellect, transcendent, profound, difficult to emulate. It had been said more than once that his idea was the culmination of human intellect, the cusp of thought, the most wondrous idea originated by the observations of a person—the idea that, in the end, might turn churches into mere historical monuments someday . . . someday.

10

"Son, have you reconsidered your position since our last talk? Remember that the fate of your own soul is at stake. Don't let bad influences drag you into the abyss of the damned."

"Dad, I think you are exaggerating. I'm just a student seeking the truth wherever it is. I appreciate your concern, but times have changed. Dogmas shouldn't have a place in a rational world."

"I hardly know you, son. You've grown apart from my wise advice. I feel I have failed in your education."

"Oh, Dad, there's nothing to regret. The way you have educated me has been excellent because your teachings have brought me other teachings. Thanks to its dogmatic orientation, I have realized there are so many other things to learn under the sun, and my curiosity . . . my curiosity has opened other avenues that, for better or worse, have helped me open my eyes to a powerful reality—I can think for myself and reach my own conclusions without others to dictate the way forward. Dad, I am free to search, to feel, to marvel at the most sensible conception of the world I can discover. And unfortunately for you, that is my absolute right. So thank you for planting the seed of doubt. It's been very useful. There is nothing else to say. See you, and . . . let me be."

THE UNKNOWN SOLDIER

Some say wars are inevitable. They are described as social phenomena impossible to eradicate because they manifest conflicts of interest between empires, nations, states, cities, tribes, and any other social grouping that supports nationalism as a collective identity and confer a sense of belonging to that particular social group.

Although wars bring destruction; disintegration of families, peoples, countries, and whole regions; arbitrary resettling of populations with all its consequences; absolute loss of property; epidemics; famines; degradation of the human condition; and all kinds of atrocious deaths as a by-product of the phenomenon, it is necessary to emphasize that war has brought about acceleration in the discovery of technologies applied to medicine, engineering, physics, and many other branches of human knowledge to develop better defense systems, an awareness of the limits of bringing destruction on the enemy, inventions that in principle have been created for combat and later become useful in civil life. However, in this dichotomy inherent in war, death is the prevailing factor—the death of combatants and civilians alike and, with it, the disruption of the future of whole human communities, giving way to lost generations.

The Unknown Soldier is a person who has once belonged to an organized community, a person who at some point has had a family, a job, owned property. Perhaps he has been a father or a mother, a son, a sibling, a friend; identified as a member of that social group; and played a role in the society in which he or she has lived. However, one of the many contingencies of war and one of the worst is that, after his or her death, the identification of the remains is not possible.

This story is about the quotidian, about a family with a military tradition and the expectations surrounding the imminent departure to war of one of its members, about the vicissitudes of that soldier facing the inescapable reality of the battlefield and a speculation beyond magical realism, about his consciousness after the conflict, and about a voice that deplores the nature of war, uncovering the harsh reality like a relief for a posterity that will not know how to stop it. The Unknown Soldier is the unthinkable product of extreme violence, the unspeakable personified injustice to the highest degree, in the end the son, father, brother, or friend who has once lived among us.

Lord, what fools those mortals be.

—William Shakespeare

The best way out is always through.

—Robert Frost

THE UNKNOWN SOLDIER

1

I have woken up in a boat, or that's what it seems. If a hypothetical being asked how long I'd been there, I would tell him a day or seven or one hundred. It's no longer possible for me to ascertain in a logical way what time it is. I will only say that I've been here for a while, and to my surprise, I don't care. Something in this environment has made me certain I can tolerate anything; it may be the environment itself. Who knows? I'll attempt to describe it the best I can.

This is some sort of boat with a sail in the center, it's made of wood, and it's about ten meters in length with a pair of oars and painted completely white, as white as a child's thought. The sail is white as a cloud, and I have the impression the boat is not being moved by the wind, and I am not mistaken. I see a thin smoke trail that comes out of the stern; it is so superficial that it vanishes within a small distance of the boat. It seems an elongated and harmless animal fading away on the surface. Suddenly, I wonder how I have ended up here in the middle of nowhere. I am surrounded by a body of water without end in sight, but again, what worries me the least is the water more than my absent and hissed presence in the middle of the boat as if I had been stuck in it since time immemorial.

2

"Please be quiet. Grandpa is going to talk. Silence! Have a bit of courtesy."

"Come on, Grandpa! Silence! Silence!"

"Yes, let Grandpa speak. Shut up those kids out there! Somebody stays with them. Children, be quiet! Grandpa is going to talk!"

"Can I talk already? Yes..? First of all . . . I want to thank God for having gathered us all here today, in this house, which belongs to all of you, our big family."

"Silence out there! Go on, Grandpa."

"Can I continue?"

"Yes, Grandpa, continue. We're listening."

"As I was saying, I'd like to thank God for having gathered us here today. It's a very special day for us and for our dear Tommy who as you know is heading for Europe tomorrow. He is going to meet his destiny as his father did when he went off to the Great War and as I did when I fought in the Civil War, being just a boy. And as many of you know, I fought for the Union, and that experience made a man of me quite early because I knew how to survive."

"And how you survived, Grandpa?"

"You can't imagine how hard it was, Abigail. But with a bit of luck and a lot of courage and applying the simplest formula for survival, I didn't allow myself to get killed—as simple as that. I told the same thing to Tommy's father when he was on his way to those infernal trenches, and he survived and best of all . . . in one piece."

"And here I am, Dad, very proud of your teachings."

"Thanks for being an obedient son. Also, I pray to our Lord Jesus Christ to bring us Tommy back again when he fulfills his mission across the ocean and becomes a real man after his baptism of fire in Europe."

"Grandpa! Grandpa! You allow me a few words?"

"Of course, Tommy. This is your celebration."

"I want to thank you for your words and tell you . . . and all of you that I'll live up to your expectations, and I'll take care of myself properly. And I want to say to Arleen, my beloved girlfriend, that we're going to have many children as we have planned."

"That's the spirit, son. Hooray for Tommy!"

"Hip, hip, hooray!"

"Now comes the blessing. Please, Reverend Johnson. Quiet down. The reverend is going to talk."

"Thanks. First and foremost, thank You, Lord, for allowing us to celebrate this day with our dear Tommy. I've known this honorable family for over thirty years, and I know better than anyone they profess Christian values—wise values that have borne fruit in terms of humanity, education, spiritual strength, and vows of obedience to the Lord, as well as abiding support for our community. And Tommy, a member of this distinguished family, leaves as a true Christian to perform the duty his homeland has assigned to him, with the boldness and courage that characterizes this family, regardless of the dangers the endeavor may hold. May the Lord bless and preserve you. Amen."

"Amen!"

3

Winds of war are blowing in the horizon for the unsuspecting Westerners. The drums that have once filled the air with cheerful and vivacious sounds now beat at the unmistakable rhythm of war chants full of dire omens. Nations against nations, sulfurous lightning and shrapnel fall on the people of the world, and nature quivers. There is nowhere to hide while the hydra of a thousand tentacles sucks Europe inside out.

Pitiful generations, doomed in life to the gnashing of teeth. It is the Teutonic revenge that flies over their heads, summoning deadly specters on green meadows; on bell towers, ghettos, parks, monuments, bridges, houses; on the wrecked lives of innocents. The ax falls evenly on the blossoming fields of mankind.

The unwary soldier heads toward the east, thinking for a moment he will participate in a feast of honor, the combat dreamed of by his ancestors, who wait impatiently for his return. He feels protected by the army men marching along with him on water in huge and still unbeaten battleships; by land on a trusting caravan of battle cars with towering canyons, a mechanized force of nature; by air on bombers, flying bricks that spit fire. And he arrives at the boundaries of his destiny to a magnificent foggy coast at the side of the channel, from where he prefigures terrible battles; and as in a bloody book, he just has to turn the page and start reading the next chapter full of surprises capable of squeezing a sigh of anguish and value out of him.

The balance of destiny glides smoothly like an unstoppable pendulum moved by the strange wills of men who have decided to fight a duel spurred by anger, pride, vanity, and greed. They will come to their senses someday, but it will be too late for those waiting at both beaches. It has always been said that nobody plays with fire without getting burned. They march on!

4

The boat glides on the water with me in its gut, which inevitably makes me think of my existence and nature's reasons to hide its imperfections, or maybe it's the opposite. What is certain is that I am surrounded by water, plenty of water; at least that's what it seems. Sometimes nothing is what it seems. I have a face (I can touch it), I have a body (complete), I have hands and feet (I can see them and move them to my whim), yet I feel that there are many things missing, and more importantly, I can't find out what it is.

Through small and medium-sized crests emerging with each undulation of the surface, I see a sort of fog that turns gray and organizes itself, forming vaporous layers around the boat. It comes and goes. At times, I think they have the effect of sleep. Since I've been here for a while, I have found the way to communicate with those strange sounds that can be heard at night, but the most distinguishable can be heard during the daytime, like fireworks very far away. There are no lights. I perceive them by staying still and counting them as if by doing it, they acquire some unknown meaning. I must point out I sleep most of the time or rather dream, and the nature of those dreams is more real than my mysterious nights adrift.

5

"Do you think we'll take them by surprise?"

"I don't think so. I know it. Not even we knew when the attack was going to happen. We were just waiting for a night like this."

"A starless night, only clouds and fog."

"A stretch of blue water separates us from the moment of truth. What's your name, boy?"

"Tom, but you can call me Tommy. And yours?"

"Call me John."

"All right, John, you know something? I am very scared of what awaits us on the other side."

"You must be. It is not for less. They've been waiting for us for a long time, but that's not enough to defeat us. They have no idea of the exact day of our attack."

"John, why are you so sure they don't know about this invasion?"

"Simple, they would've attacked us right here at this very spot. Maybe you and I wouldn't be engaged in this interesting conversation."

"Do you think they are more scared than us?"

"They should. They know we are stocked up. We'll hit them with everything we've got."

"My head's spinning. I'm so terrified that I don't know if I can go through this. Will I survive, John?"

"What kind of question is that? I think you're going to die of fear first. Listen, this is not about fear but about who attacks and defends better. At this point, you must embrace death as part of you as if it were your sister or your girlfriend. There is no return. Many of us will not see tomorrow's sunset. That's no secret to anyone, but that doesn't matter. We've already seen enough sunsets in our lives, so I suggest you move on to that beach as if it were your salvation, even if your steps lead you to death. Embrace it, love it, long for it, make it yours."

"Thanks, John. It's better to try to think positively, to stay still and see the others in their constant grinding or do what I have to do without thinking or distracting myself in this environment and helping others in their tasks. It's preferable to think about what awaits us on the other side—pain, death in life, or worse being captured."

"Tommy, you are a moron or what? You're thinking too much. That makes you weak in combat. You do not need to think. Just move and do not let yourself be killed, by the way."

"I can't help it. This is killing me."

"Well, wait until tomorrow, and your dreams will come true. Try to see the bright side in all this adversity. We can't wiggle out of this. We will cross hell, and we must do it in a hurry, says the prime minister."

"You're bad, John. If we survive, I'll show you who is the bravest. Warrior blood runs through my veins. You'll see."

"We'll know by tomorrow evening. Let's get some rest now. It's going to be a long day tomorrow."

6

Dark clouds have presaged storm among men. To the north, the white mountains have seen death in the valleys of stone and grass, where the blood of dismembered bodies has been spilled and those wounded by bones and stones made into weapons have drawn their last breath.

To the south in thick jungles and open savannas, in the middle of tropical foliage where an arrow or perhaps a spear fulfills its mission is the promise of a bloody death during endless tribal wars, the result of conflicts dating back to the dawn of civilization.

War is a complex source of advances in humankind's path. It's a the dark light on a somber road that leads to this strange radiance at the end where lifeless bodies are counted by the hundreds, by the thousands. It's a chaotic course toward carnage where the perception of death has a sweet taste almost in the face of individual fatality and predicts a future of pure oblivion, unacceptable to those heroes who have given something more than their lives.

Invaluable defense systems are created, imponderable death sortilege, colorful costumes hard as the steel forged by people wearing them but weak in the defeat, wounded by the magical gunpowder that flies with a thousand knives through the bodies of men, women, children, and the elderly without asking about their past, present, or blighted future, shattered by the will of the enemy warrior—the species of winners and losers. Everybody suffers its brutality. There is no place for futile lamentations.

7

In my dreams as in a leitmotif, I can see a beach house, and there's a family inside. I get the strange feeling the place represents my eternal and ultimate anguish. Will this vision be the unique form of the limits of my reason linked to a feeling or is a vain mental construction made of random longings? I don't know, but I have the intuition of being part of that family. Falling asleep, waking up, falling asleep, and waking up again—such is the structure of that other reality, so unknown as the one where I am on this drifting boat.

I assume I'm going somewhere or maybe nowhere. Perhaps this is a timeless voyage in space, but to be fair, I want to begin by telling the implausible stories my dreams consist in or what I have perceived through the mist at the height of that beach—I am the master. A sense of fulfillment invades the others before my presence, and I can perceive it somehow. My countenance is obtuse, I know. Feelings are gone. Later on, they look at me with blank expressions on their faces as if I didn't exist anymore in their quotidian alienated world; not even the dog roaming around under the table is curious about my presence, but I am not surprised either. After an unmeasurable moment, I wake up.

8

"John! John! I feel like I am suffocating!"
"Stay still! Look at the clouds, the sky. Don't think."
"I can't stop thinking. I don't want to die!"
"I told you not to think! I don't want to die either, but we must hang on and fight."
"How long will this last, John? I think I'm going to vomit."

"Hold on! You think I don't feel like throwing up too?"

"The noise of the cannons is driving me crazy. This damn war is driving me crazy."

"I'm going crazy too, Tommy, but . . . we're not in hell yet. The hardest part is yet to come, so be brave. We must take that damn beach at any cost! Try to be courageous!"

"This piece of floating tin is a mousetrap. I can't see the sea."

"And why do you want to see the sea? We must see the beach. We must cross it. You understand? And to kill all the Germans in our path, that is what we got to do."

"Yes! Killing Germans! I'll do that."

"And something very important, Tommy—do not get killed!"

"I already know it. The cannons will help us, right?"

"Yes. When we reach the beach, they will be decimated. You'll see. We will be everywhere. It's going to be very difficult for them with whatever they have left. We're just going to switch places. Most of them will be dead when we get there. You'll see I'm right in the end. This won't be our last battle. We're going to strike by sea, air, and land. Look! Look! Air raids. There is the Royal Air Force. You see all those planes? We are going to win the war, I assure you. Stay alive, and you will see."

"Yes, I will stay alive, I will stay alive, I will stay alive."

"Okay, okay, I know you'll do it. Do not waste more energy thinking. Your mind must be clear so you can move as efficiently and safely as possible."

"Yeah . . . did you hear that? It's the sea bottom. We are almost there."

"All right, listen, once we reach the shore, the boat doors will open, and we will kill Germans. Did you hear me? Kill Germans!"

"Yes, I got it. What the hell is that? They are shooting at us! From everywhere. Keep your head down, John! Down!"

"It's time, Tommy. Take the safety off your weapon and say Our Father. I will do it in silence. That's where I get courage from. Do it now."

9

I wake up in the middle of a dream, invaded by a fulminant twilight that gripped the heavens at some point during my dream or lethargy. I remain motionless a long time as if I had fused myself with the boat. After a moment, I decide to wake up completely and demarcate my lucidity in this new state of life or whatever this is.

I look up at the ubiquitous sky and think that to describe the endless dusk will be the perfect work for a colorist. Green and orange strokes intermix in an indescribable mauve, and toward the boundless sunset is a surreal degradation or exaltation of the yellow color, conquering the reddish orange suspended just above the horizon similar to a dazzling and unreachable portal as the horizon itself. I figure that behind that door, the mythical and nullifying death of consciousness awaits behind heaven's kaleidoscope with all the possible answers.

I have seen all that from this boat, but there's the striking fact that the only living thing here is me. I have not seen birds or a fish or one person outside the dream. Perhaps the sea is alive and the wind, with its whispers and fury; and this boat, that before me, may have had another passenger. Is it mine now? Will I arrive at some destination?

10

They depart swiftly from the wide meadows of Western Europe unannounced like a flock of crows, ominous and determined—the advancement of the great Parka, flying over greens and lavish plains cultivated for a posterity that ultimately will not be. The grim horseman rides guiding the throngs of thick boots and terrible armors toward the open space of the weakened enemy who does not expect the bloody ray that passes through him.

Bombs rain down on the east as clusters of poisoned fruits, spreading hopelessness without rhyme or reason; then to the north of their borders—like inertia, lightning strikes in the same manner—and to the rich west blinded by the rolling cannons vomiting fire in the middle of the dense forests, a useless barrier for an army stunned by greed. Nothing is forgiven in the middle of the inordinate conquest. Humiliation, anxiety, terror, power, resilience, pride—a torrent of emotions spring from the conquered and conqueror. Fear prevails on both sides like the sword of Damocles hanging awkwardly over the heads of everyone. Chance has no favorites. A pendulum of fate intertwines their fluids while generations of races are cruelly persecuted, determining another future course of history chained irrevocably to the past of a futile and senseless war for all involved.

The trajectory of the victorious arrow changes. Industrious bright cities turned into ruinous gorges, rugged and skinless. Ragged, starving beings—children of the war—hold up the broken, empty, and dirty cup of ravaged opulence. Barely alive, dragging their feet in tunnels corroded by shrapnel and puddles of blood and mud, they pour their hearts out in a tearless cry.

Battered soldiers fight in agony; up in the sky, treacherous clouds reveal their positions, the same sky where they have fought air battles successfully. Now the Spitfires have become balls of fire and smoke spiraling down, unable to protect the vast beach taken with suicidal violence by the enemy. It is total disarray. They have touched their sky of imperial illusions extended far to the west a long time ago. Everything is smoke and ashes. The stubborn leader, slumped over his own curse, clings insensibly to the lost beach. It's already too late; the poisoned arrow flies back to him hopelessly.

11

"Fucking bullets flying everywhere!"

"Run, Tommy, run! To the bushes!"

"Shut up! And keep running. Look out for the mines! To your right! Shoot there . . . more to your right! I think I saw something."

"They're coming down . . . shoot at that bunch of soldiers! I'll cover you."

"No! Those are on our side! They're looking for a less dangerous position. Shoot upward. Come on, be brave!"

"Let's fuck them all!"

"Shoot at the ones firing mortars. Come on! Quick!"

"Down! . . . John! . . . John! Shit! That was close . . . John!"

"I'm deaf! John! John! Where are you? Nooo! John! Nooo! You can't die now when I need you most. Don't leave me alone in this hell."

"Tom . . . I'm still alive. Argh!"

"Don't move, John . . . I'll get you out of here."

"No! How the hell are you going to get me out of here! Go, save yourself. I'll cover you. Keep moving."

"I won't leave you behind. I'll move you a little. Hold on. I'm going to check your injuries."

"Aargh! Go! Get moving, damn it! I'll cover you."

"I think I stopped the bleeding. I told you I'm not leaving! Also . . . you can't cover me. They won't see us from where we are. Stay calm and try not to move. The doctors will arrive soon and will take you out of here. Then I will continue moving forward. More troops are coming, and they'll get us out of here. Just stay in that position."

"Shit! I can't stand the pain! Let me die and go. They discovered us already!"

"We can't move further with this hail of bullets."

"That was close! Damn Nazis! Don't move. Reinforcements are coming. Let's kill them all! The war is over now. Soon we will be across the ocean. You will join your wife and little son. John! I see you at your job again. I promise I'll visit you. Our families will meet . . . I'm not lying to you. Arleen is the most beautiful woman in America . . . uff . . . keep your head down, John! I'll introduce you to Grandpa. I'm talking a lot . . . I know I'm talking . . . I can't hear much, John, forgive me . . . I'm nervous, just a little. They can't see us. That's good, John. Did I tell you you're going to like Grandpa? You're going to love him, I'm telling you."

"Tommy! Tommy! Try to listen! Look to your left! Left, look! They are preparing the mortar. Shoot them now! . . . Did you see that? That son of a bitch bit the dust. It was spot on. You hit him. Bravo!"

"Yeah, I did, but it won't take long for them to get the mortar ready again. They discovered our position, and we're stuck here. Fucking Nazis are everywhere. Wait . . . they're moving away!"

12

The dance of death has crossed Europe on all four sides, indifferent, unconditional. The dancers, victims, and executioners stir up their woes at the rhythm of the same pain while Earth, insensitive, rotates with all of them in its belly, guaranteeing absurd winters, unnecessary storms, and intolerable sunsets in the midst of the agony of man who—while killing—survives.

Red rivers spring from smoky streets, squares in ruins, stifled mountains, splintered forests, besmirched beaches while memory accumulates, and the intellect reasons about this singular delirium where life is dispelled like a blade of grass in a blizzard or rather as simple as drinking a glass of water carelessly.

13

At times, I'm aware of everything around me—of the wind over the sea contours, of flashes of light interspersed with water vapor, of the line of the horizon changing slightly from my perspective, and above all of the material and accomplice silence as if it were alive and part of me—while the long twilight ends, giving way to a pleasant starless night.

Sleeping and waking up alternatively, lulled by the distant sound of fantastic thunders reverberating in the air, I look above the small deck, the glow of fleeting battles among the clouds hurting my eyes like a subtle caress. And I fall back asleep hopelessly.

I have woken up in the morning strongly impressed by my last dream: I was walking casually along the beach, led by the usual inertia—the same beach, empty, crystalline, welcoming. I was walking along at a gentle pace until I reached the familiar end of the road, with the little house at the top of a small hill surrounded by unknown foliage but very pleasing to the eye. I climbed the stone steps with little effort as if I had done it using my mind instead of my body. To my surprise, I noted that the little beach house was painted bright red. At first glance, it seemed to be a different house; however, the location was the same. This fact alone had the powerful effect of imbuing my dream with lucidity. From that moment on, my perception of that reality was sharper, the colors were more intense, I was aware of my breathing and of small and pleasant tingles under my skin. Afterward, everything was very fleeting; within a few seconds, the impact of these sensations made me feel as if I'd been teleported to the boat.

I wake up regretting not having been able to hold on to that alternate reality. In that instant, I realize I have not eaten anything in all that time, nor have I felt hungry. Then I wonder, Am I already dead?

14

"After so much sacrifice . . . and so many casualties, the beach has finally been taken."

"The high command wants a meticulous report on casualties and damage—soon."

"We are working on it, sir . . . we are working on it. We have run out of body bags. Up here only, there are more than a hundred bodies, and many of them are unidentifiable. There are hundreds more all along the beach, even in the water, sir. There are dozens of soldiers drowned. Probably the weight of their backpacks dragged them down. Apparently, they didn't know how to swim and couldn't reach the shore, sir."

"It's unfortunate. The bombing of the airplanes and battleships passed over the German defense posts. And . . . we paid the price. But we must go on. The war is moving south, in all directions. So we need that report today."

"Yes, sir. We will continue collecting the remains. Some have dog tags, Captain, but others don't."

"Since when is that a problem, Soldier? Let's do this quickly. There are more body bags over there. We got to get moving!"

"Understood, Captain! Hey, Soldier, I have a headache of all hell. I couldn't complain to the captain. You tell me what to do with these two. Their heads are gone. But this one at least is holding his dog tag in his hand. His name is . . . hmm . . . John Hernandez, but there is no way on earth to identify this other one. There's only a bundle of clothes and an incomplete body, all scorched. Our superiors want us to do miracles, don't you think?"

15

Humanity is born alone and dies alone. Exhausted humankind is occupied with extinguishing itself in full view of the numinous being invoked in the darkness of reason from an isolated corner where his replies don't reach anyone, and those replies only emanate from our own distressing thoughts, offering a mysterious consolation to real sorrows in the form of an echo full of longings for what could have been but isn't because greed, the great instigator of chaotic designs, has taken care of the victors and the vanquished in due time; however, the enigma of the void is more powerful than the pain and the grief. Hope is illusion crystallized, which finally achieves to deceive reason.

The night has come to an end, clearing the lonely and cruel road traveled by humankind during wartime. The trajectory of the butterfly has created a chasm in the future, immeasurable, unavoidable. Reality is or isn't, or it listens to us, or we are alone with the sea and heaven and earth as witnesses, together, separated, embodying each other, in pain and ecstasy, in agony and pleasure, in peace and in war. The bells have tolled at the end for all the beings who are born into hope and faint facing the confusion and mystery of death when, invariably, we become unknown beings for all eternity.

16

"Have you understood what the march is all about? What does the ritual mean? The symbolism of the ceremonial steps and the immense coffin? The first thing that comes to my mind when I see it is a luxurious mass grave."

"I didn't understand much about the march, the ceremony, or whatever you want to call it, but I can tell you something—I loved it, and I think the reason is the deep respect shown for the unidentified fallen. It intrigues me that they are three soldiers."

"It got me thinking too. And it has also impressed me. The problem is I have the feeling it is overloaded with symbolism and drama."

"Yes. All this is typical of a very expressive society. I love the detail of setting the pace with stomping steps. It provides a musical touch in the middle of the silence. I really like it. And I'll tell you something, it seems to me that under the surface, the ceremony is about the cult of death, of the unknown—to the afterlife, if you will."

"Of course. We are in a cemetery. What you say is very logical, the living visiting the dead in our future abode. You know what? I liked the ceremony, and despite not understanding it at first, it has a moral—all humans have mourners and the Unknown Soldier even more."

"Then . . . in conclusion, it is a ceremony to death itself and to the nameless darkness that awaits us."

"You know, if you think about it, we all fit into the Unknown Soldier's coffin."

GALILEO GALILEI

(1564–1642)

Galileo was one of the greatest and most influential figures of the Renaissance. His work revolutionized the world of science, including engineering, astronomy, physics, mathematics, philosophy, mechanics, and other branches of human knowledge. From a very young age, he expressed the curiosity and the creative ability to break with the paradigms of his time, and that was an important point because of how dangerous it was to try to change the prevalent perception of the universe in his era, when the Inquisition exerting its power through the Catholic Church controlled what could and could not be said or published.

He was a wise man from a young age, a willful, progressive university professor with a good sense of humor, eloquent and sarcastic while being respectful. He did everything possible to break the Aristotelian paradigm of the time under which the church operated concerning observations of certain natural phenomena, having as defenders of this conceptual modality the Collegio Romano run by the Jesuits, who played an important role in the controversy regarding heliocentrism and managed, with more skill and power than reason, to ban the Copernican precepts that established that the earth wasn't the center of the universe but the sun, at least of the universe known up to that point, ideas to which Galileo subscribed, especially after studying with the telescope—improved by him—the orbit of Venus and discovering Jupiter's satellites and the surface of the moon, establishing that it was not smooth as Aristotle had claimed almost twenty centuries earlier.

Galileo lived a long life but quite unhealthy in his last years, suffering bitterly the onslaught of the Inquisition because of his stubborn position, based on his scientific innovation, that the earth was not static and that all the celestial objects did not revolve around it.

He had two daughters and a son; the first two were illegitimate because they were conceived out of wedlock, so it was necessary to send them to a convent, that of San Matteo de Arcetri. He had a constant correspondence with his eldest daughter, Maria Celeste, until she died during the plague, a scourge that isolated her time and region. The letters she sent him were kept in the Vatican Museum because the church confiscated all of Galileo Galilei's possessions as part of a house arrest sentence for life. The sentence constituted a papal grace in virtue of Galileo's friendship with Maffeo Barberini when the latter held the title of cardinal. However, Barberini was ill advised by Galileo's enemies, managing to carry out the infamous trial against him and sentencing him to life imprisonment and finally changing it to house arrest.

In this story, I dramatized some conversations he had with his first biographer and companion, Vincenzo Viviani, who asserted that the famous Pisa experiment was indeed carried out, although there was no sufficient historiographical evidence to support that claim; however, for the love of Galileo as a paramount figure in world history, I'd assume the experiment was made. I didn't think it disrespectful to fill some historical gaps with urban legends that—who knows?—could have some truth in them.

Also, I speculated about the supposed discovery of the letters that Galileo sent to his daughter at the convent, letters whose whereabouts had been unknown since the sole name of Galileo was considered anathema. When his daughter Maria Celeste died, it was said that the Mother Superior of the convent disposed of them as best she could; either she burned them or she hid them so well that they were lost forever, or perhaps she threw them into some abandoned well in the vicinity to simply get rid of that potentially dangerous material.

The name of Galileo Galilei would always represent humanity's right to search for truth through reason and dismiss superstition and dogma as the main method for searching the truths that had evaded us since time immemorial.

Our greatest glory is not in never failing, but in rising up every time we fail.

—Ralph Waldo Emerson

Every moment of light and dark is a miracle.

—Walt Whitman

If opportunity doesn't knock, build a door.

—Milton Berle

RAISING HIS GAZE TO THE SKY

1

"Ludovico! Ludovico! Don't you hear me? Tie it to the rope!"

"I need another flashlight! Get me another flashlight, please!"

"Okay, stop yelling. You're going to suffocate down there! I can scream! You shouldn't!"

"I can't see anything down here . . . and it's hot as hell. Pull me up now!"

"Stand still! I'm going to pull you up!"

"Oh, the surface. What a relief!"

"Let's take a break. I'm dead tired too."

"We'll rest later, Lucca. Let's see what we have here. It seemed to be a box, maybe a trunk."

"It is in very bad condition. It must have been down there for more than a hundred years."

"It must be over a hundred years old. It's in terrible shape. This well was dug when the convent was built, and as far as I know, that was more than seven hundred years ago, but the well hasn't been part of the convent for centuries. As I told you, it is likely that the nuns used it centuries ago. God only knows how long it's been since it dried up."

"Anyway, that doesn't matter now, Ludovico. Let's see what's inside. Get me your knife."

"Wait, put on the protection mask and be careful. Any vermin can get out of there."

"Oh, what is this?"

"Papers! A jumble of papers? And I almost choked down there!"

"Shut up. They are papers but old, very old."

"And nothing else? Take a closer look . . . give me the damned box. Where are the diamonds, the relics, the gold?"

"What gold are you talking about, Ludovico? Your mother's gold? You almost suffocated to death down there for a pile of papers. It makes me laugh."

"Let me see them. There must be something valuable here. I didn't take such a risk for this trifle. Give me the knife. I'm going to see what these papers are about."

"They are letters, Ludovico. Letters! It's so funny. Written by some jilted bride maybe? You tell me. You're the expert here, the poet."

"Shut your trap, Lucca. I'm trying to understand this hieroglyph. They're letters from a father to a daughter. Let's see. It says, 'Do not worry, daughter, I'm getting better, thanks to your timely remedy. You are an angel. What would I do without you? Thanks to your dedication, my legs hurt considerably less, and I am walking without help.'"

"Stop it, I'm not in the mood for such things. We must go back to work. Lunchtime is over."

"Wait! Wait! I can't believe it! I'm scared now! If I'm not mistaken, Lucca, this is worth more than gold. Check this out. Tell me I'm reading that name. Tell me that's the name!"

"You're losing your mind, Ludovico. I only see G.G. written there."

"No! See below!"

"Goddamn! That man is a celebrity. But can you tell me why these letters were in the center of hell?"

"What do I know, Lucca? An expert must determine that."

"What are we going to do now? This has to be a very valuable material."

"Yes. Let me think for a minute. There's no time to lose. We must clean all this up and read them carefully to see what they are about. There are many. We have a lot of work to do."

"I'm excited, Ludovico. You see, my advice was worthy. I have a knack for important findings. Just see how well they hid them in this old well. I told you."

"Yes, yes, I can't deny it. You have what is called instinct, Lucca, but I'll ask you something. Let's keep it between you and me. Did you hear me, Lucca? Between you and me, at least until we have the right information. Is that clear?"

2

Was the cosmos the divine breath in the expansive nothingness before the first moment when a chaotic flash gave birth to energy and matter? Was that universe, in wandering expansion, randomly widening in the ether in infinite bubbles ever farther away, where space-time originated in the form of particles that linked together to form suns and planets, gas clouds, galaxies, clusters and more universes without more purpose than the fact itself? Was that same universe all there was and nothing else, without awareness of its own existence other than the anomaly humans represented in this tiny blue dot called Earth?

One gaze into the starry sky in the confines of time through the hole chiseled into a cavern wall was enough for the question to emerge without language, without anguish, only the primitive admiration for the immensity of the great dark mantle peppered with luminously flashing dots, unanswered questions in the eternal night's flow. But that was way back in humankind's lost ocean of time rising every century under the infinite mantle of stars looking down, offering answers of all kinds in the dilated and serene future measured only by the extent of his reason made up of flimsy arguments at the beginning, underpinned by his ephemeral fears and pressing needs until one day the first conjecture, the fruit of reflection without passions or misleading prejudices, opened little by little a more practicable path beyond myth and legend through the effort of reason climbing toward a different type of reflection. And humankind realized at last his own capacity for unraveling the mysteries of the universe lying before his eyes. Once the first bit of knowledge was passed on, many others would follow, ever more complex and accurate.

The universe showed a faceless inscrutableness where each answer engendered more questions that would be answered in due course. He made use of numbers, geometric figures, logic, and physics, lifting veil after veil, and only when he had disposed of myth or superstition did he move upward, climbing out of the dark well where he had been. He was born with almost no chance to triumph over the forces subjugating him, including those set in motion by himself; but the fruit of knowledge was more powerful than the vile chains that bound him to ancestral designs of opprobrium, oppression, and darkness. And eventually, heroes and martyrs arose in the human endeavor already called science. One of the greatest came into the world holding a guiding torch through the wolves' dens, marking the definitive start of the great battle between the cloistered Word and the great method. His seed was planted and would not be destroyed no matter how much his enemies inflicted unjust punishments to the flesh of those carrying forward the torch for humanity. The damage was done because only the work of Cronus, in the inevitable future, would bring the house down once and for all.*

3

"We can stop now, Vincenzo. The letter to Cardinal Francesco can wait. I am not in the mood to write more nonsense than I've already dictated. I feel rather nostalgic. I'd really prefer to talk about other topics."

"Master . . . why don't you tell me a story from your youth, for example, about your experiment in Pisa?"

"Which one? I did so many in those days. Are you referring to the hydrostatic balance or the weighting pendulum? Or the cycloid one maybe?"

"No, no, Master. Do you remember the falling bodies experiment at the Tower of Pisa?"

"How to forget it? Vincenzo . . . I have a lot of time to think here and even more time to remember. In my days of youth, I felt, you know, full of vitality. Nobody could defeat me in a debate, and I already considered myself a full-fledged anti-Aristotelian. I set out to refute Aristotle's concepts concerning free-falling bodies. I think I've already told you something about that."

"Indeed, Master, you told me that two bodies dropped from a specific height, regardless of their weight, fall at the same time."

"Something similar, Vincenzo, but it is very important to add, 'In a vacuum.' For Aristotle, heavier objects fell faster because he thought those objects were above the circumstances as they appear to the naked eye if we ignored other more fundamental circumstances such as the fact that the earth is—why hide it now?—fixed or static. Yes, fixed. The earth moves with all that is in it and, at the same time, attracts everything to its center and does this just with the same force of attraction for all objects on its surface. Therefore, there is a constant of acceleration of all objects that have once been dropped from a considerable height, moving toward the center of the earth with increasing velocity. This constant is the same for all objects, be it a feather or a one-hundred-pound iron ball."

"But, Master, it could be argued that experience reveals the opposite. I still don't understand how a feather would fall at the same time as a cannonball."

"That's why I made that clarification at the beginning, Vincenzo. The phenomenon occurs in a vacuum. Air offers greater resistance to the lighter object because its mass, much smaller than the heavier object, opposes less force to the force of air in its fall."

"Do you mean, Master, that if we eliminate the air variable, the two objects would fall at the same time?"

"Naturally, Vincenzo."

"Then . . . your experiment."

"Yes, yes. Anyone would say it is totally absurd that someone like me did an experiment of that nature in the Tower of Pisa, but you see . . . in those days, I needed an audience. There were some traditionalist people who were against me and did not accept that a presumptuous and haughty young man could get away with it."

"That's why you carried out the experiment. But in reality, what could you achieve with that if the results you were trying to get wouldn't be accurate because the experiment had not been done in a vacuum. Besides, dropping objects from the Tower of Pisa would be somewhat . . . reckless."

"I know, I know, but my main motive was the experiment itself. Apart from the results I would obtain for or against my arguments, it was necessary to establish the verification of the studied phenomenon. I needed to use a standard method to establish the truth and, above all, to generalize that method. We should not continue to take the explanation of a phenomenon for granted just because Aristotle, Ptolemy, or Archimedes said so."

"Do you mean, Master, to question everything that has been established?"

"Definitely, Vincenzo. To question it in a reasonable manner, taking into account that our main aim is to get at the truth through a process of experimentation, which is possible when we carry out the experiment on equal terms with other experimenters."

"Ah, I understand now, Master. But through your method of experimentation, you could study any phenomenon of nature, and . . . would it also apply to the arts?"

"For god's sake, yes. In fact, it is being done since the Greeks. Remember Archimedes, Eratosthenes, Ptolemy, Aristotle, the Pythagoreans, and others who experimented in an empirical and, if you will, elementary way, but their influence has been enormous as you understand. But like everything else, knowledge has an expiration date. It is necessary to adapt it to other findings and observations made from time to time. There you have Copern—"

"Master, please."

"Sorry, sorry. I know that, in this convent, the walls have ears and distort reality. I don't forget my lamentable status here."

"You were talking about your Tower of Pisa experiment."

"I remember that day well, a very nice sunny day. I left the university in the middle of a great commotion I had created, unwittingly by the way, and in the blink of an eye, a small crowd of students and a few professors were following me. I claimed I could demonstrate the opposite of what Aristotle had stated. My claim was unacceptable for some people, but with the help of a handful of students, I managed to carry a cannonball of about one hundred pounds and another one less heavy."

"And how could you carry such heavy objects, Master? It seems a ridiculously long way up to the tower carrying such a heavy object even if the distance was short actually. But up to the Tower of Pisa?"

"Remember, I was young and burly, used to carrying heavy utensils, and you seem to forget that wheels exist. As I have told you on other occasions, I did a little bit of everything with metals, both light and heavy. So I embarked on the project and carried it out with utmost care and patience. I tried to ignore the tenacious skepticism I perceived in the eyes of the onlookers and expunged from my reasoning the sense of ridiculous because, in my view, what I was doing was not an act of rebellion. I climbed the tower as best I could."

"Did you do it alone, Master?"

"No, no, in fact, two students helped me get the few materials I needed up there after making the pertinent calculations, that is, the distance between the objects, taking notes on the wind speed and direction, to check that the area of the fall was the ideal one. The inclination of the tower helped me a great deal. It seemed to have been built for that experiment. The visibility was perfect, so I could see my experiment from above. Below, two students were waiting quite close to the impact area to see the result on site. Already in the belfry, which is the upper part of the seventh floor, my assistants and I dropped the two balls in unison at the bell's final toll."

"At the last toll? It must have been deafening."

"It was, but as you can imagine, we were cautious and covered our ears, of course not so much so as not to hear the sound of the falling balls. As for the results, according to Aristotle, the cannonball should have reached the ground ten times faster, depending on its weight since it was ten times heavier. However, they fell almost at the same time, much to everyone's surprise. The students below could make note of it. Well, Vincenzo, the experiment was performed. In time, I played down its importance because I was young and impetuous and actually considered it a minor experiment. I did not think it was that important. That's why I don't mention it in any of my writings. In fact, I would prefer to leave it just as it is—in oblivion."

"Master . . . would you allow me someday—no, never mind."

4

The genius was touched by an incurable curiosity. He looked up at the sky in dark times and with a strong intuition surveyed with his gaze some secrets forbidden to man, discovering moons, valleys, mountains where once only could be seen regular shapes, smooth and with no more life than the light reflected by tiny suns scattered in neighboring skies. This strong-willed genius followed secretly the path of Copernicus, his predecessor, not seeing that the trail was bound to lead him to inevitable misfortune in the not-too-distant future.

He took flight anyway, with adversity behind him. He imagined that his demeanor, self-confidence, fame, prestige, and ability for argumentation were emblems he could rub in his enemies' faces, people existing in a permanent dark night of terror, those malicious monks that in time would hatch the scheme for his martyrdom to the detriment of science and the future, but his vision was always the most real of all, with an eye set on the earth always revolving around the sun for the frustration of many unlearned people always deviating from the true sources of knowledge. Thus, his genius—revealing what had been concealed—lit the dazzling fuse of scientific knowledge by invoking a fair dose of courage in the face of an empire of lies and superstition. A man had never been closer in changing the perception of our world by raising his gaze to the starry sky and appreciating, once and for all, how small we were.

5

"Vincenzo, take me to the terrace. I want to breathe the night air. This summer, I have not had that horrible pain in my legs, a real miracle, and I am in the mood to be outside."

"As you wish, Master."

"I want you to look through the telescope for me. Direct it toward Jupiter and tell me what you see. At this time of day and at the end of September, it should appear to the west. Let me know when you get it focused, Vincenzo. Have I told you my father had the same name as you?"

"Yes, Master. I got it in my sight, but I can't focus it. Are you sure this telescope will be sent to the Collegio Romano?"

"Yes, as I told you, it's all the same. I doubt that it will be used frequently. Did you get it focused on Jupiter already?"

"One minute, Master. I think I almost got it . . . That's it. What do I do now?"

"Look closely at its moons and tell me how they are placed."

"You are going too fast, Master . . . wait. I see two diminutive objects near the planet, I believe. I see nothing else."

"It's okay, Vincenzo. You've done me a big favor. Every time I call you by your name, I remember my father, and I feel very nostalgic. You must know that, as a child, he rescued me from the clutches of the church. I was about to enter a monastery at a young age, and my father, under the excuse that I was being neglected by my then tutor, took me to Florence. If that hadn't happened, only God knows what my destiny would have been, definitely something very different from what I ended up doing in life. No experiments would have been possible, and my most beloved instrument would have remained in the hands of our enemies from the north. As you see, apparently, things worked out well."

"I think so too, Master. I cannot imagine you without the telescope and the great discoveries you have made through it. By the way, you

The Voice and the Fallen

haven't told me the story of how such an opportune device came to your hands."

"Do you think it is the right time to tell you such a tortuous and remote story? Let's see how easily you convince me, Vincenzo, to tell you my stories. Well, I was around middle age by then and living in Venice. I was working as a professor of mathematics and other subjects, and the pay was a pittance as you may know. I had worked on some inventions for the institutions of war but none of great significance, and they were not enough, so one morning one of my former students who had spent a brief period in Holland paid me a visit in my workshop. You would never believe it if it weren't coming out of my mouth, Vincenzo, but when that student gave me that information in a somewhat casual manner, it was as though something had gotten illuminated inside my head. And suddenly, I saw the future before me. Call it intuition, premonition, or simply the need to move forward with something extraordinary that providence had in store for me. At that time, Vincenzo, I realized what my true calling in life was."

"Oh, Master, you took advantage of your greatest opportunity. We're you not affected by the fact that another person had invented and patented that instrument?"

"Absolutely not. In my heart, there was no room for feelings of sorrow or guilt. I knew deep down I could create a better instrument than the existing one. Remember that I was living in Venice, where I could use the best lenses that could be obtained in the whole of Europe, thanks to the Murano quarries. I saw all this inside my head in a matter of seconds. I felt possessed by a sudden and unstoppable fever. I did not have another choice but to start immediately."

"Do you mean you stopped everything you were doing to embark on that remarkable project?"

"You can't imagine. I barely ate and slept very little. I spent two weeks making calculations, determining the perfect combination of concave and convex lenses, the right distance between them, the mirror that should be used to obtain the best effect, the tubes I needed, their material and thickness, along with a long array of details so that when it was ready, I would make a demonstration of the improved instrument for certain important people of Venice."

"I understand your demonstration was very successful."

"Naturally. No one in that city had seen anything like it. In addition, the improved telescope lent itself to military use. It had an inestimable value, and since I had had the good sense to donate it to the city of Venice, I was soon rewarded with an increase in my income and received other privileges at the university. But the telescope itself provided the greatest benefit when it was directed toward the sky. At last, it was possible to refute unequivocally Aristotle's observations concerning the moon after observing the lunar terminator."

"Lunar terminator? What do you mean, Master?"

"The lunar twilight. My observations showed that the surface of the moon was not smooth as Aristotle had claimed. This discovery filled me with great joy and, above all, confidence. But unfortunately, I did not foresee the danger that was coming."

"Yes, I can imagine, your affirmation that, you know, the earth should revolve around the sun and not the other way around."

"Exactly. It was naive of me to think I could convince the world of something that seemed so obvious to me. I underestimated the power of my enemies, many of whom I never imagined were, in fact, enemies. But you see, Vincenzo, where I am now, imprisoned in this precinct only for persevering in the pursuit of an idea, but . . . time will tell if I am right. Only time will tell."

6

Man discovered the stars in due time, that never-ending mantle of light beams lost in the distance. He cannot figure out its meaning yet but found answers through the haze of the mystery, thinking everything parted from his finite and obtuse gaze. He believed in his imagination, and that gave him wings in the erratic and dangerous flight of the mind. He believed he can know the designs of the universe by just using his prosaic knowledge, the fruit of dubious observation, and was convinced that he was the scale of everything because it was the only one he had. As a worthy disciple of Plato, he decreed what his eyes—fixed on earth—saw: this must be the center of the universe.

In the course of time, another man observed the same indecipherable sky and with logical discernment glimpsed into a truth that had been there since the beginning of time: the sun was the sovereign ruler of the surrounding space in this tiny portion of the universe. Earth, minuscule like a grain of sand, drew an ellipse around its unstoppable orbit. That absolute truth can shake the foundations of myth and the divine Word forever. The men wielding the scepters trembled; they devised terrible punishments, vainly dragging the truth to an isolated corner, but other winds would blow soon, when the method—carefully refined—would rise from the ashes of their temples.

7

A letter was found by Ludovico Totti in the well near the convent of San Matteo.

Beloved and revered daughter S. M. Celeste,

Despite being held against my will in this quiet place, daughter, I don't feel too bad. I am treated with great respect, and my caregivers take into consideration my age rather than my life achievements. I thank you once again for your great zeal in providing the best you can get on this earth to your tired and sick father. I am also immensely grateful for the efficacious remedies you have sent me. I have used them according to your wise indications, and I am happy to tell you that they have provided the relief you predicted. The pains in the knees have subsided noticeably in recent days. I don't know when I can go to visit you, but don't lose hope. I do not ask you, daughter, to do penance for me as you informed me in your last letter; but if that is your wish, I consider it sacred. Please don't forget to give my regards and infinite affection to Signor Rondinelli and tell him I wish him good fortune in his great vineyard enterprise. I am glad that the energies he has devoted to it are bearing fruit.

I will have to rest now because shortsightedness prevents me from writing everything I would like to communicate to you, but even if I do not write enough, be assured that you and your suffering brothers are always in my heart at every moment. Receive my most affectionate hug.

Your father who loves you deeply,
G.G., Sienna, 12 Nov. 1633

8

"Vincenzo, fetch the ointment my daughter sent and apply it to both of my knees, please. Today they are worse than ever. Oh, life with unnecessary pains is full. At least here, I can complain about my sorrows, Vincenzo. Can you hear me?"

"Certainly, Master. Your pain grieves me. Can I help you with something else?"

"Yes. When the pain relents, I would like to answer what you asked me in the morning."

"When you wish. I will be looking forward to it, but you can answer me another day when you feel better."

"No, I'd rather do it today. Oh, here is Maria with that miraculous ointment. Please, Maria, be generous with the oils and apply them with your usual softness and sweetness."

"I'll do so, sir. Rest assured."

"Oh, what a treat! Your kind hands relieve my pain quickly. You are an angel, Maria. Thanks for your fine attention. I feel the balm penetrating my skin, fighting off the pain in a pleasant way. Now, Vincenzo, I am free for your questions. You can go now, Maria. I don't know what I would do without your sweet caresses in my tired joints."

"Oh, Lord, do not hesitate to call me if you are in pain again. With your permission, I'll retire."

"Yes, Maria. Vincenzo, if I remember correctly, you asked me what my general impression of the trial to which I subjected was."

"Correct, Master. Has it been an inappropriate question? If you are not in the mood for talking about such a sensitive issue, I understand. Don't feel obligated by any means."

"No, no. If I told you I need to talk about it, would you believe me?"

"If you say so, Master, I sincerely believe you."

"Well . . . I never imagined that things would turn out this way. I never thought, I repeat, that my position would ever be in danger, a position gained through a great effort and an inflexible work ethic throughout my whole life in science. My doubts turned into certainties over fifty years of work, bearing fruits in my findings in astronomy, geometry, mathematics, and physics and in the methodical application of order in the search for truth. Never crossed my mind that my enemies would throw overboard all my work in the blink of an eye for only having published a book that, at the end of the day, a few people have read. And to top it off, the book was not subjected to censorship, so I was accused of disobedience for having come back to the topic of heliocentrism, which is the astronomical model in which Earth and planets revolve around the sun at the center of the solar system. No, no, that has not been the key to my sentence."

"But, Master, what you are telling me has great importance since, according to the Collegio Romano, the Congregation of the Index, and especially the Court of the Holy Inquisition, that affirmation—applied conceptually—constitutes in itself a heresy, pure and simple. Don't you think it was somewhat imprudent and even dangerous for your interests and even for your physical integrity?"

"Of course, I knew that, but I used the resource of putting it in the mouths of three hypothetical characters. And despite being based on real people, their approaches are fictitious. The most serious problem was that, in my scandalous naivete, I did not realize that one of those characters strongly resembles who would become my greatest enemy. You imagine who I'm referring to."

"It is an unfortunate fact, more so because His Holiness used to express great appreciation and admiration for you before the assumption of his current position."

"Yes. Many seasons have passed since then. Times have changed and revealed the true nature of his heart, which has always been stone cold. Having hurt his feelings has been the lever of my condemnation. Only I could have come up with that damn metaphor. During the trial, I had hopes that proved to be futile because of my naive attitude of trying to defend my point of view in a rational manner. But the ambassador of the Grand Duchy of Tuscany had the good sense to clarify that, in the Holy Inquisition Court, we were not going to debate the controversial points of the book. Rather, I had to reduce myself to accept the accusations and ask for clemency and, even more important for them, to recant the ideas exposed in the book and in so doing taking the opposite stance of which I actually professed. And here you see me, a victim of what I predict to be the first altercation between religion and science."

"The first altercation? I was unaware that there had been an altercation, but on second thought, there is no doubt that your position would call into question the corpus of the church as a whole."

"But . . . you must know that it was never my intention since my faith in the most essential precepts of the church is still intact. I do not have the heart to disappoint my daughters and all the people who hold me in high esteem. It has never been my intention to undermine the foundations of that sacred institution that, until the fateful moment in which I published my book, had only offered protection, admiration, and consideration toward me and my family. As you see, it all comes down to a misunderstanding. I can only hope that, in the future, I will be released from this prison. Although the hardships are not an unbearable sacrifice, I would naturally prefer to have my freedom. I would like to see my daughters again and lead a peaceful life in the warmth and peace of my home."

"I hope your wish will finally be granted, Master."

9

Genius had descended on the earth once more. Humanity was eager to be guided through the dark passage of history. It assumed the form of a simple human, a faithful observer, an inveterate optimist who—with curiosity worthy of his mentors, the Greek sages—climbed the ladder of knowledge at the expense of his peace of mind. He was a mere mortal in a terrible epoch, subjected to the intense tidal waves that life threw on his path; but he dominated them, sacrificing his body to the authority absorbed in the impotence of overcoming the genius. In the end, the dead word shall not rise from the grave and would sleep eternally.

Did the genius know, in his inordinate search, his inescapable future, choosing the tortuous path revealed before him? Or did the great and unsettling view from the precipice timidly revealed his truth? And once revealed, he would face the consequences as he could, a mortal and fragile human being fearful of the vile suffering he would have to go through. Knowing his destiny, he faced the consequences courageously and stoically; glory was reborn even greater because he carried on his shoulders future generations worthy of his insatiable curiosity for truth at the expense of his own vicissitudes.

10

A letter was found by Ludovico Totti in the well near the convent of San Matteo.

Beloved daughter S. M. Celeste,

I can't wait for the day of our long-awaited reunion when I get to the convent of San Matteo by my own means.

Keep the pears you promised for my return and that I like so much in a cool place, away from the sun. There is no need to send them with the ambassador's wife.

Something worries me so greatly that is a reason for constant sleepless nights, and that is your health, dear daughter. Why should you have that terrible feeling that—I cannot even mention it. Just thinking about it makes my whole body throb in pain once again. You'll see that, with the Lord's grace, you will be healthy when I return to Florence and embrace you tenderly.

I want you to know that the Holy Father, Urban VIII, has given his authorization to have me transferred to Arcetri. Finally, living in the house I have longed for! Except for not being able to receive visitors, I'll be confined in my own home. Nor will it be possible to do teaching work there. I can tolerate that; what will be intolerable is being away from you, your sister, and the rest of my family and friends. Besides, I will be in my element there, and we will take care of each other. I know you need it as much as I do.

Only if it is possible, and I think it will be, I'll continue my studies on certain research topics, of which I will give you more details later since you have shown interest in knowing what I am doing lately, so don't give up. I'll be there soon.

Your loving and hopeful father,G. G., Sienna, December 12, 1633

11

Visit of John Milton to Arcetri, Florence, 1638

"I am so pleased with your warm and kind welcome, Lord. Even though I come from afar, your research and findings have had a profound influence in my country."

"It is my utmost pleasure to hear that from you, who is, if I am not mistaken, a renowned poet and politician in your homeland."

"That's right . . . sir, or I'd rather call you Master, if I may."

"Sure. I am flattered by that compliment, which I do not think I deserve."

"You do deserve it, Master. No doubt you have earned it, considering your titles, among them mathematician, physicist, astronomer, inventor, in short a great scientist. What wouldn't we do with your expertise at Oxford or Cambridge?"

"Well, I'm . . . forbidden to teach and to receive visitors, but . . . let me tell you that your Italian is perfect, and you have mastered Latin as well."

"Yes, also Spanish, French, and Greek. My visit was made possible by the ambassador of the Grand Duchy of Tuscany."

"It is amazing that you can speak fluently all those languages. We also need someone like you in this region. My friend, the grand duke has been very kind."

"I would do it gladly, but the sociopolitical situation in my country is increasingly unstable, and possibly, I'll have to interrupt my travels for the time being. I must support the republican cause in my homeland. The Anglican Church, on the one hand, and the monarchy, on the other, have shattered the will of the people in charge of our unsteady parliament."

"I am very sorry about your situation, but as you know, in that sense, yours is a more developed nation than mine, where we are ruled by the Holy Catholic Church basically, a fact I don't deplore, but a certain level of openness in the scientific order would be desirable, given the inquisitive nature and novelty of our work, meaning the work in the sciences, don't you think?"

"Yes, very much so. Despite my Catholic fervor, just like you, I am in favor of a measured openness within our universities because, in my view, it is necessary to release the ties of man's reasoning from time to time for his own benefit."

"I have fought all my life precisely for that reason, that is to say, seeking the truth through reasoning and experimentation, but it has not been possible to carry this out in a way more fitting for science. The church keeps us in shackles, making our task close to impossible."

"Master . . . one of the reasons for my visit is to know how you are faring in this . . . unjust imprisonment. I ask you not only out of personal interest but also that of many people of a progressive mentality in my homeland who have received news of your injudicious trial and no less unfortunate sentence."

"Thanks for your kind words. It is good to know the fruit of one's work is held in high esteem in distant places."

"It is difficult to ignore the amazing discoveries you have made with your telescope, for example, the moons of Jupiter, the rugged surface of the moon, the sunspots, not to mention your studies concerning the tides and the trajectory of objects when they are launched as projectiles."

"I see you are very aware of some of my work."

"Yes, it's not for less. You have been an inspiration for many scientists in my country who, following your example, have set off through the path of scientific research without fear of the prejudices that have guided us so far, made possible by the excesses of religion."

"How much I would have liked to visit your homeland and be a firsthand witness of the fervor the sciences bring out in the individual, but sadly, that will never happen."

"Master, your words fill me with emotion. I want you to know that you are with us, and this confinement only imprisons your body in these walls that also provide shelter. Your work has been circulating freely among us for a long time. Rest assured, no priest will be able to roll back the turn you have given to the course of history."

"Oh! If I could only get up from this chair by my own means, I swear I would do the same thing all over again. I see everything clearly now. God created the thinking man just to rise one day from the dark confines of the human weaknesses that will always be part of us. Thank you for your visit, Mr. Milton."

"Thank you, Master. I will never forget this conversation."

12

The heavens had been deciphered, the starry mantle's veil of mystery forbidden to man in the era of darkness had been drawn, the dead word ceased to hold the profound meaning of the stars in their unfathomable remoteness, and the deep gaze of the man of science prevailed today, working in his corner of knowledge, taming the firmament.

Organized thought had become the method, the instrument created by man's ingenuity to unravel the hidden truths of nature, leaving behind the baggage of superstition that did not satisfy curiosity and left humankind clinging to a vaporous faith for centuries.

When the heavens were opened, the human mind took flight, and consciousness—within the physical limits of man—had at last known unsuspected pathways. The doors were finally opened to roads that, as tree roots scattered in his environment, provided infinite possibilities in the search for truth, thanks to the noble and complete sacrifice of Galileo, who fought against powerful prejudices in the midst of utter darkness. Prejudices dragged along for centuries in the slow evolution of man, having the effect of a powerful drug that annihilated the enterprising spirit without denying the ecstasy of the glorious epiphany and the strong belief that everything can be achieved by making use of a crushing faith, only to find, at the last second of consciousness, that there was no turning back when the doors had been closed, just as in the beginning, after being opened through a life that had become inevitable. And the only thing man truly possessed seemed to be this tiny interval of light to decrypt the great mystery.

13

"Are you sure this is the right place, Lucca? I don't see anyone around here."

"Yes, I'm sure. This is the only intersection that coincides with the arranged place."

"But there is no one here. Are you trying to trick me?"

"Ludovico, I'm not trying to cheat you. Don't be stupid."

"Excuse me . . . I'm kind of jumpy with all this. You were the only one who talked with that mysterious character, and the last thing I want is that someone shows up trying to be smarter than me . . . than us."

"It's okay. It is not a mysterious character. I know him well. As soon as I mentioned the letters, he was very interested. He seems to know what it is about."

"Well . . . I think any antique lover would be interested enough to . . ."

"To what?"

"Make us disappear. You have no idea what these letters could be worth."

"No. The truth is I have no idea. I'm a moron. Of course, I know they are worth a lot of money."

"Look . . . look . . . someone is coming, but it is a . . ."

"Yes . . . Who else would be interested? Hello, Mr. Menicucci. Here we are as we arranged. He is Ludovico Totti, my associate, Mr. Menicucci."

"Hello, it's my pleasure. There is a café nearby. Let's go there and talk. Did you bring them?"

"Just a few. They are very valuable, you know. It's not good to walk around with all of them. Here you are. Take a look."

"Let's see . . . interesting . . . interesting. They seem to be originals. And where do you say you found them?"

"We haven't told him yet, right, Lucca?"

"Well . . . I told him we found them in the vicinity of the old convent of San Matteo, near Florence. Don't make that face, Ludovico. We had to tell him anyway."

"Ah yes, San Matteo, in the well. Hmm, that complicates the situation a little bit. You must know that, by law, that land belongs to the Vatican. But in any case, you have the merit of having found them, and that has its price. I'll give you one thousand euros for each letter. It's a very reasonable price, don't you think?"

"This is a scam, Lucca. The letters are worth much more than that. Let's get out of here."

"Wait, I'll give you five thousand for each letter. That's my last offer. And it's a reasonable offer, considering they are stolen. I just have to make a phone call and—""Okay, we've got a deal. Lucca, calculate ten letters for five thousand euros each. That would be . . . fifty thousand euros. Do you have it with you, Mr. Menicucci?"

"Don't you get smart with me, Mr. Totti. My patience has a limit. I know there are thirty-six letters."

"And if you want to lose the letters and the money, dismiss my good intentions again. Be aware that I am not alone. You are being watched right now, so we will proceed to do the calculation again. Let's see, thirty-six multiplied by five thousand is . . . one hundred and eighty thousand euros, a reasonable sum, considering we're dealing with a stolen object."

"You betrayed me, Lucca. I told you these letters could make us rich."

"I had no other choice, Ludovico. You don't have children. You don't know what economic hardship is, going to bed on an empty stomach, not having money for medicine when your child is sick. You know nothing about that. So don't give me shit like that. I need money, period."

"You break my heart with your ambitions and financial difficulties. And if it's any comfort to you, I'll be generous and give you one hundred thousand euros to each of you for the service provided but, above all, for your silence. Know that you will be watched for a while and at the slightest misstep . . . kaput."

"Okay, your offer is surely reasonable. And since you don't leave us any other choice . . . Lucca, give me the phone. Just wait a moment . . . Geovanny . . . it's me, Ludovico. Do you remember the package I gave you for safekeeping? Yes? Take it to . . . the Piazza San Pietro and give it to Monsignor Nicolini. He will know what to do . . . wait!"

"No, no! What are you doing? Okay . . . I'll give you half a million euros! No? What is this shithead doing, Lucca? Is he crazy?"

"If you want the letters, deposit one million euros in this bank account. Once you do it, I will give you the letters at the doors of the same bank where you deposited the money. Otherwise, go on your way and forget about us."

"Okay, you win. Your friend is a good negotiator, Lucca."

"Yes, I am, Father."

14

A letter was found by Ludovico Totti in the well near the convent of San Matteo.

Beloved daughter S. M. Celeste,

As soon as the ambassador of the Grand Duchy of Tuscany, who in turn had been informed by the doctor, told me your health condition had deteriorated more and more, I immediately set out to send you these lines of encouragement and infuse you with hope and faith that, by the grace of Almighty God for whom there is nothing impossible, you will get better soon. My return to Florence is imminent, and when that happens, my dear daughter, I will go straight to visit you, even if there is a blizzard. I want you to know that, despite the bad weather, frequent high winds in recent weeks, I feel much stronger the same time last year. It must be because of the news that I'll finally return home to see you and your sister soon, and that makes me very happy. Be steadfast and put your trust in Christ. Have faith and follow the doctor's suggestions strictly.

Your dear father, who loves you infinitely,

G. G., Sienna, March 17, 1634

15

History had spoken, and justice, although delayed, had been made to the wise man through new men who carried the guilt for having sentenced him to silence the truths that flowed from the earth and the sky.

"And yet it moves"—*the chroniclers of his time had put that phrase in his mouth, an exultant complaint perhaps thought but never*

disclosed in the frightening inquisitorial tribunal, ruled by men who today toned down their positions with attenuated arguments and absurd requests of forgiveness before the insignificant grievance of delaying the advancement of science by imposing an implacable faith, bending wills to exert control, claiming divine subterfuge. But times were different now, times of change in which pure and simple evidence invariably dissipated doubts, and humankind depended less and less on the supernatural and unreal perception of unlearned people who, diluted as they were, believed that the entire world turned as if it were crazy and didn't realize that the problem lay in their head full of vain and insubstantial mist.

It was a different era. Other bells tolled new truths at the rhythm of other outlooks, the fruit of great curiosity, which was an essential part of humankind and impossible to stifle in its determined flow. It appeared in his childhood, giving as a result a genius who had served as light and support for humanity through history and would never see again the yoke of the unreal hiding its true purpose.

FRANZ KAFKA

(1883–1924)

Kafka was a writer and lawyer of Jewish descent born in Prague. He wrote all his work in almost complete anonymity, characterized by an obscure and alienated perception of the world in which he lived, reflecting a vision of humankind unable to overcome the influence of an indifferent, brutal, and disconcerting system despite his brief life. He was diagnosed with tuberculosis at the age thirty-four and passed away six years later; he was considered one of the most important writers of the twentieth century, and although he was not awarded with the Nobel Prize for Literature, he had influenced several Nobel laureates such as Thomas Mann, Albert Camus, Eugène Ionesco, J. M. Coetzee, Jean-Paul Sartre, Gabriel García Márquez, José Saramago, and literary figures of the stature of Jorge Luis Borges, J. D. Salinger, and W. G. Sebald.

His biographers agreed on the fact that he was the victim of an authoritarian father who inevitably filled him with insecurity and a sense of guilt throughout his brief existence and was strongly opposed that his son followed literature as a career; this insecurity and restlessness was revealed in many of his writings. He did not marry nor had children despite having maintained multiple romantic relationships. He devoted his whole life to literature, aided by his loyal friend Max Brod, to whom he left the terrible instruction of burning all of Kafka's unpublished works after his death, an order Brod didn't carry out fortunately.

His few novels were among the best writings in the twentieth century, which revealed a tense and dark world where the efforts of man were impeded by the imprint of a blind system indifferent to the vicissitudes of man in his daily life, emphasizing a cruel and indolent bureaucracy and the unsustainable innocence of his characters persecuted by uncertainty and fatality.

The following story made a parallel between Kafka and a character living in present times who suffered from Gregor Samsa's malady, so to speak, and had no other choice other than to redeem herself in what could be called a magical, realistic ending as well as the inability of medical science to cure her by conventional means.

The will to win, the desire to succeed, the urge to reach your full potential . . . these are the keys that will unlock the door to personal excellence.

—Confucius

THE MYSTERIOUS MR. K AND THE WORM

1

"I will give you some recommendations for dealing with my daughter. First, do not make prolonged eye contact with her. Second, always speak in the same tone of voice with her, a soft, relaxed tone. Third and equally important, never touch her. She doesn't tolerate any kind of physical contact. Oh, and I almost forgot a fourth recommendation: do not make sudden movements. She is very skittish, and you wouldn't like to see her upset, believe me. Understood?"

"Yes, ma'am. It's all very clear. We've already handled other cases."

"But not like this one. Nobody knows how she thinks, not even me."

"We understand. As my colleague said, we have treated many patients with Asperger's."

"Did I tell you my daughter has Asperger's? Because if I did, I had forgotten."

"No, no, you didn't tell us, but—""We read Dr. Thompson's report, where he suggests she has Asperger's, but we can't really tell for sure before meeting her first. Right, Gaston?"

"True. We need to meet her, and we must interview you in depth, so excuse us for having mentioned Asperger's."

"Yes, I agree. After talking to her, maybe you'll get an idea of how her mind works. It's simply beyond me. I don't know if she is delusional. At this point, I have no idea what to think. When Dr. Thompson used that diagnosis for the first time, he didn't sound very convinced. However, when he saw her again, he had more doubts than certainties. And I . . . what can I say? I do not know anything about these things. You are the experts."

"Yes, it's true, Gaston. Now that she mentions him, he was not sure of anything."

"And presented the case to us in a succinct way. I got the impression he was rather perplexed and not exactly certain because he didn't know what was going on."

"Do you think his intention was to make us share in his confusion, Lars?"

"Anyway, Doctors, or should I call you researchers?"

"As it's more comfortable for you."

"She should call us doctors, Gaston. It's better for our purposes. Ma'am, please tell us everything you know concerning your daughter's case."

"Fair enough. Well, as you know from Dr. Thompson, she is in a wheelchair not because she can't walk. She can. And when she feels like it, she crawls around like a . . . worm, yes, as you heard. She doesn't want to speak either, and she is perfectly capable of doing so. But when she utters any sound at all, she moans and talks gibberish. And do you know what the worse part is? She speaks fluently when she is alone."

"How do you know that? Have you caught her doing so?"

"I wouldn't catch her in a million years. Sorry to lower my voice. I had cameras installed in her room. I will show you the recordings in due time. But . . . going back to the issue, she acts and thinks as if she were a worm. Can you imagine? She thinks she is a damn worm! Sorry for being rude, but I can't take it anymore. You have to help me. She slides off the chair and then crawls on the floor, talking gibberish to herself. I don't know why God has given me this trial. She is my only child. If only she were crazy, I would know what to expect. I'd take her to an institution where she would be stuffed with pills, and I'd bring her back home in a zombielike state maybe but human nevertheless."

"Don't despair, ma'am. We have worked in many bizarre and unpredictable cases, and we can certainly achieve something substantial in hers."

"Lars, Dr. Thompson mentioned she has a favorite book, a very important book for her."

"What about it, ma'am?"

"She has torn off the covers, but I suspect it is by a German or Czech writer from the twentieth century."

"Any idea who the author might be, Gaston? Mann or Musil maybe?"

"I'm not very familiar with those writers, but I think it's someone who wrote about a huge bug. I think you did some work about that author a few years ago, Lars."

"It's nice that you mention that. What you know about that author could shed light on the solution of this problem maybe. It should be useful."

"How did she get the book, ma'am?"

"I don't know. She used to be quite a normal girl, although she did not socialize much like most people her age and spent hours and hours reading compulsively. But apparently, she'd never come across an author like that whose complete works she probably read in just a few days. And not satisfied with that, she started rereading it over and over again. I've come to think those writings have completely taken over my daughter's life."

"But, Lars, didn't the same thing happened to you when you read it? You only breathed K, thought like K for two years. His obsession with K's oppressive sensation took hold of him too, ma'am."

"Yes, but he did not become a filthy worm as my daughter did. I'd give all I have just to prevent her from setting eyes on that author's work. But . . . it's too late now. It's time to go in. Please remember what I told you at the beginning, and . . . good luck."

2

With a sad look in his eyes, he absorbs life, impassive on the outside, weak as the stem of a wheat sheaf moved by the wind; but in the inside, his inner being sustains him like the straight and immovable beams of the most enormous bridge that unites or separates according to the case of a fleeting reality but of abyssal depths. "A lost childhood," he will say to himself, "hopelessly lost," when he imagines a family life—wife, children, work, the love of a child, of a brother, and especially of a father. Everything fades away and alone in the distance, like a remote possibility; he caresses the light of his muse, waiting for the best moment, when the time is propitious, to pour his true anguish, his true self, on the blank page.

He glimpses his dark and insubstantial future from a desolate balcony, cold as his father's heart, like the arm of icy wind hitting his whole body. He shudders in his corner, where he has been held for infamous punishment; there, he urges his revenge toward the coarse and proud beings and more toward the incomprehensible and blind father who does not see the diamond in the making his son shelters inside, once again weakened by his implacable imprint. He does not know, and he will never know how close he has been to undoing the eternal grudge he has caused in his son, who just needs a warm hug and a good-night kiss.

3

"Oh, Max, I have all the nights of my world to think and think. There is not a moment when I don't perceive ominous things, desperation haunts me endlessly, and you are not there . . . My family is not there, only me and my thoughts, an executioner before my impotent gaze. I don't know why you always ask me the same thing again and again."

"Calm down, Franz. I only asked you why you feel like an outsider. What's wrong about my worrying a little about you?"

"My feelings are unavoidable, I'm afraid. The baths chased away my restlessness at first. The sudden trips, seeing the meadows and mountains going by swiftly from the train window—that has calmed me down, to examine closely the untroubled and logical movements of the other passengers and guessing their own futile and senseless comings and goings."

"But you have enjoyed it somehow, Franz, and it has been a learning experience because of your great capacity for observation, developed skillfully over time. I would not be able to write like you, no matter how hard I tried. You are endowed with a powerful and strange force. And as you say, you feel persecuted by it, and you can't explain it satisfactorily, but somehow it drives you forward."

"Yes. I have tried to write something sublime because of the beauty it might contribute to the world, a poem, for instance, but the essence slips off my hands, and pessimism, a sense of oppression irremediably takes over as I have told you, and no one can help me. I think all this writing will be worthless. Only I could understand it and just making the necessary effort."

"Your first writings are as fascinating as the last thing you've shown me. That is undeniable. You have the gift, and you know it. I don't understand why you resist to accept it."

"I accept it, and I don't accept it. It goes beyond me. Perhaps it is the way they have made me perceive my world. On other occasions, I have confessed to you how despotic my father has been in the past. He has been blind, deaf, and dumb to my desires and I who have consciously and unconsciously tried hard to please him, and the task has been little more than impossible."

"But you don't have to do that anymore."

"That's why I rebelled, and I wrote a letter that I do not intend to send, at least not for now. But . . . I must do it anyway. Thus, I will put an end to the whole matter."

"A letter? That sounds interesting, but I don't think I'm going to end the whole thing as you say. Up to a point, your father's imprint guides you with his dark and unfathomable threads."

"Maybe you are right, but in any case, I think it's good to conjure up the evil that creeps inside me to make it come out and uproot it as best I can."

"I am not sure you are doing the right thing, but I won't be the one to encourage you to do otherwise. It seems to me that everything you write has great value, and I mean it with all my heart."

"Thank you, but I think the value of my writings is far removed from being something tangible or worthy of the necessary attention that an average writer could draw. This is just a desperate effort to grasp an illusion that is constantly vanishing."

"But please, Franz, don't stop pursuing that illusion. It is better to continue the search even when you can't find what you want, on the way leaving your footprints so you can draw a possible route—your route."

"You will not convince me with your rhetoric, Max. I feel what I feel, and I don't think there's power on the earth able to clear my path. Everything around me is futile. Can't you see it? Why write then if the effort does not take me anywhere? If in the end I lack the strength to finish what I have started? Have you ever asked yourself that question before reading my work? Do you see any light at the end of the road? Why keep writing, I repeat, even tired?"

"Those questions don't make any sense considering what I've seen. You have an important point to make with your writing, something uncomfortable and definitely transcendent to show us. The world is not a rose garden. That is clear. You are like a judge who points out the absurdity in human nature, and humanity lacks such severe and forceful critics. The reality you portray is everyone's reality. What you mean deep down is that there is no happy ending. Otherwise, it would be an illusion, shared by many unfortunately."

"Exactly for those reasons you expound with such clarity of vision, you make me feel guilty because I am not contributing to the happiness of others, but I can't help it. I am trapped in a vicious circle. I see myself as the biblical God imparting woeful designs to my characters. That definitely is not right."

"It is not all bad either. It is necessary to show the troubled waters to avoid them. Your plight is also my plight and probably everyone's, only I cannot express it like you."

"We're talking too much about the same thing, but I'll tell you something—my big problem is that I think I understand too much, but basically, I know nothing. And to console myself a little, I tell to myself that none of us know anything in spite having information up to our eyeballs. That makes me despair."

The Voice and the Fallen

"Why choose despair when you can choose to soothe your thoughts or at least be more compassionate with yourself?"

"I cannot detach myself from the past."

"You must do it if you want to pull through."

"I may not want to, despite—"

"You will always have the future, which could be better if you set your mind to it."

"That's a half-truth. You know we have no future. We are doomed."

"We have to live with what little we have. There is no other way out. If we leave our eyes anchored in the past, it's as if the future would never exist."

"That is exactly what I feel. Otherwise, I would write something optimistic, according to a future less . . ."

"Nonexistent?"

"You are reading my mind. I'm glad we finally agree. I can already, before your eyes, continue my meaningless babblings. I finally got a guaranteed reader, and that's you. I will not disappoint you, and yes, laugh all you want. You won't be able to change my way of thinking."

"No. I am laughing because you have designated me as your official reader, and I know I will not change your thinking. Rather, you will change mine if you continue scribbling your incoherent babblings."

4

Creativity is difficult for those who do not hold art as a religion, art as a substitute for the emptiness left by the absence of God, those multicolored or grayscale paths depicted on a canvas or on the blank page capable of accepting the most improbable traces that the artist's will and emotion can make. Attaining equilibrium is the goal, his goal, and he achieves far more of what he believes to be his possibilities. He lets himself be dragged along the paths of inspiration, where ideas emerge without being looked for; they look for him, a suitable receptacle for an ancestral torch passed on by preceding artists unbeknownst to him at first. Perhaps he has never known for sure and just senses it somehow.

And the battle goes on despite his steps being slower while the shadow of death half-hides within him, that scourge that condemns him to wither quickly and impels him to shape his particularly intricate world, like a maze you can't get out of, in an amalgam of asphyxiating situations and characters tinged with dark humor and fleeting sensuality. And so those beings wander erratically through vague moorlands, side streets, labyrinthine buildings that suck the breath out of them, causing desperation and bewilderment. It is the rule, his rule, that we must respect because it represents a will in balance.

5

"Hello, Karla. I am Mr. Lars, and my colleague is Mr. Gaston. Can we talk for a moment? It won't take long. We'll ask you just a few questions. Your mother . . . your mother told us it would be important if you talked to someone. Mr. Gaston is going to ask you some questions now, if you'd be so kind."

"Yes, I know, I know. Ask away, Mr. Gaston."

"We know, Karla, that you like books a great deal and that . . . during the last few weeks . . . you've grown fond of a specific one, a special book. Isn't that so, Lars?"

"Ask away, Mr. Gaston."

"Sorry. Karla, can you tell us why that particular book?"

"What book, Mr. Gaston? This one?"

"Yes, that one. What is so special about that book? I understand it was written by—""Yes, it's a book by that author, Mr. Gaston. There is nothing special about this book or its author. I like it. I just like it."

"But . . . your mother told us—""My mother doesn't know anything, nothing at all. You don't know anything either, Mr. Gaston. Neither do you, Mr. Lars."

"Thanks for answering, Karla, and it's true. We don't know anything. That is the reason we are asking. Mr. Gaston and I would like to know if what is in that book is special for you and why. That is all we want to know."

"Mr. Lars, I already told you. I like it. And . . . do you want to know something else? I believe him. It's just like it says in the book. I think it really happened to the main character. He transformed into a—"

"Both Mr. Gaston and I know what happens to the main character, but . . . Karla . . . as far as Mr. Gaston and I know, it is about a fictional character. He isn't real. It's a metaphor. Don't you understand that? Why take it to heart?"

"Mr. Lars, Mr. Gaston, you understand nothing. For example, I became a worm. Haven't you noticed it? Can't you see my rings, my legs, my little antennae? Don't you see my whole body covered in this filthy slime?"

"But, Miss Karla, you are a human being, not a worm."

"One second, Gaston. It would be good if Karla explained to us why she feels she is a worm."

"I don't feel it. I am a worm! I don't walk like you. I crawl! I don't speak. Rather, I communicate through my antennae. One day I went to bed like every night and woke up like this as you see me. I didn't do anything to be turned into this, and yet here I am, transformed into a worm."

"What do you think, Lars? There is no way to convince her otherwise."

"You will not do it. Just understand it. It's easier for me to convince you. What I'm telling you is the absolute truth."

"Let's see. Gaston, let me do the talking. Miss Karla . . . why have you become a worm? Perhaps the book influenced you in such a way you don't see anything you don't want to see. Do you really feel so guilty?"

"I just turned into a worm. I don't feel any guilt. That's irrelevant. I have no control over what happened to me."

"But if you have done nothing wrong, then . . . why did it happen to you?"

"I have failed, Mr. Lars. Humanity has failed. What happened wasn't the result of my own actions, rather the result of the actions of all of you. I am an inevitable product of our times. There is no turning back."

"But we see you as you are, an ordinary human being, just like us."

"Mr. Lars, I clarify, you see what you want to see, but your eyes or, more precisely, your mind perceives me as one of you. But don't kid yourself. I am a worm. I can't change my state, and that's why I declare this will be my final resting place, my last . . . abode."

"I propose, Miss Karla, to take you to a place where you will be treated well and taken care of properly."

"No! I will not be subjected to the scrutiny of indolent people who will never understand my situation. Besides, I'd be embarrassed to be seen like this. You can't imagine, Mr. Gaston, the effort I have to make to communicate with you and, most of all, to be exposed like this when you obviously don't realize what's happening to me."

"Lars, I declare myself powerless in this case. I don't know what you're going to do, but I have it clear."

"No, Gaston. Don't give up. Everything will be fine. It's a case of somatic delusion, that's all."

"Listen, don't try to keep your voices down. It's useless. My antennae are very powerful. I can even sense your fear and detect the sound of your entrails. By the way, Mr. Gaston, your heart will stop soon. I can feel it. Let's conclude this fruitless talk for now. You can come back another day if you like. I'm exhausted."

6

His strength fades little by little while, all of a sudden, a strong taste of blood appears in his mouth one night. He has neither expected it nor anticipated it; he only knows he is condemned as one who awakens suddenly to a reality he has always feared. He intuits that the end will not be long in coming and will be painful. That never-ending night, his dreams fall precipitously into a void as he sees his glittering blood dripping along with an emerging and enduring agony through his whole being and writes, "I am doomed."

Another day, he decides to express his misfortune in intricate twists and turns, like a dark and indecipherable plot as if shouting at every step about the vain and miserable reality of man. He speaks through his fiction of the great impossibility of knowing the ultimate reality of man, who is caught up in the illusion of a happy ending that will never come. It is his truth and that of his characters that go out into the world, always confused, always lost in the indolence of others—evanescent reflections of a fellow human being who wants to help him but cannot given the unknown nature of the reality in which we are involved and what we wrongly call life.

7

"You don't realize how much I appreciate your visit, Max. It is not for less after receiving my last letter."

"Your testament, rather."

"Yes . . . that. What do you think about my decision?"

"You might imagine what I think. We have already talked a lot about your work, the unpublished and the published one, and . . . I have the unwavering certainty that—"

"That they are worthless."

"Don't put words in my mouth. I said nothing of the kind. You know very well what I think of your writings. They are simply fabulous."

"I'm so tired, Max, and the ghosts have returned. I thought they would not follow me to Berlin, but they are here."

"Do you mean the pain, the blood, all the bad things?"

"Yes. When I was writing, the ghosts were right there with me, and now they have returned, and I don't want them in my life. Chase them away! Burn my work! All of it!"

"Everything? How can you ask me to do such a thing? What you're asking is an extremely hard thing to do."

"Just do it, please."

"But what if I keep your writings so you can go over them later and discard what you don't consider of great value? It would be an easy task though."

"Why easy? I would have to discard whole stories and even one unfinished novel."

"You wouldn't throw anything away, believe me. Do you have any idea of what you are asking me to do?"

"I know very well. Burn everything that has not been published."

"What about the published ones?"

"There's nothing I can do about them. They are published. I can't go around seizing my books, you understand."

"What if I don't have the courage to destroy it?"

"You are my friend whom I blindly trust. I know you will do it."

"Well . . . you put me in a serious quandary. But . . . after all, I am your friend."

"Max . . . unfortunately . . . that work dies with me. I am the only one who understands it. It came out of me with great effort just to be who I'm really not. It's false because that's not me."

"But you're an artist, Franz. Despite not being you, as you say, you cannot break off it. It is the fruit of the effort of many years—"

"Wasted years. As you see, literature has been killing me in recent years, not to mention that it has been very jealous. It has kept me from having a wife, children, a family."

"Franz, please. Don't blame literature. It has been the only family you trust. That is the way it has been for some reason."

"Well, I think it has killed me slowly despite having given me some satisfaction. But in the end, the balance is negative."

"It is possible, although I don't agree with everything you say. You have expressed unequivocal and complicated truths worthy of thorough study."

"There is nothing to study. It is an agonizing work and circumscribed to my own overwhelming personal sorrows."

"In reality, your work addresses the sorrows that overwhelm all human beings. Many would feel identified with your sorrows and uncertainties. It has happened to me. Sometimes I feel like an outsider incapable of communicating with others, and everything becomes even more recognizable after reading your work. Can't you imagine how influential you can be?"

"You exaggerate. No one would feel influenced by a beetle or by an ordinary man who has become one. Where did you get that from?"

"From you, my friend. You are the most centered person I know. You were born for literature, even though you do not want to accept it now. You are literature. Now rest. You look exhausted. I will be dealing with your terrible testament in the days to come. Rest well."

8

In a race against time, he surrenders to literature, that compass he always has at hand, guiding him through unknown routes with an overwhelming rhythm, through indifferent cities and towns where absorbed characters never find what they are looking for with great determination. Perhaps the search is unnecessary because they might never find the coveted truth. He, in his creative efforts, reveals his true nature—reason, victim of his own captivating power.

He knows he will be defeated absurdly by an increasingly weakened life and the fear that grips him before the only possibility hanging over his head—the stony reality of impending death. He does not feel completely dejected and dreams of a happy life; it is his right to follow a dream, there in a battered world full of longings. Death is moving closer, but he is determined not to let it break his fortitude, so he holds on to his inspiration as the only weapon against destiny.

9

"She slid a message under her bedroom door, and it's for you. Apparently, she is becoming human again because she has decided to communicate through writing."

"Interesting. Hopefully, the delusion is letting up. No doubt the medication we prescribed is already taking effect. What do you think, Gaston?"

"It's a good sign. Maybe communicating with Karla will be less complicated now. Keep in mind she has used her hands to communicate and not the dozens of legs she thought she had."

"Hmm. Don't get your hopes up, gentlemen. It has been impossible for me to administer the medication because I have had to prepare her meals in the bedroom, and she only takes a few bites without taking her eyes off my face as if trying to guess my thoughts. She is very smart."

"I don't like that at all, Lars. We must find a different method."

"Well, it is what it is. We'll see what we can do after this second interview. It's time. Let's go in. You'd be so kind as to introduce us to Karla again, ma'am?"

"Yes. Karla! Karla! Mr. Gaston and Mr. Lars are here to talk to you. Did you hear me?"

"Yes, yes. Let them in, please, Mother, and stop the chatter out there. I can hear you perfectly. Let's see . . . come in, Mr. Gaston and Mr. Lars. I've been waiting for your visit anxiously. I've got some news. I am still a worm but more developed than the last time you were here and—""Could you be more explicit, Miss Karla?"

"Don't interrupt me, Mr. Lars, please. As I was saying, as you may have noticed, I am a more advanced worm now or rather more evolved. So my antennae are more sensitive. I can sense your deepest fears, your anguish, your most secret desires and dislikes and anger before they show on your stupid faces. Do you think I was not going to find out about the medication?"

The Voice and the Fallen

"Eh . . . well . . . you know that it was absolutely necessary to make you rest. It's been a long time since you slept properly. You look exhausted. On the other hand, Karla—and you can ask Lars if you want—we humans can perceive some of the inner complexities of other people without having antennae."

"It's true, Karla. We also possess those skills you mention in one way or another. That's why we have the ability to reason, make complex judgments about our surroundings, and assess potential risks in our interaction with other living beings. And . . . we haven't seen the antennae you claim to have."

"Can't you see them?"

"No."

"Not at all."

"What about these? Can you see these?"

"Yes. Those are your hands, Karla."

"Yes, we only see your beautiful human hands, with five fingers on each."

"I don't see hands. I see pincers that can easily kill any prey."

"It's a kind of metaphor, Lars."

"Karla, do you really think they are pincers? Can't you see more than pincers where your hands are supposed to be?"

"That's right, genius."

"Gaston . . . it seems to me that this is a very unusual case of species usurpation. It's definitely not a metaphor. Karla, let me ask you another question. Have you been eating the food your mother cooks for you every day?"

"Where is that coming from, sir? Of course, I've been eating the plate of fresh green leaves that my mother gives me every day. Do you think I'm so stupid?"

"And the usurpation is total. It has affected all her senses. I've never seen anything like this, Gaston. It's an extremely rare case, and we must study it thoroughly."

"I'm really sorry to interrupt you, gentlemen, but this will be the last time you'll see me. As my organs become more complex, in that same measure, the life force escapes from my body. I will die soon. No one can save me. I have aged fifty years in the last week. It can't be helped."

"But, Karla, you are still so young. Your face doesn't even show any trace of old age."

"You need to rest, to sleep for long hours, and then wake up from that nightmare in which you evidently find yourself."

"It's not a nightmare, Mr. Lars. This is my cruel destiny. Now I am a worm, but it could've been worse. Why did this happen to me and not to you? I have no clue. Nobody knows the laws that govern this process. We are just guinea pigs in this random experiment. I have no strength left. When you leave the room, tell my mother I never stopped loving her. Goodbye."

"No, Karla, don't say goodbye. We have a lot to talk about. We've just started our conversation, and I think we can help you."

"Yes. We can provide relief and lessen your distress. As for the physical side of things, it's necessary you have some tests done and get special treatment. You look sick, Karla. Please cooperate, and you'll see how quickly you recover."

"I have already cooperated enough, and the most important thing for me was to convey the message about my condition and say goodbye to my mother. It's impossible for me to communicate with her and to be indulgent with you. I will take the medication. I warn you, though, if I take it, I won't wake up, so this is goodbye. It's time for me to meet with him. I need to be left alone—now."

"Thanks, Karla, for granting us this interview. You've been pretty clear."

"Oh, and before we leave, Karla, could you tell us, who are you going to join?"

10

His stories come and go in an incessant flow full of mysterious metaphors and paradoxes, a bestiary of inferior beings, possessors of man's reason and always troubled by the complex vicissitudes of life or death. They are talking dogs, famous monkeys, snakes distressed by their concerns for survival, artists of hunger and death always lurking around hyperbolic characters in their bubbles of anguish—prisoners awaiting horrible tribulations before the impatience of the executioner, doctors on impossible trips after a spectacular cure, characters lost forever in large and impersonal cities or ostracized in semifeudal towns where God is equated to the enigmatic lord of the castle as absent as the being they pray to, and men persecuted by an invisible law and tried by equally invisible judges taking the sentence to its ultimate outcome, in short an improbable insect weaving the fate of an unhappy and petty bureaucrat as if a cruel fate delighted in causing suffering to all humanity through a torment of antennae, scores of legs, and empty walls. There is no escape for these characters, one more anguished than the next by their uncertain future.

But he fulfills his mission through the written word that hides the tribulations and uncertainties in a time of ominous forebodings. Death has come early, silencing his perplexed voice before the ever-cruel and dark reality of humankind. No other voice has revealed the grim face of reality so insistently, going beyond the streets of his old city; no other gust of wind has dragged the rubble of its own time as he has done with his unselfish writings.

11

"Love . . . is it day or night?"
"Day, dear, a cloudy day."
"It's cold."
"Yes, it's very for this time of year. I made an infusion. It'll be good for you."
"I don't feel like it now."
"But you have eaten almost nothing in the last three days."
"I have you, and that is enough for me."
"What do you say, love?"

"That I ha—"

"Don't talk too much, love. You will catch a cold again. Take a sip, please."

"Well . . . argh!"

"It hurts a little, but it is necessary."

"I can hardly swallow."

"Don't talk anymore."

"But I want to talk . . . at times, I feel as if I'm going, but I just fall asleep."

"Yes. When you sleep . . . do you dream of something?"

"I may dream, but . . . I don't remember my dreams. It's like I'm dying, and then I wake up and realize I'm alive."

"Yes, love. You are as alive as I am. Take another sip."

"No, I'm not as alive as you."

"Love, you break my heart when you say that."

"But it's true. Sometimes I think I'm already dead. I would like to look outside, but I no longer have the strength to get out of bed."

"I know. It's not worth it. It's an ugly day, and . . . love, don't ever say you're dead."

"You say it to comfort me."

"I say it because it's true. It started to rain now."

"I want to listen to the rain. It brings me . . . good and bad memories. There are many things I want you to know about me."

"Don't strain yourself. You can tell me when you feel better. I opened the window a little so you can listen to it. I'd like to hug you now."

"I'd like to hold you in my arms too, but better not do it."

"You know I'll do it sooner or later."

"No, stay there . . . don't get closer . . ."

"Franz? Did you fall asleep?"

12

Rivers of ink about his life and work have flowed, discourses, eulogies, analyses for someone who—unknown during his lifetime—has filled the world with dazzling metaphors and allegories, the literature of a whole era influencing ill-fated times, the scholar and the laborer drinking equally from the fountain of his art. A coarse death is not enough to bury his legacy because his imprint, free and imposing, has sent the message to a world thirsty for meaning and sensibility. His life has been brief, although his courage and discipline have been sufficient to stamp its truth on the art of prose writing, a truth that fulminates time and space.

13

"Who died?"

"I don't know. I'm just the gravedigger. I just bury people, no questions asked."

"Right, there's no reason for you to ask. I'll ask someone else. Hey, sir, who died?"

"A young man. He didn't have any children. It is a pity."

"Yeah, it's a shame. I wish I could have met him. Maybe I could have become his wife."

"What do you say, girl? His wife? You have too much imagination. But you know something? You can still get to know him, figuratively of course. He was a writer and a great one. I was his best friend, and now I say goodbye to him with great pain."

"I'm very sorry for you, sir, and also for him."

"You'd have been a good wife, and he would have loved you."

"You believe so?"

"Yes, I do. Do you like beetles?"

"No, I like worms better. Why do you ask?"

"He turned into a beetle long before he died. He was very young then."

"Well, I'll become a worm, come to his grave, and . . . I will eat him."

"He will like that. That way, you'll become his wife."

"Someday."

"Yes, someday. Goodbye."

"Goodbye."

CARL GUSTAV JUNG

(1875–1961)

Carl Jung was a Swiss psychiatrist, creator of the method of analytical psychology. At the beginning of his career in psychoanalysis, Sigmund Freud—whom he met in person in 1907—influenced him. Initially, their friendship was very intense in terms of their respective views on the depths of the human psyche; however, because of their great differences in the role-played sexuality in their theoretical framework, they broke up their personal relations in 1913, and Jung stepped down from his position as president of the International Psychoanalytic Association, although Freud had considered him the principal heir of his intellectual legacy.

After his break with Freud, he intensively investigated for decades the inner workings and mysteries that underlay the unconscious of people in general, of his patients and his own, as the collective unconscious. At the core of his research, he developed concepts such as archetypes, archetypal images, and complexes (in the psychological sense); extraversion and introversion; the shadow (related to the repressions of the personality) and the collective unconscious; synchronicity, a term that alludes to the paranormal without falling into a pseudoscientific interpretation; the self and individuation, the latter related to the goal of every person to achieve his or her greatest potential through inner search, among many other phenomena of depth psychology.

He traveled the world studying indigenous cultures and putting into practice his deep knowledge of the collective psyche of precivilized cultures, observing their similarities with European societies in terms of beliefs and behaviors. He studied extensively the symbolism of dreams, his own and those of his patients, achieving a great understanding in a subject so subjective and an untapped potential for scientific research.

He lived in Zurich practically his whole life, where he treated his patients. He maintained a close professional and sentimental relations with two women: Sabina Spielrein and Toni Wolff, who were very influenced by his particular way of penetrating the human psyche and who in turn influenced him in a similar way, especially Spielrein.

He built a house on the shore of Lake Zurich, in the middle of which he built a sanctuary, which only he could access, and he depicted his dreams in the form of pictographic symbols in there. He also had a stone brought where he carved many of the symbols that represented the content of his unconscious.

This story covered important moments in his life and relationships and a final interview, as well as the interaction between a married couple who made a pilgrimage to the world of Carl Gustav Jung and their particular divergence of views around some psychological theories of this student of the human mind, considered at the time of his death the most renowned psychologist in the world.

Words have no power to impress the mind without the exquisite horror of their reality.

—Edgar Allan Poe

There is only one journey. Going inside yourself.

—Rainer Maria Rilke

AT THE LAKE HOUSE

1

2013

"Here we are, Hannah. All we have to do now is to follow the path that leads to the stone."

"It's a beautiful view of the lake, don't you think? See how quiet the surface is. And to think he spent his best moments in this place."

"I think so. This lake would inspire anyone. It'd be a dream place for a poet."

"Also for a psychologist. It's a shame the lake doesn't have all the answers."

"I don't want to talk about that right now."

"Hmm, I think it is inevitable to talk about that. We agreed on doing it before taking the train."

"Please. Let's get to the stone, and then we'll see."

"But anyway, consider it done. We get to the stone, you look at it all you want, and then . . . you'll give me the pleasure of talking extensively about what I have to tell you."

"All right. We are almost there. I think it's around here that they told us it was."

"Yes . . . there it is. Look how big it is."

"Yeah, it's huge, and it seems perfect. I want to touch it. May I?"

"Well . . . since we're finally here after such a long trip, it would be stupid not to do it. I'm going to touch it too. Is anyone looking at us?"

"I don't think so. Oh, I'd like to take it home."

"Don't exaggerate. You can take all the photos you want. Only that way you can take it with you. And even if he comes out of his grave and gives it to you, still, you can't take it. Man, what an imagination!"

"It's beautiful. Look at the inscriptions. He carved them just by himself. He had brought it across the lake, from a quarry not far away. Originally, he ordered a triangle-shaped stone, and they brought him this one, cube shaped as you see, and he loved it."

"The truth is I don't see what is so fascinating about it. Please, it's just a huge stone placed in an environment it does not belong to."

"Hmm . . . I see where you're coming from. But you got to admit you were curious to see it. If you knew what it meant to him, it wouldn't seem so aberrant."

"Yes, yes. It has many inscriptions and symbols he himself engraved on the stone. I could accept that it is a kind of work of art, a very personal one by the way. Getting into its meaning is something else. Don't think it's the Rosetta stone. His followers would love to be able to make that comparison. In addition, not all of us are willing to delve into the meaning of all those strange symbols and quotations in Latin. Who do you think I am?"

"It's no big deal. If you are angry with me, I understand, but these inscriptions are very interesting and represent a lifetime of study. It exemplifies the consummation of his knowledge, nothing despicable, I must add—scientific knowledge, even if you find it difficult to accept."

"Do you think the study of the unconscious is very scientific? How could you replicate something as subjective as dreams? They are so personal. And as Calderón de la Barca would say, 'And dreams are only dreams.'"

"He wouldn't put it that way, you know. He spent his life analyzing the dreams of many people and also his own, reaching surprising conclusions and best of all healing people whose minds were sick, especially making them understand themselves a little better."

"I could not say the same. It seems more like an innocent deception. I believe that the unconscious simply doesn't exist. It's only the reflection of a void we all have inside where we can throw in all the garbage we want. Maybe that emptiness is a fundamental flaw of our imperfect brain."

"Oh, now you really got it all wrong. How can you say that the unconscious doesn't exist if it has been studied so extensively? The classic definition holds that the unconscious is the part of our psyche where the acts and desires we have forgotten or repressed from our conscious life go. The unconscious has a life of its own inside our psyche. It operates without us perceiving it and inevitably dominates us. Afterward, the man who carved this stone expanded that concept to include the collective unconscious, referring to the psychic forces that have been transmitted with our species through time and manifest themselves in a more . . . powerful way."

"Well . . . if he says so, you only have to believe it, and that's it."

"But I told you it results from a lifetime of observation, of over sixty years to be precise, and so you know he proved many of its hypotheses through his method of study, and his therapy work focused on the complexities of dreams. And evidence of that is the concept of an archetype, one of his great discoveries."

"Oh yeah. It's surprising you had not mentioned it yet. You know what? I think it is not more than a very elaborate explanation circumscribed only to what is convenient for him to point out."

"However, I do not see a more convincing and elegant explanation of the phenomenon. He said that the archetypes are patterns we have inherited throughout our peculiar evolution. In other words, they are automatic and generalized cross-cultural acts, for example, the archetypes related to death and its rituals; the archetype of the gods or God, as the case may be, which is present in all the cultures on the planet; the hero archetype; the trickster or the villain; and a long et cetera. The most brilliant part is how this leads us to the notion of the collective unconscious and how it operates in most of our actions. Do you find all that unconvincing?"

"You're only describing a given situation observed in the middle of a theoretical tour de force. I could analyze it from a different point of view but no less important. For instance, you know about our humble evolutionary origin well. What man observes can only be measured by the only scale he possesses, which is his own reasoning, assigning a category of pure reality to his observations, totally limited by the insufficient capacity of our brains to fully understand natural phenomena. Just as matter disappears as we enter it, studying the atoms and the myriad subatomic particles, so also the ultimate reality of what we call consciousness eludes us. We think we understand it, but deep down, we only understand the game we have invented. Sorry to disappoint you, but in there, ultimately, there is nothing fully demonstrable. If you don't believe me, ask your dear Plato."

"I think you have diverted the conversation to where suits you best. You are being very unfair to human brilliance in general. We have inherited a great wealth of knowledge in the last three thousand years, and you are narrowing it down to say that 'everything is nothing.' I think your attitude unworthy of someone who calls herself a scientist. What you think and do must have a personal root. I just don't share your nihilistic point of view about the sciences and life in general. I think our differences in this matter are irreconcilable."

"If you think so, there's nothing else to say."

2

He has to start with a question directed inward, in the dark of the night, in the middle of the dense forest or between the wet cracks of a mountain wall, or in the shade of a tree lost in the hostile savanna—a question whose answer he has seen reflected in the transparent surface of the river when his face appears on it. "Who am I?" asks the primitive being, spear in hand and fatigued by tearing off another day from death.

"Who I am?" he repeats, getting only echo for an answer, empty like the immense space over his head.

"Who I am?" he screams, desperate and finally exhausted, with a lone and uncertain path before him, waiting for his steps to lead him inevitably to it.

But he will never only get an answer in the dream that sears his being at night. Flashing and hyperbolic images will populate that incomplete world by traversing the space behind his eyes as he sleeps peacefully on the soft surface of the earth. He does not yet know that this other world is full of meaning and unknown omens, predicting the small battles he has to fight in everyday life. He falls asleep and goes into his own caverns that, one day, he will explore, like a seafarer navigating oceans of unfathomable and ghostly depths. He only knows that they lead him to some destiny, but far from grasping its meaning, he remains asleep, even though he is wide awake because the unconscious, if it's real, will be inaccessible forever.

3

1919

"I'm glad to see you again, Carl. It's been so long since the last time. Do you remember that afternoon at the lake?"

"How could I forget it? Are you still living in Vienna?"

"Yes but not for long. I feel as if I am being segregated there. One breathes such a masculine air. Besides, everything—absolutely everything—revolves around him. I don't think I can take it anymore. Since you sever your ties with the movement, I am not regarded favorably by some members. And although he has not told me, he feels a little . . . uncomfortable with me."

"I'm sorry to hear that. If you stay there, keep your expectations low. The schism that separated me from their ranks has not been the first, nor will it be the last. Now after several years, I can say that I am cured of that failed friendship with him. However, I must admit that it affected me for a long time. But at the end of the day, I have not only cured myself of that illness. I can tell you that my research into the issues that resulted in our break up has borne fruits."

"I know. Nonetheless, it is still excellent news coming from you, although you were not very clear in your last letter. Have you already unraveled the question of repression and the death instinct?"

"No. That is your subject. And he has taken on blatantly without giving you the well-deserved credit."

"That does not bother me anymore. I can't deny at that time it really did, but that is in the past now. I'm more interested in what you're working on at the moment. Can you tell me more about it?"

"Sure. After my rupture with him, I began to tread my own path. And from my point of view, it was strictly necessary to continue the endless search for the unconscious but analyzing myself as you well know. I analyzed my dreams as intensely as those of my patients. It was not an easy task at the beginning. I felt that I was falling apart inside, but despite the difficulties, I continued until it was finally revealed to the full extent of what my own limitations allowed, that dream that years ago I had naively told to him."

"Yes . . . I remember. How his analysis of it dismayed you. It did not seem worthy of him."

"That's right. After several years, I grasped its significance in all its magnitude, thanks to my studies of mythology, anthropology, comparative religion, and the study of ancient and modern cultures."

"I must confess how amazed I am because someone like you had the courage and good sense to expand psychology's field of study beyond its known limits."

"You flatter me, but . . . everything was there. I only put the pieces together. One thing took me to the next, and so observing certain patterns in nature and in ancient cultures, I discovered the archetypes, picking up an ancient concept of Plato's. You see, from a very tender age, the pattern that will govern our thoughts, feelings, and actions is preestablished in our psyche."

"But . . . that contradicts somehow the concept of the tabula rasa established by Locke."

"In the light of the archetypes, there is no such thing as a tabula rasa. Just as an oak seed harbors within itself the information of becoming a robust tree, in the same way, we have preestablished patterns of response to the surrounding phenomena, both outside and inside our being. That is what I have called archetype, which is composed of complex and simultaneous perceptual patterns throughout all known cultures."

"Regardless of the time or region of the planet where a person is?"

"Correct. Thus, you will find the archetype of God or gods in a homogenous form in most cultures, numerous death rites, manifestations of sexuality as the pattern for reproduction and recreation composed of the most complex rituals that express instinctively the mechanics or modus operandi of life after death, very similar in diverse cultures distant in time and space."

"Impressive. From that perspective, the archetypes can explain the way humans think and act."

"And we sublimate our deepest worldly desires and make them acceptable to our consciousness. He would say from his evanescent throne in Vienna, 'I, for one, maintain that those patterns of response underlying the depths of our psyche move to the beat of that great orchestrator I call archetype.'"

"Would you define it as a categorical assertion?"

"I would go further. It is not necessary to be categorical with something sufficiently clear and applicable to the subject of study."

"It then becomes like a kind of unit of measurement as in physics."

"Unfortunately, psychology is not a hard science, and we cannot or rather should not confuse our factual mechanisms of reaching concrete conclusions established in the study of psychology with those in those sciences, that is to say, although the archetypes are similar patterns of perception and reaction, they don't necessarily constitute measurable units. They are rather theoretical constructs to bring us closer to a more comprehensible way of dealing with the phenomena we have been talking about. It all comes down to understanding what is intrinsic within patterns of collective behavior."

"It is an even elegant way to understand it, and it is not only reduced to the individual but to the whole conglomerate."

"You have put it very well, Sabina, and talking about conglomerates, behind the archetypes hides the collective unconscious, which becomes the mechanism of action for the archetypes."

"And did you prefigure that in the analysis of your dreams? Didn't you?"

"Yes, I deduced it from the dream I asked him to analyze while we were on our way to America, the one I already told you about."

"The powerful way in which your unconscious revealed itself on that occasion is a sign you are on the right track. It's always been said that practice makes perfect."

"I think so. Had I not analyzed my dreams, the unconscious would not have revealed itself as it did at that moment. I was truly on the right path."

"How would you summarize the different aspects that form the collective unconscious?"

"Simple. We all inherit that pattern of responses I have already explained, to which I referred only in its form or structure as an archetype, but none of us can remember our ancestors' experiences other than in the legacy originally transmitted to us orally and after the written language and the artistic expression appeared. That legacy has become more concrete. Well, the spirit of those ideas, the abstract corpus of that great ideological legacy, has been transmitted in that parallel dimension that exists within us and that we call unconscious. The concept of the collective unconscious refers to that wave or flow of information embodied in the culture through the imaginarium that our species has compiled through thousands of years and does not die out with individuals. You might wonder why now, and I would answer that probably the collective unconscious had already been discovered, but apparently, it had not become a seriously and methodically followed subject of study."

"You have cleared all my doubts. What remains to be done now, with the permission of the two women who rule your life, is to give you a kiss. May I? Only one kiss."

4

Dreams are a mysterious and elusive tangle, part of life, uncertain and abundant, ethereal and fleeting, like a flash of light that travels from the inside toward the senses represented in the deepest part of the mind, the biochemical mechanism that balances life day by day. Will human beings be able to open the door that leads to the creative matrix of dreams? To that forge that evades meanings about shooting stars in their remoteness? Will dreams be that unknown reflection of the universe that extends over and inside our heads, incapable of grasping the essence that escapes like a shadow that will never be touched except in a flight of the imagination?

A lifetime is not enough to open the gates of wisdom that dreams enclose, that riddle that has escaped humanity's full understanding through time. Nevertheless, he tries; and in his struggle, he believes with an ardent illusion to glimpse a flash of light, but he doesn't realize that he is only looking through a window, the infinite precipice that lies before him, and puerile questions are the fruit of his indefatigable illusion when faced with the vastness of the enigma enclosed in the dark region that makes up dreams. But this does not discourage him; he is optimistic and pursues his chimerical endeavor through the course traced by the maze of his ideas and will not rest until death surprises him. And perplexed, he will not find his way back, where the rest of the living wait for his answers on this side of the river of life.

5

2013

"Are you going to be mute much longer? Hannah . . . say something, please. Your silence is cruel, and it hurts me. We agreed on coming to this place. I know you like this city a lot. It was your dream to come to Zurich. I was the one who didn't want to take this trip. I had the intuition this would happen. Deep down, I saw it coming. You know why? You do know . . . I consider it my sanctuary because he lived and worked here all his life, and I did not want that fact to antagonize you. That's why I didn't want to come, although I was dying to do so. Well, you succeeded in making me happy and unhappy at the same time, all in one day. If only I could go back in time and undo what is already done, I swear I would do it just to see you happy again, make things as they were before. Please say something."

"I have nothing to say. You are happy because you visited your idol."

"No, no, you are the one I idolize."

"Lie! You idolize him. You have always said it, since I know you."

"With more reason you should understand me."

"I do not intend to waste my time understanding you. You are as you are, and that's it."

"But what I feel for you is unique, different from what I feel for him, for his work. That is called admiration. What I feel for you is love, passion. I have chosen you as my partner."

"Ah, you have chosen me. Coincidentally, right? Among how many? Tell me! Among how many?"

"Please . . . I didn't mean that. I love you, and I think I've shown you how much."

"That's not enough. Also . . . your patients are very special, more than me actually. I'm just one of many. I know what's going on between you and some of your patients. Just look at my—"

"What? What are you implying?"

"I don't know. You tell me."

"What the hell are you talking about? Where did you get those ideas? Are you losing your mind? How can you insinuate such a thing?"

"Now you want to make me believe you're offended. Do you think I don't know what's happening? You love your idol so much you follow his steps even in this way. Like father like son. You have become a master just like him."

"So that's how it is. This is the real Hannah, the one I'm in love with. But right now that we're here, in my sanctuary, in one of my happiest days, you decide to release all the repression you've been keeping bottled up for who knows how long. Now I understand your coldness these last few days. But . . . you, who are so scientific, should prove your theory with facts, don't you think?"

"There's nothing to prove. It's in plain view, no explanations needed. I never intended to change you or just make you feel bad on a whim today, your . . . happiest day."

"So be kind. Go easy on me. You have been very rude since the day we went to see the stone as if you wanted to hurt me in my weak point. You have an adamant position about all this, and I'm making an effort to understand your point, but unfortunately, there are parts of your position I just don't share, and I doubt I'll ever do. For example, I can't accept when you say we are empty inside, that our life has no purpose, and that death is purely and simply the absolute end of everything."

"You're starting on the same subject again. It seems that you don't learn your lesson at all, or you are evading the main issue. What will I have to do to make you understand me?"

"If I have to make the greatest effort of my entire life to do it, I'll do it because I love you, and . . . I'm not evading anything. You may not believe me, but I accept you the way you are, including your radical ideas about the self."

"What self? What do you mean by that? Wait . . . wait . . . let me finish. You don't understand when I tell you that there is nothing enduring inside our skulls. And if there is something, we don't know what it is. Consciousness is given by our particular biology, and that makes us perceive the world around us in the only way that our brain allows it, but think of other species, any of them, and you will get to the conclusion that their world and perceptions are different, and the main point for our little debate is the voids of consciousness."

"But you will not deny that some animals have consciousness."

"That is yet to be proved. Ethologists don't agree on that point, but what is striking is their emptiness."

"Right, we are superior animals. I maintain that we have a consciousness and a subconsciousness or a region of our psyche we know as the unconscious."

"That is a way to disguise our ignorance on the subject, dear, in an elegant and convenient way, but the reality is that we give names to the void only as a point of reference to our species. Just look at the quintessential point of reference—time."

"That is another matter. You think then that we try to fill the void with convenient answers as an easy way to aid our understanding, but in reality, there is the nothing."

"Nothing enduring."

"And what is there then?"

"Just fog and then the abyss from which no one returns. And do you know why no one comes back from there to answer the questions that torture us?"

"I'm listening."

"Because there is nothing to say. None of that is important for the universe. And if you don't understand this point of view, as simple as terrifying, it is because you can't separate yourself from your limited human conceptions and appreciate the reality outside the box you are in, until someday you will have to walk the last trail. We'll all do it sooner or later, and it will lead you to a tunnel with a bright light at the end, and it'll be the last light your brain will register."

6

1926

"What a splendid sunset. This time of day and the beautiful setting sun are so suitable for us to continue with the analysis of dreams."

"Carl, how do you link your intuition to your own reality, the latter being well known to you because it lies in that part of you which is conscious?"

"Through my dreams and thoughts, Toni, and the common thread that connects them and guides them."

"But . . . do you constantly resort to the self-analysis of your thoughts, actions, and feelings? How can you do it?"

"Well, I spend most of the day alone. When I'm not immersed in reading, researching, I am with my patients, analyzing their dreams and lives, and it is inevitable that what I find makes an impact on me, thus affecting my self-analysis. That is why the patients are my own reflection basically. When I analyze them, I see myself in them."

"Aren't you afraid of losing your mind?"

"That is the point. There have been occasions in which I have lost it, recovering it again after a short time. It is definitely risky but necessary to find oneself."

"It is a dangerous and inadvisable task, I would say.

"I give you that, Toni, but . . . if you manage to overcome the barrier posed by creative illness, you will come in contact with the unconscious and may establish an active and lasting connection with it."

"I believe you, but let's start from the beginning. Was it through a dream you discovered the collective unconscious?"

"Correct."

"Can you tell me what happened as you remember it?"

"Certainly. That night, I went to bed early. I was very tired, and after some time, I had this dream: I was in a house I felt I did not know, but it was my house, and I was on the upper floor in a room furnished in the rococo style. I did not know what the floor below was like. Down there, everything was much older. I estimated that part of the house must have been from the fifteenth or sixteenth century. The furniture was medieval with a red brick floor. I went from one room to another, thinking I should explore the whole house. I found a heavy door and opened it. A stone stairway went down to the basement. There, I saw a beautiful vaulted room that seemed ancient. The walls were from Roman times. The floor was made of stone slabs, and then I discovered a metal ring for pulling up one of the slabs, so I opened the hatch and saw a very narrow stone staircase leading downward. I descended and entered a cave. There were scattered bones and broken pottery on the dusty floor, the vestiges of a very primitive culture. I discovered two enormous skulls, probably archaic, half disintegrated. Then I woke up.

"It was clear that the house represented a kind of image of the psyche. The room represented the conscious. It had an atmosphere of having been inhabited. The lower floor represented the first level of the unconscious. The deeper I went, the stranger and darker the scene became. The Roman basement and the prehistoric cave mean past times and previous stages of my unconsciousness. My dream evidently marked the bases of culture and history in successive layers of knowledge and made up a kind of structural diagram of the human psyche. It was the first collective sign under the personal psyche."

"Wonderful. I suppose that the understanding of your own unconscious became easier from then on."

"To tell you the truth, I don't see it that way. I think it got exponentially more complicated."

"Explain yourself, please."

"I'll do it in exchange for something."

"What could it be?"

"Just say yes, and I'll reveal it to you at the end of the session."

"It will be like making a deal blindly, but you have me so intrigued that I have to agree."

"Good. Over time, I had other dreams concerning catastrophes that would happen in Europe. I am referring, of course, to the period before the Great War, maybe one or two years prior, right after my break with the movement. It was a very hard phase in my life because I had to deal with patients, but the most difficult part was dealing with myself. Everywhere, I could see the shadow subtly taking over everyone, and that took its toll on me. I began to dream of rivers of blood crisscrossing all Europe and one in particular where a great flood on the continent that reached the Swiss Alps themselves, and those dreams filled me with confusion because people couldn't foresee the war yet. Later, in hindsight, I attributed them to my patients' collective unconscious and their underlying fears and to the fact that their unconscious vibrated at the same frequency without nobody knowing it. That was something new. We have the ability within us to predict personal and collective tendencies. Do you see it more clearly now?"

"Of course, Carl. How didn't other great investigators of the mind think of it? Him, for instance."

"Hard to know. I can only say in my favor that, to a large extent, the discovery of the collective unconscious has to do with an unusual curiosity that led me to the conclusion that if I wanted to understand this great particularity of our species psyche, I should stop thinking like a European and think of myself as a human, unconstrained by nationalities or cultures, so I could see the whole picture to get to the roots of what we all are."

"Interesting. I never would have seen it that way. But how not being a European if you are in the center of Europe?"

"In fact, I had to leave this continent and explore distant cultures and time. I visited Africa and the American Midwest, looking for those common traits that had the diverse indigenous cultures of those regions. And to my great astonishment, I discovered that their respective collective unconscious had inescapable similarities in relation to the great issues of survival and belief systems. After my travels, I did not harbor the slightest doubt—the psyche works in the form of fundamental archetypes independent of the race, the culture, or the geographical region in which it has developed, and not only that. I would speculate, beyond my field of study, that the way the archetypes operate applies equally to all natural phenomena and even the universe. I see you are surprised."

"You've left me speechless. But on second thought, it's not that easy to accommodate your findings, say, to Newton's mechanical physics, to the theory of relativity, not to mention the latest discovery, quantum physics."

"Unfortunately, that is research that surpasses my range of action. However, in that sense, I have received strong support from intellectuals and physicists who do not detract from the merits of my work."

"It's no wonder. If you set yourself to the task, you can dig deeper into this subject as long as you have any breath in your body. You have shown a great ability to push further your topics of study. After everything you have told me, you only need to keep the promise of revealing your great secret now."

"Yes. I'll tell you without preamble. Give me a kiss."

"Only one?"

7

2013

"Can we stay in bed all afternoon? It has not stopped snowing the whole morning, and I don't feel like going in any of your excursions. I have pleased you in everything, love. You owe me one. Come, get closer. And if you behave, I'll tell you a story."

"Hmm, you've convinced me. And when you set your mind to it, you're pretty good at it. It's better to stay in here, warm. I'll call room service to have lunch brought in."

"I love it when you're so docile. Get closer."

"Oh . . . Hannah, you take me to the valley of joy."

"And you, Roberto, to the valley of tears, but I like it. I'm a bit of a masochist, you know. Or haven't you noticed? We think so differently, but I'd rather have that a million times than nothing."

"Well . . . I don't know if to feel flattered or just the opposite, but I always want to be with you despite not being able to cure you of the illness of emptiness, so to speak."

"You won't cure me, but rest assured that we will have fun during the treatment. Come closer, even more. Yes."

"Maybe you want me so close to you so I can't escape?"

"Yes. Because I'm cold, and you're the only coat I see in the room. Kiss me."

"Mmm . . . I seem so full of life. We need no philosophizing for this, and there's no science to explain the axioms of passion."

"Do you want to hear the story now?"

"Now? Why not later?"

"Because I want to tell it to you now. I got you a little treat for later."

"Agree. Now then."

"I will tell you briefly the story of my maternal grandmother who died before I was born. She was born in the Christian faith, just like you and me, but at some point in her life, still young, she stopped believing. Don't ask me what happened. I don't know the details, but she got up one fine morning and decided that God would not be part of her life anymore. Then she began her philosophy studies. She lived here in Zurich, and being very young, for some unknown reason, she decided to visit your idol."

"How come you never told me that story before? It's right up my alley."

"Don't think I've told you even one-tenth of my family's stories, and I have told you many."

"But capriciously . . . even malevolently, you had this one under lock and key. Keep going, please."

"The fact is that she visited the famous psychiatrist, and according to some relatives, she became quite dependent on him after a while. Won't you say, by chance, an occupational hazard perhaps?"

"No way. Keep going."

"He apparently penetrated her unconscious in such a way that, in her dreams, she felt him as her God, the God she had left behind. Seemingly, he cured her neurosis, that is, urged her to find herself to where she clung to a feeling of the numinous. Unfortunately for her, that was temporary. And eventually, she felt an emptiness even greater than the one she had experienced before visiting the therapist. Remember, she was studying philosophy. She was clinging to him and to nothingness. She eventually stopped seeing him, and finally, shortly after his death, she committed suicide, my mom being a little girl at the time."

"But you don't mean to imply he had something to do with her death, do you?"

"Not exactly. But . . . that tragedy changed our lives—I mean, his great influence affected us in the long run."

"You must know in such a situation, everyone is responsible for their actions. I don't mean to be harsh with your grandmother, but we should examine the context in which the events took place."

"It's not worth it. It's been over fifty years since it happened."

"And how do you know that story? Did your mom tell you?"

"No. My grandmother left a diary."

"And . . . will you show it to me someday?"

"No!"

"Sorry. I didn't mean to offend you. I just wanted to know what he did wrong."

"Maybe he did nothing wrong. And it's impossible to read the diary now because my mother threw it in the fire. Now . . . if after hearing that sad story you still want the treat, I won't deny to you."

8

1957

"The confusion you're feeling now is usually the product of manifestations of the unconscious still to be uncovered inside you, especially if you use dreams as tools to reach your unconscious mind."

"But, Herr Doktor, dreams escape me. As much as I attempt to remember them, I only retain fragments, and they make little sense if any at all."

"That is how the unconscious expresses itself, in such a way that you ignore its motivations, mechanisms, or the reason for its contents. Otherwise, they would be in the conscious part of you. You only need to retrace the memory of your dreams. It will be some effort, but you can do it one at a time. Then we will do our best to decipher them. Do not despair. We will do it together. Start writing the diary of dreams I assigned you from the beginning of our sessions, and once you have some practice putting it on paper the best you can, when you least expect it, you will be in control of the content and connections in your dreams. It is like slowly and methodically unraveling a skein of subtle and sensitive threads."

"But what you suggest is not an easy task."

"And what is easy in analysis? You must pay close attention to what happens to you day to day at the university, in the interactions with your family, and especially in dealing with strangers. Then when you feel ready for this exercise, your unconscious will reveal itself in an unstoppable manner."

"Unstoppable? Do you assure me, Herr Doktor?"

"Naturally. I have it for a fact. Sometimes it is almost impossible to translate dream images into words, but it works better for me when I draw them."

"No, Herr Doktor, the method of drawing the images does not work for me. However, I would feel comfortable writing my dreams."

"Do what suits you best. Now I propose an exercise. Last week, you told me several fragments of dreams related to me. I think I deciphered them."

"Oh, I'd love to know your explanation. I could not understand them."

"You know that I consider you a brilliant student of philosophy, with an analytical capacity superior to that of many. I would not have expected for you to identify me with a father figure, but it was very surprising to me when you let yourself be carried away by that type of delusion."

"Do you consider it a delusion, Herr Doktor? But you have told me that this type of phenomenon is part of the therapist-patient dynamic."

"Anyway, you surprised me but in the good sense of the word. So in cases like this, as a therapist, you inevitably resort to dreams to establish a direct dialogue with the unconscious."

"Allow me to interrupt you for a moment. That you are not my father is clear, and I didn't pretend that. However, for some reason unknown to me, it is as if you were, as if I depended on you in every way."

"Therefore, it was imperative to analyze that series of dreams where I assumed the role of your father, in which you appeared sitting on my lap, safe in my arms, and I was a tender father with that little girl you were."

"That dream is embarrassing, Herr Doktor. Perhaps the fact that I was an innocent girl sitting on the lap of a kind and enormous father personified in you excuses me somehow."

"I was the giant father, and you were my little girl secured in my hands like a fragile bird."

"Besides giving me shelter, you conveyed me a peace that is not of this world, I assure you."

"I believe you. In another of your dreams, I was in a huge wheat field ready to be harvested, caressed by a gentle and constant wind, making waves on the whole field. And along with the wind, I was rocking with you in my giant's lap at the wind's rhythm as if I would put you to sleep. Did you describe it that way?"

"Yes, exactly. And with your gentle movements, I felt I was in the arms of a god."

"I must confess, in the light of your special feeling revealed in that dream, that the harvest within you was already ripe. What you have projected onto me, because you are not aware of that, is the basic idea absent from your conscious mind, that I was a deity. Therefore, you see that deity in me. What do you think of my analysis?"

"I'm speechless, Herr Doktor."

"It always happens, especially in a case like yours. After going through an intense religious education at first and then receiving an increasingly secular education, eventually, your relationship with God ceased to exist at a conscious level."

"I don't regret that because my university education became more complex, and it played down the role of the supernatural in the explanation of natural phenomena. It was no longer enough for me to simply attribute all the wonders and tragedies of the world to an absent god."

"However, your unconscious does not see it that way. The idea of a deity is an archetypal, nonintellectual idea that appears in the great majority of ancient cultures. Therefore, it is an idea that is attached to our species. It has different names, different qualities."

"So, Herr Doktor, if I have understood correctly, my idea of a deity embodied in my unconscious is only an archetype. Is that what it's all about?"

"Yes. It is an image of that archetype, a god of nature, of vegetation. The spirit of wind and wheat manifested itself in you. You had a direct experience with the archetype. That, dear friend, is not something you see every day."

"Oh, I never would have imagined that something like this was happening inside me, Herr Doktor. For the first time in my life, I feel I am not as empty as I thought."

"And your unconscious has projected it on me, so I became the conduit to transmit its existence. Isn't that wonderful? You have had an experience of the numinous that dwells in you, and that makes you feel liberated and makes you whole. Now you are on the path of your own individuation, and someday if you don't forget this daunting experience, you will become what you are called to be by human nature from the beginning of life."

"Please never leave me, Herr Doktor. Without you, I will not reach that wonderful destination."

9

The inner search has not been easy; it has taken him a lifetime trying to know what appears to be there within the reach of everyone and anyone at the same time. Like an unfathomable sea, it embraces him, contains him; but in the long search in those chasms, he succumbs, being amazed by a brief glance toward the unknown. It is necessary for him to delve into the diversity of culture and civilization to define the still new path for humanity. When he observes carefully his inner being, he sees the outline of caverns, glimpsing what he longs to find through dreams, and it seems to reverberate in an eternal moment, consciousness, after the last breath. But it seems to him he isn't misguided when claiming to know God exists instead of just believing in His existence. God lives inside him in the form of beings that swarm in his and everyone's unconscious, ancestral archetypes that give meaning to this mundane life where we all share the same fate—being forgotten in the flow of time.

His legacy is to have opened an infinite path in the depths of mankind, and his work, unfinished by necessity, offers novel ways in the search for the elusive unconscious. He knows that his long life has not been enough to lift the veil of ignorance, but he is confident that others will follow his path, synchronizing, typifying, reading between the lines, digging into the meaning of dreams, and through all that, through the process of individuation turning an insignificant oak seed in a huge and leafy tree. Only he knows if he has completed his adventure of knowledge in the dense forest mind's phenomena. Let's ask him again.

10

2013

"Are you satisfied with your trip—sorry, our trip?"

"Yes. Seeing the stone up close was very moving, but even more so, seeing the lake house—it was like having been through a mystical experience."

"I can imagine."

"But you don't look satisfied but rather sad. That mysterious face betrays you. It doesn't seem you've enjoyed this trip."

"I enjoyed it, but . . . now that I think about it, it would've been better if I hadn't come . . . so you've come by yourself."

"Why do you say that, love? We solved our differences. We decided to accept ourselves as we are and respect our beliefs without trying to convince each other. That was the deal, wasn't it?"

"Yes. But . . . I haven't told you everything. There is something you should know so you can understand me."

"You're scaring me, love. Now the mystery has become an intrigue. I'm ready to hear what you have to say. It's a long train ride, and I assure you that the landscape won't distract me."

"It's a long story, but I'll tell you the essential. I already told you that I did not know my maternal grandmother. She committed suicide a few days after giving birth to my mother, more than fifty years ago. She took to the grave her real reasons for doing it, but many people said it was because she was raped. I see that you are in shock. Indeed, she was raped, and nobody knew who the rapist was. But as a result, my mother was born, whom she abandoned to her fate when she killed herself. My grandmother's family raised her for a short time. Time went by, and when my mother was about twelve years old, she was told what had happened, including the fact that her mother committed suicide the same year her therapist died, whom, according to family gossip, she idolized."

"I'm so sorry for you and your family. Tragedies like that—"

"They should not happen in any family. It was devastating for my mother. It marked her forever. After knowing what had happened to her mother, her innocence literally evaporated. No one could have anticipated her reaction. She became a very solitary, suffering person for many years."

"But I guess she received psychological help."

"From a whole army of psychologists, and in the end, they didn't achieve much."

"I suppose they took her out of Switzerland."

"Yes. They took her to France and England, and as an adult and by her own means, she went to America."

"They must have spent a fortune."

"That's right. Only time and her studies achieved what so many psychologists and psychiatrists couldn't."

"I wonder what the reason was for so much medical failure."

"Well . . . we're talking about the seventies. There were no modern treatments. At the time, they diagnosed her with chronic melancholic depression."

"Melancholic depression? But there was already pharmacological treatment by that time."

"Right, but she stopped taking the medication somehow, and the depression returned as if it never had left."

"It's a frustrating story, especially because she got professional help. Maybe your relatives gave up trying by traditional means at some point."

"Take into account that, in the family, there was already some frustration with psychologists and psychiatrists. As you know, the best psychiatrist of her time treated my grandmother."

"But didn't she took her own life after his death?"

"Yes. He was the last one who had a very positive effect on her. He made her another person—more complete and more self-confident. According to what I've heard, she was a person full of peace, serenity, and with many important projects. But . . . the rape not only changed the course of her life but that of my mother's and therefore mine as well."

"How come you had never told me that story before? I'm a little disappointed because you didn't trust me enough to tell me but just a little. It's just that I love you so much. Come here, we both need a hug. Cry. Cry all you want, I'll always be here."

"But . . . maybe if he hadn't treated her and filled her with so much confidence, perhaps she wouldn't have had such a radical destiny. She would not have been raped."

"Impossible to know. On the other hand, your mother would not exist and you."

"I know where you're coming from. We wouldn't be here in this cabin about to make love either. I know. I know you."

"You tell me. You are the philosopher. What would we call this situation?"

"We'd call it the lake house effect."

11

1960

Brief monologue

Life here is apparently simple. I live completely alone in this house. After working on the stone for a long time, I inevitably turn my gaze to the lake. I stare at it for some time, maybe for a few minutes or for long hours. It depends on my mood at that moment. There, reflected in the serene and glaring surface, I see tiny flashes of light;

and suddenly, some of my dreams come up, and often I speak only with my memories or with those beings with whom I have shared the walk of life in the last fifty years, faithful companions whom I've gotten to know but not to understand.

I light my pipe constantly, a mechanical but pleasant gesture, and I let myself go. I unlock the only door that belongs to me, and then I enter my world, protected by the echo of my steps, already dragging because of my age. Despite everything, I feel energetic; and like every day, I light the fireplace before evening falls. And regardless of being alone, a sense of bliss flows through me precisely because I am alone with my thoughts. I will not deny that I love being by myself since I was a child, when I hid my precious talisman and then sat on my first stone. I always reflect on those things. For what is life when it is longer than expected if not to remember the past while I smoke my pipe in the present.

Sometimes sitting by the fireplace or at the window's shelter, I hear the soft roar of the lake, and I think that everything will remain the same when I'm not here anymore, when I am gone. I suppose that thought should be painful, but it is not. I reflect a little, and I conclude that it must be because of my mandala. My mandala is in the center and at the back of the house. It is a space tailored to my personal requirements. I am the only one who can enter. That space is me. It is closed almost all the time, whether I am inside or outside.

I find myself through my dreams and reflections. It has not been an easy task, but I can assure that they have brought me an understanding that will be impossible for me to put into words; that is why I use the images that come spontaneously from my unconscious. It is as if I lived several lives at once with my body and my mind, and I think once again that life will always be short when you decide to take the path of the unconscious because it is inexhaustible. The only way I have to bring beings from the unconscious to life is to paint them. The walls are full of them already, my eternal companions.

If life has a meaning or an aim, I have validated it here in my precious mandala. What is the meaning of life? It is the task of each *person to seek it; otherwise, that meaning will go over their lives surreptitiously, and maybe, just maybe, all their life will be in vain.*

12

1961

"Herr Doktor, how would you define your life if this were the last chance you had?"

"You ask me a complicated question, young man, because I could not define it with a simple answer. Suffice it to know that, in my personal balance, after eighty-six years of life and having plumbed the depths of the psyche of so many people, it has been a very fulfilling life. And if there are any complaints, I suppose it is the natural incapacity to live another eighty-six years to continue my work on people's unconscious and my own."

"Interesting. Doesn't the ability to learn and discover new things become increasingly limited with age?"

"In theory, I guess. But at this point in my life, I'm still learning and writing, and I have not perceived what we might call a drain of my intellectual creativity."

"Surprising. I would call that being gifted."

"No, no, don't exaggerate, young man. All human beings could potentially have that capacity. The secret lies in cultivating curiosity and exercising it all the time and to know that the key to aging well is to prevent devastating diseases by taking good care of one's health, but as you and I know, it is a lost battle. However, the medical sciences do the work of extending our lives as long as possible. In the distant future, there will exist, perhaps, the possibility of . . . avoiding death."

"Avoiding death? Forgive my daring, Herr Doktor, but that sounds like science fiction. I don't believe such a feat would be possible."

"What I mean, young man, is prolonging consciousness after death through some unknown scientific advancement not yet at our disposal."

"It still sounds like science fiction, Herr Doktor."

"But as you know, for people in the sixteenth century, flying was more than impossible or curing certain diseases, and now they are our bread and butter as the saying goes. In fact, we do not know for a fact if consciousness is still active after we die. It is just that we do not have a way to find out."

"Probably because there is no such thing as the prevalence of consciousness after death. Maybe death is simply an irrevocable and irreversible step that means the ultimate and definitive end of life, with no more repercussions for the physical world than the disintegration of the body."

"I see that you have gotten in the field of improbabilities, young man. In other words, you mean that life is totally improbable in any form after the death of the person."

"Correct, Herr Doktor. I'm afraid that there is nothing beyond death."

"Or in any case, we cannot determine the phenomenon."

"From that point, we can ask one last question. Since man through science has penetrated deeply into the nature of so many phenomena that happen not only on Earth but also in the universe at large, an achievement by the use of reason, do you think we will unveil the mysteries of death one day?"

"As I have said in other interviews and even in some of my writings, I am sure that in the next hundred years we will not be able to determine what happens to consciousness after death. As people, we are not capable of determining our postmortem reality a priori by our own means because we can't expect a useless machine to work, assuming that there is no soul without a body."

"But a body is without soul once it succumbs to death."

"Moreover, as a species, we have always looked for what I call archetypal answers to the phenomenon of death. If the answers we give to ourselves for the sake of our own satisfaction have the faculty of being categorical, that would prove nothing."

"Therefore, any attempt to explain the afterlife has no practical value because we don't have the tools to perform such a feat, and nature is indifferent to our ignorance."

"That's correct. You just said it. We cannot know. There won't be any results. Let us wait for what future generations have to say about it. Thanks, young man, for your kind and deep questions."

"Thank you, Herr Doktor."

LEONARDO DA VINCI

(1452–1519)

Leonardo da Vinci was the greatest representative of the Renaissance in the late Middle Ages. He was considered by many as the man with the most wide-ranging curiosity in history. In addition to being a painter, he was an architect, designer of all kinds of mechanical gadgets, scenario decorator, musician, and above all one of the most influential characters in history. Despite having painted relatively little, all his pictorial works were considered masterpieces; standing out among them were The Last Supper, Mona Lisa, Virgin of the Rocks, Adoration of the Magi, The Virgin and Child with Saint Anne. Among his most famous drawings was The Vitruvian Man.

He never married, nor had children of his own but adopted children, who after his death divulged many of his works, especially his innumerable notebooks containing a considerable amount of drawings and sketches that stood out for their impressive attention to detail, inventiveness, and variety of subjects.

In Florence, Milan, and finally France, he was supported by powerful patrons who saw in him the great and unequaled genius of the arts and technology, especially his facet as an architect and designer devices for warfare.

His most valuable work, the Mona Lisa, also known as La Gioconda, was according to many of his biographers his personal favorite. He began working on it in 1503, and it was said to be unfinished because he continued to retouch it, trying to perfect it almost until the end of his life.

It was said that Prince Guiliano de' Medici, son of Lorenzo the Magnificent, commissioned the portrait; however, he never separated from it. The painting ended up in France, and since it was already in that country long before Leonardo's death, it was considered a national heritage of the French nation. For that reason, after being stolen by an Italian citizen on August 21, 1911, the portrait became extremely popular, seizing the imagination and feelings of the French. Never before the steal of a work of art had been so unsettling for a people who had learned to idolize it and felt deeply its absence created on the wall of the Louvre Museum after its mysterious disappearance.

This story reproduced in a somewhat novelistic way the repercussions of that infamous theft, regarded until then as the steal of the century. On the other hand, some details of the execution of the painting and the motivations that led to its creation were depicted, as well as Lisa Gherardini herself, whom he immortalized with the name of Mona Lisa or La Gioconda.

You can look at a picture for a week and never think of it again. You can also look at a picture for a second and think of it all your life.

—Joan Miró

Art is never finished, only abandoned.

—Leonardo da Vinci

Everything you can imagine is real.

—Pablo Picasso

A true masterpiece does not tell everything.

—Albert Camus

OBSESSION

1

If you look carefully, it will leave an indelible mark on the chosen ones. Astonishment is not enough; the portrait will never leave that viewer's heart and mind. It will trap him. He will think of numerous reasons for that: the saga of the painting through time, its tiny and enigmatic cracks drawn as if by an invisible hand, its perfect geometry, the depth of that nebulous scenario calculated exhaustively—blurry mountains in the distance, a meandering river without a riverbed, a desolate bridge, and a kind of dark lake full of shadows tangled with an unreal but alluring sky like the depths of his creator's thought.

But the most captivating part is the foreground, so powerful and yet so simple, unknown, full of mystery as if that transcendent face spoke of struggles, romances, wisdom, perhaps arrogance, perhaps innocence, with an impenetrable smile that could not be a smile at all anyway. It is impossible to be sure. Hands crossed, a mourning dress, or maybe the garment hints at complacency . . . at lust . . . at power. But above all is the unparalleled hint of a smile, indecipherable, with her eyes on you, challenging, an accomplice of virtues or of . . . who knows what. Only he, the only human capable of deciphering it, could determine it by catching his thought, which in the end will be the thought of the viewer subjugated by his own troubles. Woe to you, miserable viewer, who is about to know the hidden motivations of the master.

If you have looked properly and you are among the chosen ones, you will fall under her influence and will no longer be able to take flight; and like others, it will drag you into her atmosphere of strange provocation. "Let it go," you will say to yourself. "It is just a painting, a work of art hanging on a museum wall, shielded by past struggles and the intense anguish of a people who almost lost it forever."

2

My name is Vincenzo Peruggia, and I am Italian from Dumenza, Lombardy, and very proud of it. I've been living in Paris for two years and working at the museum for several months, thanks to a cousin with good connections and my profession. I am a painter and decorator, and I understand craftsmanship very well; in addition, I have mastered the art of preserving paintings using the glazing technique. That's precisely why I work at the museum. My routine usually starts in the mornings, when I do the work assigned to me.

I don't presume to know as much about art as some of my superiors, but I know more than many stupid French people who have no idea of the value of the treasures they safeguard in their museum. Those undesirables, who refer to us Italians as macaroni, really don't know us, ignoring perhaps, with the arrogance that characterizes them, that we have given to the world more works of art and of equal or better quality than them. But I won't waste my precious time talking about them anymore.

Through my work here, I've managed to familiarize myself, to a large extent, with how the museum works, especially regarding security matters. I don't pretend to be smarter than all of those who work here, but I think I've found the solution to a problem that has been growing in my mind for some time. I have been obsessing about this idea to the point of feeling fully capable of carrying it out. When I finish an assignment on the lower or upper floors of the museum, I don't lose sight of any detail, any wall, any door or corridor, any work of art. I have memorized completely the layout and premises of this great palace converted into a museum and most of the works that adorn it, and I know which are the most visited room and which are the less visited, and that gives me a great advantage. I laugh to myself when I think how easy it could be to take away the work of art of my predilection; of course, if I do it by myself, I will be limited by the size of the work I choose. So the only trouble is making the perfect choice and choosing the right moment.

That moment will come soon. I can feel it. For those strange turns of fate, I no longer work at the museum every day; however, I still have access to it. By wearing my customary uniform, I will be as invisible as any other worker. After much thinking about the matter, I've made my choice already, and I think it is the right one. At first, I've thought it will be more feasible to subtract a beautiful Mantegna that hangs from a certain wall, but my silent inquiries make me think the Mona Lisa is much more valuable, and not only that—I think that taking away the Mona Lisa would be more hurtful to the conceited French, who mistakenly believe that work is their property. But they are delusional. That painting has been stolen by the greatest thief of works of art, Napoleon B. So finally, justice will be done. I will retrieve it and take it to the town, where it belongs. Just thinking about it makes me shudder. I will do something in my life that my compatriots will be grateful for. I will become a hero. I'll take the painting to Florence. These stupid Frenchmen will see what this useless macaroni is capable of.

3

"Good morning, dear Master. You give me great pleasure visiting our mandatory refuge here in Venice."

"The pleasure is all mine, dear Prince Guiliano. I always remember you as a child in our beloved Florence, next to your father, Lorenzo de' Medici, 'the Magnificent.' You were a graceful child and then a bold young man full of promise. I was very sorry about your departure."

"So it is, my dear Leonardo. As soon as I heard of your gracious presence here, I decided to come and pay my respects to your immense genius and charisma."

"I do not deserve your words of praise, esteemed Prince, but I accept them in good taste."

"My admiration for your work knows no limits, Master. My great admiration goes back from my childhood. And I long to appreciate your most recent works, which I have not seen because of this absurd exile."

"Unfortunately, dear Prince, I have left some along the way, but I have here some sketches I would like you to give me your informed opinion about. You are a connoisseur of the fine arts."

"Now you flatter me, Master. I hope to be worthy of your words and enter your workshop."

"Come right ahead. What do you think of these drawings?"

"Lord of the heavens! They are wonderful! The attention to detail is astonishing. How do you achieve it, Master? And that one . . . maybe it's who I think it is?"

"That's how dear Guiliano is. It is a sketch of the marquise Isabella d'Este."

"Marvelous. Look at the pose . . . and that face, just perfect. You can guess by her bearing she possesses great austerity and wisdom. And the position of her hands, it's a stroke of genius, Master. It adds a certain mystery to the whole and completes masterfully the harmony between the head and the bosom."

"Thanks, Prince. Excellent observation. I knew you possessed the gift of art criticism. It is not for less being the son of the Magnificent, Lorenzo de' Medici."

"Master, you are always well remembered by our family despite all the misfortunes that have befallen us. Men like you make us love Florence even when we are away and in spite of the contempt to which we were subjected. But . . . Master, seeing this incredible portrait, although it's unfinished, reveals without a doubt your genius, and anxiety arises in me, and it will only depend on your magnanimous will—""Prince Guiliano, the debt I owe your father and your family is infinite. Don't think for a moment that I would not grant you a request."

"I knew you were still our beloved master Leonardo, your usual self. So without further ado, I will talk about what arose in me moments ago. You probably remember my aunt Nannina, who is married to Don Bernardo Rucellai, and perhaps you remember Camilla, his niece."

"Sure, how couldn't I? Remember that in our beloved Florence, we all know each other more or less or almost everyone."

"Well, you might also remember that Camilla, a highly inventive woman, is married to a rich merchant who lost his wife years ago in a terrible way. Well, Camilla is the stepmother of a young girl named Lisa, Lisa Gherardini."

"Of course, I know her. She is the wife of Don Francesco del Giocondo, a wealthy cloth merchant."

"I see you make things easier for me, dear Master. I must confess that Lisa was the love of my youth. At the moment of our exile, she and I dreamed that we were the princes of Florence. Not a night went by without my wings flying to her window in the form of my thoughts. She reciprocated my love in the same way, but it was an impossible love marked by the tragedy that was to affect my family, so without saying goodbye, the love of youth was taken away from me. And now to my great sorrow, she is married and with children. Now you will understand better the assignment I have for you. I ask you to paint a portrait of her, but first of all, I beg to keep this whole affair between us since it is not my desire to hurt the sensibilities of her honorable husband, who has been a faithful friend and associate of my family for a long time. If you accept, you will be appropriately remunerated in advance. If destiny does not bring us together again and I do not see the fruit of your creation, it won't matter. I only wish to fix her image in time as a symbol of a love that by chance went nowhere and that it is precisely you, great Master, whom I admire so much, who paints it. I will imagine her portrait as I remember her from that time, and she will remain that way for me. Having confessed all that, do you accept my personal and sensitive commission?"

"Yes, I do, esteemed Guiliano. I do."

4

Today, Tuesday, August 22, 1911, I confess that I am afraid; but at the same time, I feel an indefinable joy. From being only a thought fed by anger, now it has become a harsh and cruel reality for many French people, perhaps for all French people, because I have taken their precious Gioconda or rather our dear Mona Lisa, and the strangest thing is that fear has invaded me here in the safety of my room. I don't even want to see the painting. Just thinking about it makes my hair stand on end. I look around and can't find a safe place to put it. It's still in the wrapping. I don't want to touch it. I don't want to look out the window. I don't think I'll go out on the street this week, and if someone knocks on the door, I'm not willing to open it. I haven't slept a wink last night, and I'm so alert today that I doubt I will be able to fall asleep. I can't trust anyone either until I make my way to Florence, but I will have to wait a long time . . . a long time.

As I have thought, the subtraction—I refuse to call it theft—has gone on as I have planned: I have gone to the museum Sunday afternoon, and I've stayed to sleep there; the next day, everything will be easier because the museum does not open to the public on Mondays. I have been dressed in a white smock just like everyone else. God knows that I don't lie when I say I have been unfaltering all the time, sure footed, all my movements calculated. I have gone directly to the room where the painting has been and only come across one person, who apparently, did has not recognized me at all. Since I have worked in the glazing of the painting, it has been very easy for me to disassemble it and, in a matter of seconds, extract it from the frame and put it under my smock.

I have walked naturally. Who among the people there will have imagined that this insignificant being has under his arm their precious treasure? There has been a small problem; when I've wanted to go out through one of the side doors, I have not realized that it is locked, but God . . . God is merciful and good when it comes to justice, and one of the locksmiths, a very old gentleman whom I have seen in the corridors occasionally, has appeared. To my surprise and with no hesitation or suspicion, he has opened the door for me with one of the many keys he carries. It has been the only time I have felt my heart missing a beat but only for a few seconds. When I've left the scene with the painting under my smock and understood that there is no return, I have walked and walked, and the people crossing my path have not even set their eyes on me, a humble worker staring vacantly into space, going along the bank of the Seine with his precious invisible item.

I can't say that my steps have been calm at this point but not too hasty either. My sweaty hands have betrayed my so-called tranquility, but nobody has noticed it. I have stopped in a random place and bought bread, cheese, and wine for a couple of days. Now that I think about it, it has been a risky but necessary move, and I've had the intuition that the people in the museum will not notice the absence of the painting until the next day, that is, today. That's why I have felt calm deep down walking through the streets of Paris with probably the most precious artwork in France, but my serenity will not last long without the danger of being discovered.

When I have finally arrived in my little room, no one has noticed me; however, the whole weight of my action and the presence of the painting itself have made that moment unbearable, and I don't know how to explain it, or maybe I do—the fear and the joy of being able to contemplate at my leisure and in absolute solitude the wonderful Mona Lisa, painted more than four hundred years ago. I have not slept in two days; I can say for sure those have been the most distressing forty-eight hours of all my existence.

5

It is an oil painting on a poplar panel of 77 × 53 cm executed between 1503 and 1519. As it has been typical of the artist, the painting is unfinished, although he has kept working on it off and on until his death. The technique is sfumato, Renaissance style. The first official owner is King Francis I of France at the beginning of the sixteenth century. Since then, it has been the property of the French state. Napoleon has possessed it for some time. It shows a moderate level of deterioration due to the ravages of time, and several layers of varnish have been applied in later centuries. At present, it is on display in the Louvre Museum in Paris, where it is being preserved under the proper environmental conditions. Having said that, let us go over the soul of the painting.

If we take a peek into the artist's workshop, it reveals more mystery than certainty. Is he looking for beauty? Is he looking for harmony between the landscape and the Madonna? Does he try to catch a thought and make it indecipherable at the same time? Or perhaps his intention is to confuse us with the genius of one who knows himself to be unachievable? Does the hint of the smile goes or returns from one of those unknown places in the background? Is she the hostess of gloomy places, half hidden in her intentional gaze? Or is the pose of the lady a reflection of the buried underworld in the artist's mind, of his memories or the trace of a vain contempt he has been subjected to in a distant past, of his parents who have not known how to do their job raising him? Or rather, will this be his revenge on the world of those who will remain alive as if to say they are doomed to see and not understand anything because feminine nature is like the waves, like the wind, like water that spills between your fingers, like death? A deep but simple mystery.

6

"Welcome to our home. You grace us immensely with your presence. This is my beloved wife, whom you already know. Lisa! Lisa! Dear, Master Leonardo is here."

"Thank you, Don Francesco del Giocondo. The honor is mine. Madonna, it is a pleasure to see you again."

"Welcome to our home, Master. Make yourself at home. This is your house too. Would you like some wine selected from our Chianti harvest? You will love it, I guarantee you."

"Happily, dear Madonna. I appreciate that wine very much. It would be a delicate pleasure for your humble servant's palate."

"Come, make yourself comfortable, Master, and let your faithful assistant do us the honor. Let us talk about your interesting assignment."

The Voice and the Fallen

"I suppose your dear wife is already aware of the reason for our visit."

"Yes, Master. She is very excited, a little scared too. She had no idea she would be asked to be a model for an embellishing work that will fill us with, Master Leonardo."

"I am pleased to hear you approve gladly, illustrious Francesco. I will not deny that the whole thing had me a little worried, but I know Prince Guiliano and you are united by a great friendship."

"That's so, Master. We have had a business relationship and a friendship for many years with the Medici family, and for us, it is a great honor to serve you once again and without reservations in your important assignment. You only need to tell us when you want to start the work."

"Would you mind, Mr. Francesco, if I started as soon as possible in my workshop, where I have everything ready? We would only have to coordinate the most convenient time for my distinguished model and me to begin. It is necessary to pay attention to the vagaries of the weather and other minutiae so that our work yields the expected results."

"It will be when you order, Master. Lisa, do you agree? Are you feeling ready for this great task?"

"Sure, my lord. I already have the garments and jewels you ordered for this occasion."

"Madonna, I would prefer a simple apparel. Without luxurious clothes, I would achieve the desired effect. I wish to exalt your natural grace, and for that, I will need you to be yourself. Fancy garments would stand out more than necessary. You won't need them, you'll see."

"Master Leonardo, I see you have liked our wine. Be kind to accept a selection of Chianti wines from Antonmaria di Noldo Gherardini, Lisa's father, who will be honored that the great maestro Leonardo tastes his lauded product."

"Yes, my father will be proud if you take with you some of our fine wines."

"Since you insist, Salai will come to pick them up in a few days. It will be a real pleasure for him, more than for me. The infirmities of age do not allow me to enjoy it as often as I would like to."

"Going back to the matter of the garments, Master, what do you suggest? We have everything in our stores."

"Thanks for the excellent offers, but I have decided to dispense with luxury this time. I would prefer something dark that, without giving the impression of mourning, somewhat lends itself to that possibility."

"Given that guideline, let Lisa choose what she would wear on this illustrious occasion."

"So be it. Madonna, I know you will surprise me, your humble servant, with your natural beauty and an appropriate selection."

"Master Leonardo, you put me in an awkward position, but I will appeal to providence to help select the most appropriate garment according to your requirements. Now I must attend to household matters. I ask your permission, beloved husband, to retire. Master Leonardo, it has been an immense pleasure to have you in our happy abode."

"The pleasure and honor are all mine, Madonna, Mr. Francesco. We are also leaving. Salai will come very soon for the wine."

"See you soon, Master, and thanks for your visit."

"Ah, I almost forgot. Give Prince Guiliano our most affectionate greeting when you see him."

"I shall do so, Mr. Francesco."

7

From the beginning of its creation, back in 1503 in Florence, this work has not ceased to amaze everyone who has set his or her eyes on it. It is said that Leonardo himself has completely been taken with it until his death in 1519. It's impossible to imagine the perplexity of its creator when he senses that he has created an absolute masterpiece. Let's imagine him alone, focused on a subtle brushstroke he thinks is missing, a detail only he can perceive. He wants to recreate more than one thought in the face of the Madonna. It's been years since Lisa Gherardini has posed for him, and he has lost touch with her because he lives in another city; however, for him, she is right there— the eternal woman, the housewife, neither a princess nor a duchess, dressed in rich vestments, and wearing fine jewels. It is just her and him, she a mother, wife, lover, friend, and confidant; he the creator who becomes the son of his creation. Alone, he lives for her. Only death will separate them.

Inevitably, he wonders what will happen when he is gone forever. Will she be gone too? Will an opulent impostor come to take away his muse, his Madonna? At times, he becomes desperate, and a dark and odd question crosses his mind: What if he destroys it when death begins tugging at his elbow? It will be easy to deprive the future of its presence, undo the work with his own genius. But no, he is not that selfish. He has made peace with his past, and in any case, her elusive but powerful smile like a sudden lightning intimidates and intoxicates him at the same time. But he finally wonders how to kill a child you love madly; how not to share with posterity his greatest achievement; how not to go to his grave, pleased at the prospect of being immortalized through a piece of wood full of colors, technique, and all his senses put onto it.

So he finally agrees to sell it to that sovereign who has given him shelter in a strange but gentle country. With firmness and detachment, he decrees, "Francesco Melzi, give it up for sale to King Francis I. That is my final decision, after I'm gone, of course."

8

"How do you like the background music, Madonna? I had the musicians brought to awaken in you the sense of tranquility required to sit for the portrait. I know how tedious it can be for you to stay in the same position for such a long time."

"Oh, Master, it has been very propitious. It fills my spirit with serenity and joy in a very special way."

"That was the intention. Allow me to lower the window curtains a little. So much light is unnecessary for what I intend to achieve. Stay still in that position. Now please tilt your face to your right a bit, a little more . . . good . . . that's fine. Lift your head a little, only a little."

"Will you start with my face, Master?"

"Yes, Madonna. Try to smile but not widely. Yes. Look directly at me."

"Oh, Master, I'm a little embarrassed to look into your eyes."

"Remember the smile. Don't worry, look at the midpoint between my eyes. That way, you will feel less intimidated. See? It's better now. I just need you to keep that posture for a moment. Stay still and do not talk for a while. Let me speak only to myself."

"So be it, Master, but I'm a little nervous."

"It's okay, this part will not take me long. I will reveal to you some elements of the technique to capture a chiaroscuro effect. You have noticed that I have placed myself so that my line of sight is between the illuminated part and the shadows of your body. Don't forget the smile . . . like that. I want to capture the natural beauty of your face, and for that, I have placed you in a somewhat dark space of the room. Doing so, I will achieve the chiaroscuro effect reflected on your face. And then through the illuminated part, I will be able to get its reliefs on the painting. Thus, I will capture certain reflections not perceived in a first impression, which will be magnified. Perfect."

"Master, forgive me for breaking the silence, but . . . why me? I mean, it is known the models for your paintings are counted among the highest in the ranks of society."

"Interesting question, Madonna del Giocondo. You are a woman who should not envy those models who only enhance their beauty with luxurious and extravagant clothes. I am tired of those pretentious models. The true and mysterious beauty of a woman is possessed by a woman like you, a devoted wife and mother with extraordinary natural attributes. Besides, in all my years in this profession, I can assure you that, in your face and especially in your eyes and smile, beauty and mystery are combined in a woman as never before. And I have seen many faces in my life. It is not a coincidence that Prince Guiliano had appreciated those unique qualities in you."

"Master Leonardo, your words flatter me, although I think they do not correspond with reality as you or Prince Guiliano believe with respect to my personal qualities. I would believe it if it came from my husband, Francesco, who took me for a wife for reasons of the heart."

"Don't be mistaken, Madonna. Beauty flows naturally from you, and my humble job is to show the world that someone like you exists and that it would be an unfortunate twist of fate that your countenance and deportment are not immortalized for posterity. So that wonderful beta of charm, embodied in your person, should not fade away. It must stand the test of time and never . . . wither away so people not yet born will surrender to you defenseless, Madonna."

"Strange words, Master Leonardo. Do you really think so?"

"I do, Madonna. No important or simple phenomenon of nature has escaped my observations so far. As you know, I'm not just a painter."

"You are full of surprises, Master, but I consider myself a simple woman after all and not the possessor of all those qualities you confer on me."

"The painter's look reveals something very different. Now it's time to end our break. I want you to cross your arms for me."

"Like this?"

"No, allow me, please. Your right hand on the left. Spread slightly the index finger, your hand in a straight line with your face."

"This way?"

"Perfect. Mr. Francesco del Giocondo has done me a nice big favor by following my suggestions about the dress. It has been an excellent choice."

"Master, excuse me, but I chose it myself."

"Oh . . . yes . . . great choice . . . sorry for my mistake. I forgot it. What a fool I have been. It has been your best choice . . . Let this fold rest over your left shoulder. Breathe gently . . . calmly. Today I will only sketch your entire figure. In other sessions, I will define the contours, but you must understand that it is a process, and this is one of the most important parts of the work. Feel free to talk. I am working on your torso now."

"Thanks, Master. I already feel more comfortable with the position. At first, I thought I could not hold my gaze, much less the smile. Is the smile okay?"

"Clear as water. It was perfect."

"For a moment, I thought I could not hold it. I hope I didn't look very sad."

"Absolutely not. The smile could not have been better. Remember, I am doing the sketch work now. I'll attend to the details afterward. I think I've managed to fix your face in time."

"Do you know I've never posed for a painter before?"

"Yes, I know. And you have done it very well. I apologize for having subjected you to such torture, keeping you static like a statue all this time. But I am afraid other days like this will come until I finish the work."

"Don't forget, Master, that this is a small effort I am doing, which is well worth the eternity, don't you think?"

9

It's been so long since I have her with me. I have learned every tiny brushstroke, every little crack, every proportion by dint of contemplating her every day; and always, she incites me to sigh. I've been with her for three months now, and sometimes I fall asleep looking at her as if she were all mine, and suddenly, I cry because I can't share her. No one should witness my sighs when I'm with her.

One afternoon I got a knock on my door, and I felt like dying; I began to sweat like a sow, and it was midfall. I thought it was the police again because, in the first week of the robbery, they investigated all those who had been employed at the museum; but as expected, they couldn't find my secret hiding place. Once again, I didn't know if my nerves would give me away. I did not want to answer. I was about to throw myself out the window, but I pulled myself together and came to my senses in time. The painting was on my bed, and I took it quickly and put it in my secret hiding place. A little resigned, before the possibility the police might be on my doorstep, and without opening the door, I asked, "Who is it?

"Open the door, sir," replied the landlady. I owed two months' rent, and since I still hadn't gone out to look for a job, I was saving every penny I could. Obviously nervous and without opening the door, I yelled she shouldn't worry because I would pay her that night, that I would take the money to her house, and that she should excuse me for the inconvenience. She left muttering something I couldn't understand, nothing good for sure. Only when I heard her fading footsteps echoing on the wooden floor did I calm down and go back to bed, but this time, I did not take out my treasure from the place I had it hidden.

I am in so much fear of being discovered that days go by. And I do not get out of bed, not even to admire her as I usually do. I have no idea how all this is going to end, but I need much more time to take our masterwork to our land, where it belongs.

Spring is here. I've had it in my possession for more than six months, and a lot of things have happened. The poor French must be resigned to their definitive loss. They don't know what else to come up with. I have recently bought a chocolate bar, and the wrapping paper has its figure printed on it, and I have laughed for the first time after the . . . retrieval.

I go out more often. I visit my cousin who keeps promising to get me a new job but never does; at least he takes me along to do some work with him sometimes and gives me some money, but the truth is I hate to separate myself from her. I feel she belongs to me; that is my property, and that's why I can't stay away from her.

One afternoon I imagined that the witch of my landlady had evicted me, and she inevitably had found the painting. I ran across the city frantically, down the Rue de Rivoli like a madman. I couldn't stand the subway's slow pace. I ran and ran desperately, fearing there would be a police contingent already surrounding my little apartment. But no, everything was in order. It was necessary to catch my breath in the desolate street. After a while and with my nerves shot to pieces, I got to my doorstep without being noticed. Once inside, still nervous, I went to the stove, and there she was, waiting for me just as a faithful lover would do—passive and without complaint, with angelic eyes and that smile. I took her to bed, and we stayed together until the next day.

More than two years have passed since the subtraction, and the most surprising thing of all is that they don't have the slightest idea of her whereabouts. In their stupidity, they have blamed two renowned artists, clearly innocent; and that has given me great satisfaction, being a run-of-the-mill worker who, without intending it and according to newspaper columnists, has made the steal of the century. I'm overflowing with joy. I have the impression I will be considered a hero in my beloved Italy. Sometimes I daydream and see I am welcomed with cheers and parties everywhere in Florence, where the painting belongs, but then doubt assails me.

The sacrifice I have made can't be paid with cheers and parties. This effort must be paid with gold; that is why I have compiled a list of probable buyers, but I must be very cautious. I'll make the choice at the last minute. I prefer to get my reward in cash. It is a paradox that I, the great Vincenzo Peruggia, with a treasure like this in my hands, am going through economic hardship. That's why I decided to go to Italy.

The time has come. I will choose the perfect buyer carefully there. I will take the train inconspicuously and hide the painting behind the lining of the suitcase with no problem. The fear of being caught has vanished already. So let's go, Vincenzo.

10

"The end is near, Francesco. My limbs are not responding anymore. I just can whisper now and do not feel like having more of Mathurine's soup."

"Don Leonardo ... dear Master, I am here for you, and I will always be. Life has given me the privilege of being one of your children. As long as there is a breath of life in you, I will be your legs, your eyes, your arms."

"I know, dear Francesco, and you mean so much to me, the king too. He has given me protection and, more importantly, kindness. I want you to keep all my writings, paintings, including other personal items as well as the remainder of my pension."

"If you wish, Master, I will put your belongings to good use and guard them with my life."

"I will bequeath my gardens to Battista and Salai and ... some money to my stepbrothers in Florence. Ah ... a fur-lined cape to Mathurine. I know she will like it."

"Rest assured, Master, I'll take care of everything. Allow me to remind you that the king wishes to have Lisa's portrait."

"Well, he deserves it, but it will cost him. It's a shame I can't take it where I'm going. I have never been apart from it. That painting is part of me as my own soul, if there is one. I will never reach that look ... that smile. I see her eyes in my dreams, and its meaning vanishes like a vaporous cloud. If only I could take it with me."

"Master, it will always be yours. You are squeezing my hand as you talk about her. It's a clear sign that portrait gives you life. The end is not near when in your mind is ... your Mona Lisa."

"But my life is fading ... Francesco Melzi ... fading. It is inevitable. I will enter the wide sea soon."

"We will meet there someday, dear Father ... Leonardo. Your voice still vibrates. You can speak. As long as you speak, you are here with me, among the living."

"My soul . . . son, I leave it in my works but especially in that portrait that had me on my head all these years and, like sweet thorn stuck in one's heart, alleviated the pain of not having painted more, having been able to."

"Do not grieve, please. You have done more than most."

"But . . . I have been negligent and wasted some valuable time. I should have done more."

"But your legacy will be immense based on your observations on all things worthy of an inexhaustible curiosity. I will make sure that posterity will be a witness to your great ingenuity."

"My soul, Francesco . . . I leave my soul in my works. That is my legacy. Give my most precious painting to the king so it will be properly preserved over time."

"Your will shall be done without question. Now I will bring your soup. Mathurine is knocking on the door. You have to make an effort to have some . . . beloved Father."

"I don't feel like it, Francesco."

"You must have some. You will recover."

"No, please. I beg you. I don't need it now. Just help me get up a little and bring me the painting. I want to feel it since I cannot see it anymore. I'm losing my sight . . . as the rest of my body. Bring the painting, please."

"I will tell Mathurine to bring you the soup later if you prefer, but promise me you will eat some."

"Yes, I promise."

"I will lift you a little now so you can feel your work."

"Yes . . . yes . . . I'm fine now. Bring it, I beg you."

"Here it is, Master. What do you feel?"

"I feel life, Francesco. I feel my whole life in this work. Would you let the fire devour it if it was my last will? No . . . forget I said that, please. Dark thoughts assail me at times because, with every breath I lose, I feel I am losing it as if my ship were sinking. Play some music for me, please. That way, I'll feel closer to it."

"As you order, Master. Music gives you life. I see it in your eyes, which half-closed shine like little suns. Is it because of the portrait?"

"Yes, it is. Let me touch it one last time."

"Take it with you, Master. Take it to that place from where there is no return. It's yours."

"As much as I wanted, it is not. It belongs to you and to those not yet born. Yes . . . it belongs to all of you."

"So it will be, dear Father. Your soup is here. Thanks, Mathurine. I will feed it to him."

11

A walk through the museum will be enough to change a life, seeing the fruits of genius hanging from centuries-old walls. Endless corridors will uncover the magic of immortal artists' steps throughout the world, creators who have left their soul here before leaving for the wide sea, each more precious than the next, priceless treasures, unrepeatable feats of artistic endeavor recreating worlds and faces lost in time. However, one of these works stands out among the rest; its imprint is the mysterious face that depicts, captivating and enigmatic at the same time. It has taken flight beyond the painter's brush and taken on a life of its own. Maybe the creator does not know it and has only sensed it. That work of art could only belong to the whole of humanity. It is not his. I repeat, it is ours, humble and ordinary passersby who lay our eyes on it, eternally fascinated; its name is made up of two simple but inspiring words that open a crack to the past that will never be penetrated other than with the serene look and the hint of a smile.

This is the way things are: You get to it after contemplating relics as if through moments frozen in time, guiding us to the real treasure hidden behind a transparent and impenetrable window. The crowd will not let you appreciate it until it's your turn, and your visit will end there; if you are one of those who know the mystery that keeps the message hidden throughout time, things will be different from there on. If you have the gift of deciphering its symbolism, you won't be able to put it into words, and you will only know it when you stand in front of her and let her observe you and whisper to you the secret she has kept for centuries. Suddenly, you won't hear or feel the little mass of people around you; you will wish to stay a moment longer, a second longer at least, because her stare feeds you. She contemplates you, and you will see the smile. And then in the middle of the flashes and murmurs, she will possess you completely, and you will not be the same again—but only if you're one of the chosen ones.

12

"Where do you say it is, Mr. Geri?"

"Where we are heading, the Tripoli e Italia Hotel. This person calls himself Leonardo. What do you think? See for yourself the letter he sent me. He claims to have the Mona Lisa in his possession."

"Hmm . . . everything is possible. Thank you for calling immediately. I have told no one in the gallery the reason for your visit, but this is true and not some lunatic taunting us. It will be necessary to contact the police right away. Do you get me? This is beyond our personal desires or interests."

"I agree, Mr. Poggi. I have no objection. You are the authority in these matters who can certify that it is the real painting. This is the place. He is in the living room. It must be that person, the one with the big mustache."

"Hello, sir. Are you Mr. Geri? Pleased to meet you. I am Vincenzo Peruggia."

"Yes. My pleasure, Mr. Peruggia. The director of the Uffizi Gallery, Mr. Giovanni Poggi, he will certify the authenticity of the work."

"It's a pleasure to meet you, Mr. Poggi. Follow me, please. This is my room. I want you to know that . . . I'm a little nervous. Nobody else has seen it these last two years. I have kept it as if it were part of my own body. It doesn't have a single scratch. I have taken care of it as if it were my own life. Let me remove this wrapper, please. I love the color red for the cover."

"Go on, Mr. Peruggia. The director has canceled an important meeting to be here.""This is incredible. Give me that magnifying glass, please. Mm-hmm . . . mm-hmm . . . incredible. Yes, it's her. This is the Mona Lisa, Mr. Peruggia. How did you get your hands on it? What do you want?"

"Well . . . I need . . . you know . . . I've kept the painting for so long. I think I've gotten sick because of taking care of it. I have neglected my health, and I need . . . money . . . a lot of money—a good buyer, you know."

"Do you want money, Mr. Peruggia?"

"Did you say you want money?"

"Don't you think I could sell it? Don't you believe so? Well, if I can't, I'll take it back with me."

"No, no, calm down, Mr. Peruggia. We can make the arrangements with a simple phone call. Just wait a moment. Mr. Geri, stay with Mr. Peruggia while I call the gallery. I'll be back in a few minutes."

13

Sometime later and after being taken on an emotional tour through some Italian cities, the portrait of Lisa Gherardini has returned to its original place, and the thief has been sentenced to seven months behind bars; he has been considered a hero in his native country for a short time to be inevitably forgotten later on. Some say it is the steal of the century, but others who will never reveal their names have said that the whole truth is that the portrait itself has executed the theft.

Oh, unsuspecting chosen one, you have ignored the most resounding and mysterious truth of all; you have overlooked the subliminal imprint that flows through that unparalleled portrait that subjugates beings like you. It has bent your will perhaps; you have realized it, but it's too late now. Her gaze has caressed you like an ethereal and sweetly malignant current. Some dark characters claim she has subjugated his creator in the same way, trapped in the magic of his work, and then kings, an unwary and volatile emperor, and finally the will of an entire people who, after the theft, have mourned her absence, going in droves to the museum only to see the empty frame hanging on the wall.

Hidden voices declare it is she who has stolen something from you, incautious and transient mortal. She has stolen your will. It is no coincidence that they have confined her in an impregnable bulletproof glass cage equipped with the best alarm system in the world since that fateful Monday so that the day you visit the museum, you do not become the next chosen one, an innocent victim of her invisible influence, stealing your will by inoculating the poison of obsession.

ACKNOWLEDGMENTS

Peter Watson (Newton, Galileo, Darwin, Nietzsche), Henry Lincoln, Michael Baigent, Richard Leigh (Newton), Allan Prior (Hitler), Frank Brady (Bobby Fischer), Irving Stone (Freud and Vincent van Gogh), Dr. Julio Francisco (Don Celito) (Trujillo), Werner Ross (Nietzsche), Ernest Miller (Hemingway), Marguerite Yourcenar (Mishima), BBC London (J. F. Kennedy), Tim M. Berra (Darwin), Dava Sobel (Galileo), Max Brod, Pietro Citati (Kafka), John Kerr (Freud and Jung), Charles Nicholl (da Vinci) —these authors have helped me delve into the stories of these men all through the process of research and writing; for that reason, I express my infinite gratitude to them for opening the way in this long and tortuous journey.

ABOUT THE AUTHOR

The author was born in Santo Domingo, Dominican Republic, in January 1968. He had published El secreto de Vincent in Spanish, later translated to English as Vincent's Secret, both in Amazon. Also, he had published three short stories in La revista cultural de Tabasco.

His other works in progress are a suspense novel and a novel based on memoirs. He lives in Santo Domingo and works as a psychiatrist.

www.ingramcontent.com/pod-product-compliance
Lightning Source LLC
Chambersburg PA
CBHW021423070526
44577CB00001B/31